FOR MY STUDENTS
AT THE UNIVERSITY OF MASSACHUSETTS,
AMHERST

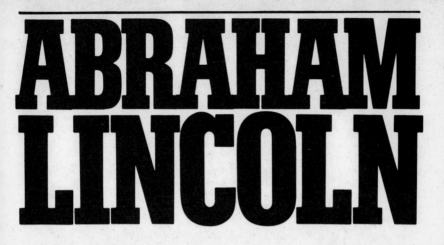

ABRAHAM LINCOLN

THE MAN BEHIND THE MYTHS

STEPHEN B. OATES

A MERIDIAN BOOK

MERIDIAN
Published by the Penguin Group
Penguin Books USA Inc., 375 Hudson Street, New York, New York 10014,
U.S.A.
Penguin Books Ltd, 27 Wrights Lane, London W8 5TZ, England
Penguin Books Australia Ltd, Ringwood, Victoria, Australia
Penguin Books Canada Ltd, 10 Alcorn Avenue, Toronto, Ontario, Canada,
M4V 3B2
Penguin Books (N.Z.) Ltd, 182–190 Wairau Road, Auckland 10, New Zealand

Penguin Books Ltd, Registered Offices: Harmondsworth, Middlesex, England

Published by Meridian, an imprint of New American Library, a division of
Penguin Books USA Inc.

First Meridian Printing, April, 1985
7 8 9 10 11 12

This is an authorized reprint of a hardcover edition published by
HarperCollins Publishers, Inc., and simultaneously in Canada by
Fitzhenry & Whiteside Limited, Toronto.

REGISTERED TRADEMARK—MARCA REGISTRADA

Library of Congress Cataloging in Publication Data

Oates, Stephen B.
  Abraham Lincoln, the man behind the myths.

  Reprint. Originally published: New York: Harper & Row.
c1984.
  Bibliography
  Includes index
  1. Lincoln, Abraham, 1809–1865. 2. Presidents—
United States—Biography. I. Title.
[E457.016 1985]   973.7′092′4 [B]   84-22596
ISBN 0-452-00734-8

PRINTED IN THE UNITED STATES OF AMERICA

*The lack of a sense of history
is the damnation of the modern world.*

ROBERT PENN WARREN

*Those who deny freedom to others,
deserve it not for themselves.*

ABRAHAM LINCOLN

CONTENTS

In 1984, when this book appears, Abraham Lincoln will be 175 years old. This is certain to cause an eruption of flatulent utterances about the sanctified figure and a shameless parade of scissors-and-paste Lincoln books with more pictures in them than print. Since in *With Malice Toward None* I immodestly undertook to write a Lincoln biography for this generation, I thought I might help commemorate his birthday by publishing a serious volume, one I have been writing in my head ever since my life of Lincoln came out. This is a biographical study, not a true biography in the grand manner, evocative and comprehensive, with a narrative sweep that carries the Lincoln story from birth to death. I have already tried that in *With Malice Toward None*. No, this is a more modest outing, an exploration into special moments and meanings of Lincoln's life. Still, I hope my narrative conveys some sense of him as a living man, for I wrote it in a style that seeks to describe as well as to analyze, to feel as well as to comprehend.

The thing about Lincoln is that he keeps growing and changing. After I completed my biography and went on to a life of Martin Luther King, Jr., who understood Lincoln and carried on his vision and work, I still found myself talking about the Civil War President on the lecture circuit. In one public address in the Midwest, I found myself discussing both Lincoln and King as "Builders of the Dream"—*troubled* builders, I should have said, given the pain and suffering both went through. In addition, I kept contributing articles and reviews about Lincoln to various publications.

As I continued to read, write, lecture, and talk about Lincoln, I realized how much I wanted to correct or clarify some of my earlier interpretations, realized how much more I had to say. Hence this book. In it, I have probed the galaxy of Lincoln myth and countermyth, a celestial world I find fascinating. Why has he become our greatest mythical hero? And correspondingly maybe our greatest mythical demon? What do such myths tell us about Lincoln's significance? What do they tell us about us? Moreover, how does the historical man compare with these mythic creations? What is the place of both in our literature?

Such questions are the *raison d'être* for Part One, which deals with the three major myths about Lincoln and against which I orchestrate the rest of the book. There I attempt an approximation of what Lincoln was like in the days he lived, taking care to discuss him in proper historical context. In specific, Part Two addresses certain themes in Lincoln's personal life—his depression, for example, and his difficulties with affairs of the heart until after he wedded Mary. Because a person's private and public selves are inextricably linked, I have searched Lincoln's inner conflicts, and described how he sought to resolve them, in hopes that this might afford a deeper understanding and appreciation of the whole man.

Another section examines Lincoln's rise to prominence in the turbulent antebellum years and his emergence as the foremost political spokesman in America for the liberating impulses of the age. Here I venture an explanation for why scholars still rank Lincoln as our best President—which would doubtless amuse him, since he preferred a seat in the national Senate to the White House. In this and in the section on the war years, I try to elucidate Lincoln's vision of the historic meaning and mission of his young country in the progress of human liberty in the world. He fought the Civil War with that uppermost in his mind, and I attempt to discuss all his momentous war measures—particularly emancipation—in terms of his vision and core of unshakable beliefs. I've given special attention to Lincoln's troubled and troubling attitudes about slavery, in part because it was the source of the conflict (as Lincoln and his associates repeatedly stressed), in part because what he did about slavery in his own view was the most important measure of his presidency. Too, my narrative seeks to capture all the passion that bondage aroused in Lincoln and his entire generation. A final section attempts to clear away some of the popular misconceptions and elaborate fantasies that surround the assassination, and to suggest the meaning of that shattering and final act. The book ends with what I hope is a fair and compassionate portrait of Mary Lincoln, surely the most misunderstood First Lady in our history. Because her whole life was bound up with Lincoln, Mary's desolate years alone constitute a tragic coda to the Lincoln story.

On the lecture circuit and in the classroom, I have been asked all manner of provocative things about Lincoln, which attests to the powerful hold he still has on our imaginations. In this volume, I endeavor to answer some recurring questions. How, for instance, did Lincoln's log-cabin origins affect him? How did he relate to his father and real mother? What was he like as a lawyer, a husband, a man? Was he really a country fellow who cracked jokes at the village store? On that point, can the Lincoln stories told by Carl Sandburg be believed? What in fact are we to make of Sandburg's immensely popular biography? Was Lincoln a lifelong white supremacist, as many blacks and whites contend today? Did the Emancipation Proclamation free any blacks? Did Lincoln steal the glory of self-liberating slaves by issuing it? Was he tender-hearted when it came to reconstructing Dixie? Would reconstruction have been different had he lived? Was there a conspiracy on the part of Secretary of War Edwin M. Stanton and the so-called Radical Republicans to have Lincoln assassinated—an allegation enshrined as fact in several books and a recent motion picture and periodically reported in the popular media? There is much more here about Lincoln's public and private selves, but I have told enough: perhaps some of you are teased enough to read the book.

Inevitably, I have covered some points and used certain facts here that are also found in *With Malice Toward None* and in a couple of essays in my book, *Our Fiery Trial*. In truth, the present discussion of emancipation considerably refines and elaborates on an argument I first made in one of those essays. Given the persistent misunderstanding of that crucial event, I thought it necessary to make the argument longer and more precise. Nevertheless, in approach, emphasis, and purpose, this is an altogether different book from its predecessors. I've offered much new material here, new ideas and insights, all of which I hope adds up to an original and spirited portrait.

In shaping it, I benefited enormously from a growing library of modern Lincoln studies. In fact, the last couple of decades have witnessed a veritable renaissance of Lincoln scholarship. Modern specialists have reexamined almost every aspect of his life and career, producing new treatises on his inner meanings, his humor, love of language, and ideology, his economics, law practice, work in the Illinois legislature and Congress, his rise to the presidency and his presidency itself, his relationship with his wife, with his generals and Cabinet Secretaries, with his so-called Radical Republican colleagues, with Negroes and abolitionists, even with his southern adversaries. But because much of this scholarship inhabits technical monographs and journal articles written by scholars for one another, it hasn't reached a broad literary audience. I am addressing that audience, because I want lay readers to rediscover Lincoln as the scholars have, to take a renewed interest in his life and work, to understand what they still mean for us. And there is no better time for that than Lincoln's 175th.

S.B.O.

Amherst, Massachusetts
August, 1983

Part One

MYTH

❧❀❧

Myth fulfills in primitive culture
an indispensable function: it expresses,
enhances, and codifies belief; it safeguards
and enforces morality; it vouches for the efficiency
of ritual and contains practical rules for the
guidance of man. Myth is thus . . .
a hard-worked active force.

BRONISLAW MALINOWSKI

1: Man of the People

In 1858, against a backdrop of heightening sectional tensions over slavery, Abraham Lincoln stood in the Great Hall of the Illinois House of Representatives, warning his countrymen that a house divided against itself could not stand. Across Illinois that year, in a series of forensic duels with Stephen A. Douglas, this tall and melancholy man addressed himself boldly to the difficult problems of his day: to the haunting moral contradiction of slavery in a nation based on the Declaration of Independence . . . to the combustible issue of Negro social and political rights . . . to the meaning and historic mission of America's experiment in popular government. This same man went on to the presidency, charged with the awesome task of saving the Union—and its experiment in popular government—in the holocaust of civil war. In the end, after enduring four unendurable years, he himself became a casualty of that conflict, gunned down by John Wilkes Booth just when the war was won and popular government preserved for humankind the world over.

The man who died that dark and dismal day had flaws as well as strengths, made mistakes and suffered reversals just as surely as he enjoyed his remarkable achievements. But in the days that followed his assassination, the man became obscured in an outpouring of flowery orations and tear-filled eulogies. As the seasons passed, Lincoln went on to legend and martyrdom, inflated by the myth makers into a godly Emancipator who personified America's ideal Everyman.

Before proceeding, I had best try to define myth as I am using it here. Above all, I do not mean some preposterous story. Nor do I mean a story that is uncontaminated by life. Myth, as I am using the term, is a grandiose projection of a people's experience. As X. J. Kennedy has put it, "Myths tell us of the exploits of the gods —their battles, the ways in which they live, love, and perhaps suffer—all on a scale of magnificence larger than our life. We envy their freedom and power; they enact our wishes and dreams." In other words, the grandiose dimensions and symbol-building power of the myths we create reveal our deepest longings as a people. And this is especially true of the myths we Americans have fashioned about the powerful figure who presided over the Civil War, our greatest trial as a nation. Our extravagant projections of Lincoln in myth suggest a great deal about the spiritual and psychological needs of our culture ever since.

As historian David Donald has noted, two traditions of Lincoln mythology developed after the war. The first began on "Black Easter," April 16, 1865, when ministers across the North portrayed the slain President as an American Christ who died to expiate the sins of his guilty land. For them, it was no coincidence that he had fallen on Good Friday. Did not the times of his shooting and death—just after ten in the evening and just after seven-twenty the next morning—make on the clock an outline of the crucifix? "Oh, friends," cried the Reverend C. B. Crane from the pulpit of Broadway Tabernacle, "it was meet that the martyrdom should occur on Good Friday. It is no blasphemy against the Son of God and the Saviour of men that we declare the fitness of the slaying of the second Father of our Republic on the anniversary of the day on which He was slain. Jesus Christ died for the world, Abraham Lincoln died for his country."

Blacks, too, viewed Lincoln with uninhibited reverence. "We mourn for the loss of our great and good President," a Negro soldier wrote his fiancée. "Humanity has lost a firm advocate, our race its Patron Saint, and the good of all the world a fitting object to emulate. . . . The name Abraham Lincoln will ever be cherished in our hearts, and none will more delight to lisp his name in reverence than the future generations of our people." In truth, black Americans came to regard Lincoln as a perfect, personal emancipator and kept pictures of him pasted on the walls above their mantelpieces. "To the deeply emotional and religious slave," as one man explained, "Lincoln was an earthly incarnation of the Saviour of mankind."

And so one body of writings depicted him in the ensuing decades. Typical of this school was Josiah Gilbert Holland's *The Life of Abraham Lincoln,* which appeared in 1866 and sold more than 100,000 copies. Holland's Lincoln is a model youth and an impeccable Christian gentleman. When war clouds gather in 1860, he supposedly tells an Illinois associate: "I know there is a God and that he hates injustice and slavery. I see the storm coming, and I know that His hand is in it. If he has a place for and work for me—and I think he has—I believe I am ready. I am nothing, but truth is everything. I know I am right, because I know that liberty is right, for Christ teaches it and Christ is God." For Holland and other writers, ministers, and orators of this tradition, Lincoln was a martyr-saint, as pure and perfect a spirit as the Almighty ever created. He was "savior of the republic, emancipator of a race, true Christian, true man."

Sheer nonsense! thundered William H. Herndon, Lincoln's nervous, besotted law partner, when he read Holland's book. This prettified character was not the Lincoln he had known in Illinois. That Lincoln had never belonged to a church. He was *"an infidel,"* a prairie lawyer who told stories that made the pious wince. Determined to correct Holland's portrait, Herndon set out "to write the life of Lincoln as I saw him—honestly—truthfully—co[u]rageously—fearlessly cut whom it may." He jotted down his own impressions and interviewed old settlers in Indiana and Illinois who remembered Lincoln. They spun yarns about "Old Abe" that made Herndon's eyes hang out on his shirt front. Their Lincoln was an Illinois Paul Bunyan who could hoist a whiskey barrel overhead, a prairie Davy Crockett who roared that he was "the big buck of the lick." No historian, Herndon embraced such tales as zealously as he did actual fact. As a consequence, *Herndon's Lincoln: The True Story of a Great Life*, which came out in 1889, brimmed with gossip, hearsay, and legend, all mixed in with Herndon's own authentic observations of Lincoln in their law office, in Springfield's muddy streets, in courthouses and on the platform.

In sharp contrast to Holland's Christian gentleman, Herndon's Lincoln is a Western folk hero, funny, ambitious, irreverent, and sorrowful by turns. He is born in a "stagnant, putrid pool," the son of a shiftless poor white and "the illegitimate daughter" of a prominent Virginia planter. Though he rises above his impoverished origins, Herndon's Lincoln still has the stamp of the frontier on him: he plays practical jokes and performs legendary feats of strength. Still, he fears that he is illegitimate, too, and that and other woes often make him depressed. In New Salem, Herndon's Lincoln has the only love affair of his life. This is the Ann Rutledge story, a chimerical story which Herndon popularized and which subsequent biographies shamelessly repeated. In Herndon's telling, Lincoln falls deeply in love with Ann and almost goes mad when she dies. As she lies in her grave, he moans miserably, "My heart is buried there." If his heart is buried there, then he cannot possibly love Mary Todd. Herndon certainly bears her no love; in fact, he detests the woman; she is *"the female wildcat of the age."* What follows about Lincoln and Mary is mostly malicious gossip. In Springfield, Herndon's Lincoln does promise to wed Mary, only to plummet into despair. How can he marry this nasty little woman? Still, his sense of honor torments him. He has given his word. Sacrificing domestic happiness, Herndon's Lincoln goes ahead with the marriage, and Mary, a "tigress," "soured," "insolent," "haughty," and "gross," devotes herself to making Lincoln miserable. For him, life with Mary is "worse punishment . . . than burning by the stake." He finds escape in law and politics, and through adversity rises to "the topmost rung of the ladder." No haloed saint, Herndon's Lincoln in sum is a product of the great Western prairies, a religious skeptic, open, candid, energetic, trusting, and brave.

Herndon had promised that his *Lincoln* would "cause a squirm," and he was right. From across American Christendom came a fierce and unrelenting cry, "Atheist! Atheist! Herndon's an atheist!" With that, Herndon's partisans took on those of the Holland school in what David Donald has termed "a religious war." And so the two mythical conceptions—one portraying Lincoln as a frontier hero, the other as a martyr-saint—battled one another into the twentieth century.

By 1909, the centennial year of Lincoln's birth, the two traditions had begun to blend into "a composite American ideal," as Donald has said. But it remained for Carl Sandburg, in his epochal *Abraham Lincoln,* to combine the saint and folklore Lincoln and capture the mythic figure more vividly and consistently than any other folk biographer. In truth, Sandburg's became the most popular Lincoln work ever written, as a procession of plays, motion pictures, novels, children's books, school texts, and television shows purveyed Sandburg's Lincoln to a vast American public, until that Lincoln became for most Americans the real historical figure.

Yet, ironically enough, Sandburg did not set out to write an enduring epic. When he began his project in 1923, he intended only to do a Lincoln book for teenagers. He had collected Lincoln materials since his days at Lombard College in Galesburg, Illinois. Now he read voraciously in the sources, particularly in *Herndon's Lincoln.* And he retraced Lincoln's path across Illinois, chatting with plain folk as Herndon had done, looking for the Lincoln who lived in their imaginations and memories. As he worked, Sandburg strongly identified with "Abe" and even dressed, acted, and physically resembled the figure taking shape in his mind. "Like him," Sandburg said, "I am a son of the prairie, a poor boy who wandered over the land to find himself and his mission in life."

Both were commoners from Illinois, both champions of the underdog, both great storytellers, and "both poets withall," as Stuart Sherman said.

As it happened, another poet had the most influence on Sandburg as a Lincoln biographer. This was Walt Whitman, who before the Civil War had actually anticipated the kind of mythic Lincoln who subsequently emerged. In the rollicking preface to *Leaves of Grass*, first published in 1855, Whitman's Poet Hero was "the equable man," simple, generous, and large, who spoke for the common people and for national union. In 1856, with uncanny foresight, Whitman asserted that "I would be much pleased to see some heroic, shrewd, fully-informed, healthy bodied, middle-aged, beard-faced American blacksmith come down from the West across the Alleghanies, and walk into the Presidency, dressed in a clean suit of working attire, and with the tan all over his face, breast, and arms." Four years later, Republican campaign propaganda depicted the rail-splitter candidate as almost exactly such a man.

In February, 1861, Whitman saw the President-elect as he passed through New York City on his way to Washington. Lincoln's "look and gait" captivated Whitman—"his dark-brown complexion, seam'd and wrinkled yet canny-looking face, his black, bushy head of hair, disproportionately long neck, and his hands held behind him as he stood observing the people." Here was a hero fit for the author of *Leaves of Grass*. From that moment on, Whitman idolized Lincoln and insisted that only the combined genius of Plutarch, Aeschylus, and Michelangelo— "assisted by Rabelais"—could have captured Lincoln's likeness. A true portrait, in other words, must have the dimensions and powerful symbols of myth.

"He has a face like a hoosier Michel Angelo," Whitman wrote three years later, "so awful ugly it becomes beautiful, with its strange mouth, its deep cut, criss-cross lines, and its doughnut complexion." Then he wrote something that was to affect Carl Sandburg enormously: "My notion is, too, that underneath his outside smutched mannerism, and stories from third-class country bar-rooms (it is his humor,) Mr. Lincoln keeps a fountain of first-class practical telling wisdom. I do not dwell on the supposed failures of his government; he has shown, I sometimes think, an almost supernatural tact in keeping the ship afloat at all, with head steady, not only not going down, and now certain not to, but with proud and resolute spirit, and flag flying in sight of the world, menacing and high as ever." Here was the mythic "equalizer of his age and land" who inhabited Whitman's *Leaves of Grass*, a poet leader who in peace "speaks in the spirit of peace," but in war "is the most deadly force of the war."

In Lincoln, Whitman saw the archetypical Captain who was destined to lie "fallen cold and dead." And after Lincoln did fall, the poet poured out his grief in "When Lilacs Last in the Dooryard Bloom'd," a melodic farewell to the leader he loved, "O powerful western fallen star," "the sweetest, wisest soul of all my days and lands." In 1886, broken down from a stroke, this "tender mother-man" with whiskered face and luminous blue-gray eyes, smelling of soap and cologne, wearing his gray felt hat tilted straight back, gave a memorial lecture about Lincoln which he repeated almost every year until his death in 1892. It was a ritual reenactment of Lincoln's assassination, a poet's celebration of a "sane and sacred death" that filtered "into the nation and race" and gave "a cement to the whole People, subtler, more underlying, than anything in written Constitution, or courts or armies."

In Whitman's writings, Sandburg found the central themes of the life he wanted to tell. He was already publishing verse that reflected Whitman's influence and would soon be known as his heir, describing him as "the only distinguished epic poet in America." But it was Whitman's mythic vision of Lincoln that most captured Sandburg's imagination, setting many of the expectations in treatment, mood, and archetype, as Justin Kaplan has pointed out, which Sandburg would try to satisfy in his biography. "In Lincoln," Sandburg himself wrote, "the people of the United States could finally see themselves, each for himself and all together." And he intended, Sandburg said, "to take Lincoln away from the religious bigots and the professional politicians and restore him to the common people."

Sandburg became completely absorbed in his Lincoln enterprise, so much so that at times he "felt as if in a trance, saw automobiles as horses and wagons, and saw cities of brick and stone dissolve into lumber cottages and shanties." What began as a teenagers' book swelled into a massive "life and times" that took fifteen years to complete and ran to 3,765 pages in six published volumes: the two-volume *Prairie Years*, which appeared in 1928, and the four-volume *War Years*, which followed in 1939. Sandburg's was a sprawling panorama, the literary equivalent of a Cecil B. DeMille motion-picture spectacular, with Lincoln himself alternately disappearing and reappearing in a rush of crowded scenes and events. And the Lincoln that emerges is not only a composite of the patron saint and Western hero; he is democracy's mythic hero, a great commoner who rises to the White House from utter obscurity, an "All-American" President who personifies the American ideal that "a democracy can choose a man," as Sandburg writes, "set him up with power and honor, and the very act does something to the man himself, raises up new gifts, modulations, controls, outlooks, wisdoms, inside the man, so that he is something else again than he was before they sifted him out and anointed him . . . Head of the Nation."

Sandburg's *Lincoln* captured the hearts of an entire generation of Americans, a generation that came of age in the cynical twenties, with its gang wars and brassy speakeasies, unbridled speculation and declining moral values, and that struggled through the Great Depression of the thirties, the worst crisis of American democracy since the Civil War. Small wonder that Sandburg won near universal acclaim. For poet Stephen Vincent Benét, Sandburg's "mountain range of biography" was "a good purge for our own troubled time and for its wild-eyed fears. For here we see the thing working, clumsily, erratically, often unfairly, attacked and reviled by extremists of left and right, yet working and surviving nevertheless." For Henry Bertram Hill of the Kansas City *Star*, Sandburg's Lincoln was "an apotheosis of the American people as well as of Lincoln as the greatest exemplar of their essential worth and goodness." For historian Henry Steele Commager, poets had always understood Lincoln best, and so it was "fitting that from the pen of a poet should come the greatest of all Lincoln biographies." For playwright Robert E. Sherwood, it was "a monument that would live forever."

Yet, as some critics pointed out, Sandburg's Lincoln could not be regarded as authentic biography, as an approximation of the real-life Lincoln based on accurate detail. No, Sandburg was not after that Lincoln. He was after the mythic figure—the Man of the People who had always fascinated him the most. And proven fact and sound documentation did not impede the poet in his search. "He suggests," as one critic said, "a bard sitting before a rude fireplace, chanting his hero tale with a poet's repetitions and refrains."

As *The Prairie Years* open, we find the future Head of the Nation born of ordinary pioneer stock on the cutting edge of the Kentucky frontier. What follows is a gripping story, a poetic story, and it abounds in fictional scenes and lyrical apocrypha. As a boy, Sandburg's Lincoln shucks corn from early dawn till sundown and then reads books all night by the flickering fire. He kisses Green Taylor's girl. He once fights William Grigsby and cries out (as did Herndon's Lincoln), "I'm the big buck of this lick." He lifts barefoot boys so they can leave muddy footprints on the ceiling of the Lincoln cabin. Later, as a New Salem clerk, he walks six miles to return a few cents a customer has overpaid on her bill. And, of course, he loves Ann Rutledge with an aching heart. "After the first evening in which Lincoln had sat next to her and found that bashful words tumbling from his tongue's end really spelled themselves out into sensible talk, her face, as he went away, kept coming back. So often all else would fade out of his mind and there would be only this riddle of a pink-fair face, a mouth and eyes in a frame of light corn-silk hair. He could ask

himself what it meant and search his heart for an answer and no
answer would come. A trembling took his body and dark waves
ran through him sometimes when she spoke so simple a thing as,
'The corn is getting high, isn't it?' " Which prompted Edmund
Wilson to remark, "The corn is getting high indeed!"

When Ann dies, Sandburg's Lincoln, like Herndon's, is
stricken with a lover's grief: he wanders absently in the forest; he
makes his way to the burying ground outside New Salem and lies
with an arm across Ann's grave. "In the evenings it was useless
to try to talk with him," Sandburg writes. "He sat by the fire one
night as the flames licked up the cordwood and swept up the
chimney to pass out into a driving storm-wind. The blowing
weather woke some sort of lights in him and he went to the door
and looked out into a night of fierce stumbling wind and black
horizons. And he came back saying, 'I can't bear to think of her
out there alone.' And he clenched his hands, mumbling, 'The rain
and the storm shan't beat on her grave.' "

Though he eventually recovers from Ann's death, Sandburg's
Lincoln never forgets the love he felt for her.*

As he grows to maturity, Sandburg's Lincoln is indigenously
American, utterly shaped by the sprawling, unruly, pungent democracy of his day. He is simple, honest and ambitious, practical
and wise. Professionally he is a homespun village lawyer and politician, always dressed in a rumpled suit and an old stovepipe hat.
It is noticed among men that he has "two shifting moods," one
when he lapses into "a gravity beyond any bystander to pene-
trate," the other when he recounts a "rollicking, droll story,"
usually to illustrate some point about people or politics. In the
company of his male friends, he can tell off-color jokes, too, and

*There is not a scintilla of evidence for Sandburg's scenes about Lincoln and Ann.
In fairness, though, Sandburg did delete a lot of this material in a one-volume
condensation of the *Prairie* and *War Years*. But even there he persists in suggesting
a romance between Lincoln and Ann and even quotes Edgar Lee Master's ridiculous
poem about how Ann Rutledge, "beloved in life of Abraham Lincoln," was wedded
to him in her grave. Later Sandburg was sorry that he had fallen for the legend. He
should have known it was out of character for Lincoln, he said.

indulge in an expletive like "son-of-a-bitch." He is a colorful and yet mystic man, a kind of prairie Socrates brimming with wilderness wit and prairie sagacity. Above all, his heart beats with the pulse of rural, working-class America, and he loves the common folk and revels in daily contact with them.

But behind his bucolic plainness is a profound and mystical spirit awaiting its call to greatness. And that call comes in the grim and terrible years that follow the Kansas-Nebraska Act of 1854. Now Sandburg's Lincoln is a ghost on the platform, explaining to the people that the Revolution and freedom really mean something and reminding them of forgotten oaths and wasted sacrifices. In his great debates with Stephen A. Douglas, Sandburg's Lincoln is always one with the people, thrilling them with his "stubby, homely words." For the folk masses, he is both "the Strange Friend and Friendly Stranger." He is "something out of a picture book for children"—tall, bony, comical, haunted-looking, and sad. Already stories about him are spreading among the plain folk, and many sit brooding and talking about this "fabulous human figure of their own time." By 1861, history has called him to his tragic destiny: his is "a mind, a spirit, a tongue, and a voice" for an American democracy caught in its greatest trial. As he leaves Illinois for Washington, the presidency, and the war years, voices cry out on the wind, "Good-bye, Abe."

When he wrote *The War Years*, Sandburg abandoned poetical imaginings and produced a kind of symphonic documentary of the war and the man at its center. Though marred by a plethora of unauthenticated scenes and stories, the four volumes are full of the blood and stench—the sound and fury—of Civil War. And they capture all the immense tumult and confusion through which Lincoln day by day had to make his way. When we see the President, in between extensive passages on military and political developments in North and South alike, he is entirely an external Lincoln, an observed hero filtered to us through the vision and sensibilities of hundreds of witnesses who called at his White House office, from generals and politicians and office seekers to the infirm, the destitute, and the ordinary. By revealing Lincoln through the observations of others and relating him to almost everything that happened in his shell-torn land, Sandburg is trying to demonstrate that "the hopes and apprehensions of millions, their loves and hates, their exultation and despair, were reflected truthfully in the deep waters of Lincoln's being," as Robert Sherwood said.

In the "tornado years" of civil war, Sandburg's Lincoln is both the hero and the instrument of the people. He is the umpire of an embattled Union, patiently sticking to the cherished middle way. When it comes to emancipation, he always follows the pulse of the people: with a genius for timing, he issues his proclamation only when that is what they want. Now "a piece of historic drama" has been played, and across the world, among the masses of people who create folk gods out of slender fact, there runs the story of "the Strong Man who arose in his might and delivered an edict, spoke a few words fitly chosen, and thereupon the shackles and chains fell from the arms and ankles of men, women, and children born to be chattels for toil and bondage."

As the war rages on, Lincoln's "skilled referee hand" guides the ship of state through cross winds of passion and cross plays of hate. Throughout he has the folk masses behind him. He is still their Friendly Stranger in a storm of death and destruction. Even during his lowest ebb in 1864, he remains the people's President: he retains their love and loyalty even as Republican leaders raise a howl against his renomination and reelection. And he wins in 1864 because the wisdom of the people prevails.

Moreover, in the last long year of the war, Sandburg's Lincoln does battle with the so-called radicals of the party—vindictive cynics like Charles Sumner and old Thad Stevens, who in Sandburg's view want to exterminate the South's ruling class and convert Dixie into "a vast graveyard of slaughtered whites, with Negro State governments established and upheld by Northern white bayonets." But a mild and moderate Lincoln refuses to go along with them. He is now in his grandest hour, this Lincoln of

The War Years, as he plans to reconstruct the South with tender magnanimity. He is the only man in the entire country who can peaceably reunite the sections. But, as in a Greek tragedy, Lincoln is murdered before he can bind up the nation's wounds and heal the antagonisms of his divided countrymen. In North and South, common people weep aloud, realizing the painful truth of the old folk adage that a tree is measured best when it is down.

"To a deep river," writes Sandburg, "to a far country, to a by-and-by whence no man returns, had gone the child of Nancy Hanks and Tom Lincoln, the wilderness boy who found far lights and tall rainbows to live by, whose name even before he died had become a legend inwoven with men's struggle for freedom the world over." There was the story of how Count Leo Tolstoy, traveling into the Caucasus of czarist Russia, encountered tribesmen demanding to know about Lincoln, the "greatest general and greatest ruler of the world." Says Sandburg: "To Tolstoy the incident proved that in far places over the earth the name of Lincoln was worshipped and the personality of Lincoln had become a world folk legend."

Sandburg ended his narrative with Lincoln's funeral in Springfield. But others have added an epilogue implied by Sandburg's story. Without Father Abraham, the epilogue goes, the nation foundered in the harsh years of reconstruction, as an all-too-mortal President succumbed to "vengeful radicals" on Capitol Hill. Alas, how much better reconstruction would have been had Father Abraham only lived. How much more easily a divided nation would have set aside the war years and come together again in a spirit of mutual respect and harmony. There would never have been an impeachment trial, never a radical reconstruction, never an army of occupation, never a Ku Klux Klan, never all those racial troubles to haunt later generations, if only Father Abraham had not died that terrible day in 1865.

And so Lincoln comes to us in the mists of mythology. Still, I have no quarrel with this Lincoln, so long as we make a careful distinction between myth and history. Myth, after all, is not an untrue story to be avoided like some dread disease. On the contrary, myth carries a special truth of its own—a truth, however, that is different from historical truth, from what actually happened. In the case of Lincoln, the myth is what Americans wish the man had been, not necessarily the way he was in real life. That is why Sandburg's Lincoln has such irresistible appeal to us. He is a "baffling and completely inexplicable" hero who embodies the mystical genius of our nation. He possesses what Americans have always considered their most noble traits—honesty, unpretentiousness, tolerance, hard work, a capacity to forgive, a compassion for the underdog, a clear-sighted vision of right and wrong, a dedication to God and country, and an abiding concern for all. As I have said elsewhere, no real-life person has ever risen to such mythic proportions, to epitomize all that we have longed to be since 1776. No real-life person can ever rise to such proportions. So we have invented a Lincoln who fulfills our deepest needs as a people—a Father Abraham who in the stormy present still provides an example and shows us the way. The Lincoln of mythology carries the torch of the American dream, a dream of noble idealism, of self-sacrifice and common humanity, of liberty and equality for all.

Our folly as a nation, though, is that we too often confuse myth with history, mistake our mythologized heroes for their real-life counterparts, regard the deified frontiersman as the actual frontiersman. As a consequence, we too often try to emulate our mythical forebears, to be as glorious, as powerful, as incapable of error, as incessantly right, as we have made them. As journalist Ronnie Dugger has reminded us, those who live by the lessons of mythology rather than the lessons of history—as Lyndon Johnson did in the Vietnam era—are apt to trap themselves in catastrophe.

This is not to say that myths have no function in our cultural life. On the contrary, if we Americans can accept our myths as inspiring tales rather than as authentic history, then surely myths can serve us as they have traditional myth-bound societies. Like fiction and poetry, they can give us insight into ourselves, help us understand the spiritual needs of our country, as we cope with the complex realities of our own time. In that event, the Lincoln of mythology—the Plain and Humble Man of the People who emerged from the toiling millions to guide us through our greatest national ordeal—can have profound spiritual meaning for us.

2: ARCH VILLAIN

From the flames of civil war rose a countermyth of Lincoln as villain—corrupt, depraved, and diabolical. This "anti-Lincoln tradition," as historian Don E. Fehrenbacher has termed it, has never commanded a large following in the United States, but it has persisted. In 1932, at a time when most Americans—even members of the Ku Klux Klan—were trying to "get right with Lincoln," a prominent old Virginian was still fighting a personal war against him, condemning the martyr President as a "bad man" who brought on "an unnecessary war and conducted it with great inhumanity."

The countermyth of a wicked Lincoln had roots back in the Civil War, when the beleaguered President caught abuse from all sides. Northern Democrats castigated him as an abolitionist dictator, abolitionists as a dim-witted product of a slave state, and all manner of Republicans as an incompetent charlatan. In truth, Lincoln may have been one of the two or three most unpopular *living* Presidents in American history. Assassination, though, chastened his legion of critics and brought them swiftly into the ranks of the glorifiers. Historian and Democrat George Bancroft, who had damned Lincoln during the war, made "scholarly, ringing tributes" to him in the funeral services in New York City. And

the intemperate New York *Herald*, which had once denigrated
Lincoln as "the great ghoul at Washington," now referred to him
as "Mr. Lincoln" and claimed that historians a "hundred years
hence" would still be astounded at his greatness.

The Lincoln-as-demon theme stuck harder and longer in embattled Dixie. After all, southerners had seceded from the Union
to save their slave-based social order from Lincoln's grasp. They
hated the man. In rebel eyes, he was the black-hearted radical who
had fomented the war. He was a Yankee Attila, a mobocrat, a
lunatic, the biggest "ass" in the United States, the evil chief of
the "Black Republican, free love, free Nigger" North out to
drown the white man's South in rivers of blood. When Lincoln
issued his Emancipation Proclamation, the Confederate press pronounced him a "Fiend" who wanted to incite a race war in Dixie;
Jefferson Davis considered the proclamation "the most execrable
measure recorded in the history of guilty man," and rebels everywhere vowed to fight all the harder against the monster who had
issued it. When Lincoln was assassinated, many southerners regretted the manner of his death, fretting that the Yankees would
blame them for it and punish them cruelly. But many other
southerners rejoiced at the news. "All honor to J. Wilkes Booth,"
a Louisiana woman said, "who has rid the world of a tyrant and
made himself famous for generations." Exclaimed the Houston
Tri-Weekly Telegraph: "From now until God's judgment day, the
minds of men will not cease to thrill at the killing of Abraham
Lincoln."

After the war, southerners who grieved bitterly over the Lost
Cause continued to hate Lincoln for what he had done to them.
For Elizabeth Avery Meriwether of Mississippi, the northern
deification of Lincoln was more than she could stand. "Is it
insanity or pure mendacity," she cried, "to liken a man of this
nature to the gentle and loving Nazarene?" Was Lincoln tender-
hearted, she wanted to know, when his legions devastated the
South, laid waste to Georgia, and drove thousands of women and
children from their homes? "Did he once, during the four years

of the cruel war, utter or write one kind word of the people on whom *he* had brought such unspeakable misery?" An ex-Confederate bureaucrat, after reading a northern biography of Lincoln, sneered that "the whole story of his career from beginning to end is so dreary, so wretched, so shabby, such a tissue of pitiful dodging and chicanery, so unrelieved by anything pure, noble, or dignified, that even to follow it as far as we have done, has well-nigh surpassed our limits of endurance." For Charleston poet Paul Hamilton Hayne, Lincoln remained in 1871 a "gawky, coarse, not-over cleanly, whisky drinking, and whisky smelling Blackguard, elevated by grotesque *Chance* (nearly allied to *Satan*) to the position for which of all others, he was most unfit;—and whose memory has been *idealized* by the Yankee fancy, & Yankee arrogance, in a way that *would* be ludicrous, were it not *disgusting,* and calculated, finally, to belie the facts of History, and hand down to future times as Hero and Martyr, as commonplace a *Vulgarian* as ever patronized bad Tobacco and mistook *blasphemy* for *wit.*"

In 1909, with most southerners joining the North in celebrating the centennial of Lincoln's birth, a Confederate veteran told a diehard band of ex-rebels in Richmond that the whole Lincoln story *"amounts to a patent perversion of the truth, and a positive fraud on the public."* The historian-general of the Confederate Southern Memorial Association, one Mildred Lewis Rutherford, thought so too. In the 1920s, she led a crusade to get pro-Yankee histories out of southern schools and to tell southern kids the truth about Lincoln—namely, that he was a slaveowner, that he tried to starve American troops as a quartermaster during the Mexican War, and that he gave $100 for John Brown's heinous raid against Harpers Ferry in Virginia. In 1959, after the Brown decision and the Montgomery bus boycott inaugurated the civil-rights movement in Dixie, the son of a rebel veteran launched a neo-Confederate attack against Lincoln, pummeling him as the country's first dictator whose radical policies had annihilated the "civilized, beneficial, humane" arrangement wrongly known as "slavery." "The real monument to the Great Emancipator is the maiming of the United States Constitution," the man wrote, "and the imposition upon the nation of a Negro race problem that progressively grows."

The countermyth, of course, was hardly confined to the southern states. In *Lincoln: The Man* (1931), Edgar Lee Masters, a Chicago lawyer and poet, portrayed Lincoln as an undersexed, "slick" and dastardly demagogue who could have avoided war, but instead crushed the South into submission, in the process obliterating state rights, destroying "the principles of free government," and clearing the way for industrial monopolies and rampant corruption. More recently, a California political scientist served up a psychoanalytical study which revealed a "demonic" Lincoln driven by vengefulness, self-hatred, and a lust for power. Because the constitutional fathers had "preempted the field of glory," Lincoln took revenge against them: he became the "very tyrant against whom Washington had warned in his Farewell Address, a tyrant who would preside over the destruction of the Constitution in order to gratify his own ambition." He unleashed his "malignant passions" on the southern rebels, whom he forced to start the Civil War at Fort Sumter, and then became a virtual dictator. Worse still, in his posturing as God's instrument to save the Union, the satanic Lincoln bequeathed a disastrous legacy to twentieth-century Americans: the ideological rationale for their efforts to save the world.

In part, the extravagance of such countermythology comes from the size of the god it seeks to destroy. Yet not all Lincoln critics have seized the countermyth to bring Lincoln down to size. Plenty of Lincoln scholars have questioned the man, exposed his shortcomings, without denying his essential idealism and humanity. But there is a class of gossipy iconoclasm that falls in between critical scholarship and the extremes of countermythology. A good example of that class is Gore Vidal, novelist, essayist, and talk-show personality, who recently announced in the Los Angeles *Times* that he had the angle on the "real" Lincoln. And it was not "the Sandburg–Mt. Rushmore Lincoln," a "gloomy cuss, who speaks in iambic pentameter, a tear forever at the corner of his eye—the result, no doubt, of being followed by the Mormon Tabernacle Choir which keeps humming 'the Battle Hymn of the Republic.' " The real Lincoln, it turns out, was a shrewd and crafty politician. But he had a serious problem. Dredging up and embellishing one of Herndon's raunchier tales, Vidal maintained that Lincoln caught syphilis in his youth and that this accounts for his fits of depression: he infected poor Mary, who later came down with paresis, and three of their children, who died prematurely. Such prattle tells us more about Vidal than about Lincoln, for there is not a shred of truth to it.*

3: WHITE CHIEF AND HONKY

There is another countermyth of Lincoln—one shared by many white southerners and certain black Americans of our time. This is the myth of Lincoln as bigot, as a lifelong white supremacist who championed segregation, opposed civil and political rights for black people, wanted them all thrown out of the country. This Lincoln is the great ancestor of racist James K. Vardaman of Mississippi, of Bull Connor of Birmingham, of the white citizens' councils, of the Knights of the Ku Klux Klan.

This Lincoln, growing out of post–Civil War Dixie, derived

*Nor is there any truth to the persistent gossip that John C. Calhoun (or possibly Henry Clay) was Lincoln's real father. After my life of Lincoln appeared in 1977, I received several letters chastising me for not stating that the great Calhoun had authored Lincoln. Where else could he have gotten his political skills and eloquence? This assumes, of course, that somehow, somewhere (a haystack in Virginia or Kentucky?), Senator Calhoun and Nancy Hanks fooled around and the result was the future Head of the Nation. Of all the fanciful notions about Lincoln, this is the most preposterous. Thomas Lincoln was Lincoln's father, period.

from the principle that a foe of Lincoln's dimensions was best converted to a friend. Undertaking a highly selective examination of Lincoln's antebellum utterances, many southerners happily concluded that he stood with them in matters of race. The leading proponent of this Lincoln was Thomas Dixon, Jr., the scion of an old North Carolina family, a spellbinding preacher and practicing novelist, as tall, gaunt, and dark as the rail splitter himself. In novels like *The Clansman* (1905) and *The Southerner* (1913), Dixon elevated Lincoln to a Christ-like hero, southern-style. What ennobled him was not his humanity or his faith in democracy. It was his belief in the purity of the white race. In Dixon's hands, Lincoln is a fine southern gentleman who is certain that "this black thing"—the Negro—cannot possibly be a man because "no real man would grin and laugh and be a slave." Like his southern brothers, Dixon's Lincoln adamantly opposes amalgamation, which means Africanization, the supremacy of "the big nostrils, flat nose, massive jaw, protruding lips and kinky hair" over "the proudest intellect and the rarest beauty of any other race." When the Civil War ends, Lincoln, "the Great Heart," is determined to prevent racial catastrophe: he sets out to reconstruct his native South with kindness and understanding; he hopes to "heal the bitterness of the war and remove the negro race from physical contact with the white." What a blow to the South, then, when Booth guns him down in Ford's Theater. "The Angel of Death," Dixon writes, now "called him to take the place he had won among earth's immortals and left to us 'the gentlest memory of our world.'"

During the Wilsonian era, a growing number of southerners embraced Dixon's Lincoln as a true son of Dixie. Kentucky-born D. W. Griffith, the son of a Confederate cavalryman, popularized that Lincoln in his epic motion picture *The Birth of a Nation*. And Senator James K. Vardaman of Mississippi, the dramatic "White Chief" who dressed in white, wore his dark hair to his shoulders, and mesmerized white Mississippians with his strident defense of segregation, informed the United States Senate that Lincoln was as racist as he. Vardaman quoted what this "wise and wondrous" man had said in Charleston, Illinois, in his 1858 debates with Stephen A. Douglas. "I will say then," Vardaman sang out, reading from Lincoln's speech, "that I am not nor ever have been in favor of bringing about in any way the social and political equality of the white and black races,—that I am not nor ever have been in favor of making voters or jurors of negroes, nor of qualifying them to hold office, nor to intermarry with white people; and I will say in addition to this that there is a physical difference between the white and blacks races which I believe will for ever forbid the two races living together on terms of social and political equality. And inasmuch as they cannot so live . . . I as much as any other man am in favor of having the superior position assigned to the white race."

Never mind that Lincoln had said this only after Douglas had persistently accused him of desiring Negro equality and intermarriage in white-supremacist Illinois. Never mind that in those same debates Lincoln had declared that the Negro was a man, that he was entitled to the same inalienable rights as whites, and that he was equal to anybody in his right to the fruits of his labor—all of which were radical remarks in the Illinois of 1858.

Disregarding all that (as Dixon did), Vardaman declared that it was "the hope of Lincoln that physical segregation of the races might be brought about for the good of both races." For Lincoln understood, as Vardaman did, that the Negro had "never built a monument, created a civilization, or added one truth to the sum total of human intelligence," that "equality at the ballot box means negro domination," and that "for the good of all the races the white man must rule this Republic and he must rule it absolutely."

In more recent times, the tradition of Lincoln as Negrophobe found near hysterical expression during the civil-rights movement of the 1950s and 1960s, when Martin Luther King, Jr., shook the segregationist South to its foundations. Because King gave his lyrical "I Have a Dream" speech at the Lincoln Memorial in

Washington, because he repeatedly quoted Lincoln and tried to convert President John F. Kennedy into a modern emancipator, enraged southern whites bombarded him with letters purporting to set King straight about "Abe." Invariably they cited his speech at Charleston. *See,* they ranted at King, *Lincoln hated niggers too. He too wanted segregation. He too believed only in the white race.* A Georgia white who sent King a list of Lincoln quotations said "it should do you lots of good to read and reread this and thoroughly digest it. And, if you are as brilliant as YOU think, you will cease your agitation of the white people who are without a doubt reaching a point of disgust." Another Lincoln quoter was more direct: "I don't believe in lynchings, but before I start living together with niggers, before I sit next to them in movies, before I see intermarriages, before I send my children to school with blacks, before I am forced by the Supreme Court with its communistic decisions to socialize with you people, I'm getting my gun."

Among blacks, meanwhile, an astonishing metamorphosis was taking place as far as Lincoln was concerned. Heretofore blacks had almost universally idolized him as one white leader who had cared for them. Heretofore they had almost always found inspiration and hope in the Lincoln story. In the South, they celebrated every January 1, Emancipation Day, with stemwinding oratory. One Negro leader recalled that while growing up in Chicago in the 1940s he read all six volumes of Sandburg's *Lincoln.* It "overwhelmed me," he said—"the images of Lincoln's poverty, the agony of social change. In the days of reading those volumes, I walked through the cold park, thinking and pondering about the meaning of life. Sandburg's book absorbed me for weeks." When the civil-rights struggles broke out in the 1950s and 1960s, black spokesmen like King found Lincoln a powerful ally. Established black scholars like Benjamin Quarles and John Hope Franklin, while admitting that Lincoln had once been ambivalent about Negro social and political rights, nevertheless admired the man and wrote sympathetically about his travail as President. They pointed out that Lincoln had always hated slavery, that his views of blacks changed dramatically during the Civil War, and that his Emancipation Proclamation (as Quarles said) was "one of the most far-reaching pronouncements ever issued in the United States."

But in the mid-sixties, with cries of "Black Power!" and "Black is beautiful" sweeping their ranks, a younger generation of Negroes wanted "none of that Emancipator shit." They were furious at the glacial pace of desegregation, furious at the broken promises of white America, furious at all the racial violence in Dixie and the searing poverty in the northern ghettoes. Out of their disillusionment with America, out of their own quest for black identity and black pride, came a black fist that knocked Lincoln off his pedestal. In *Look Out, Whitey! Black Power's Gon' Get Your Mama!* artist-activist Julius Lester caught the new mood when he asserted that "blacks have no reason to feel grateful to Abraham Lincoln. Rather, they should be angry with him."

And angry they were. In a sensational 1968 article in *Ebony* magazine, Negro writer-historian Lerone Bennett, Jr., mounted an all-out attack against "the myth of the Great Emancipator." Marshaling evidence as selectively as Dixon and Vardaman had done, Bennett offered up a racially repugnant Lincoln who never rose above the anti-black environments in which he was born and raised. Bennett's Lincoln is a rank opportunist who cackles at Negro dialect jokes. He is not opposed to slavery, Bennett asserts; he is opposed to the *extension* of slavery. But not because of any compassion for suffering Negroes. His sole concern is the welfare of white people. His speech at Charleston reveals his attitude about black social and political rights, and his vaunted eloquence of the 1850s is aimed at saving "the white man's charter of liberty," which is what he calls the Declaration of Independence.

Bennett's Lincoln does grow during the Civil War, but he doesn't grow much. On every issue relating to the black man, he is "the very essence of the white supremacist with good intentions." Indeed, he spends the first eighteen months of the conflict "in a desperate and rather pathetic attempt to save slavery," because that is where his heart is. Blacks to him are "unassimilable aliens," and if he has an emancipation policy, Bennett contends, it is to drive them all out of the country.

When the pressures of the war force Lincoln to move against slavery, he issues a "cold, forbidding" decree "with all the grandeur of a real estate deed." But the slaves, and subsequent generations of Negroes, have been duped. The Emancipation Proclamation, so celebrated in song and story, actually frees few if any bondsmen, since it applies only to rebellious states beyond Lincoln's authority.* In fact, Bennett says, Lincoln may have issued this anemic document to outflank congressional "radicals" and forestall definitive emancipation. White supremacist that he is, Bennett's Lincoln announces a reconstruction policy that will put whites only in power in postwar Dixie. And to his dying day, he promotes colonization to solve "the Negro problem."

So much for the "Massa Linkun" myth. "In the final analysis," Bennett writes, "Lincoln must be seen as the embodiment, not the transcendence, of the American tradition, which is, as we all know, a racist tradition. In his inability to rise above that tradition, Lincoln, often called 'the noblest of all Americans,' holds up a flawed mirror to the American soul."

Delete "flawed," and there is nothing in Bennett's remarks with which Dixon, Vardaman, or King's ranting correspondents would disagree. That angry blacks and white segregationists should embrace the same Lincoln myth is one of the great ironies of modern race relations.

By the 1970s and 1980s, Lincoln as honky had become the conventional wisdom among younger blacks, particularly in the academies, and among disillusioned whites too. The most impassioned debunking of the Great Emancipator came from the pen of Vincent Harding, a black historian who had marched with Martin Luther King, taught at Spelman College, and plunged

---

*A view held by certain white scholars, too, but for a different reason. For them, this illustrates his admirable conservatism and legalistic approach.

into the radical black-studies movement that had burst forth on college campuses. In 1982, Harding published *There Is a River* to rave notices from prominent black and white Americans. The "river" in the title is a metaphor for the black struggle for freedom, a self-liberating struggle in which blacks themselves had defined their freedom, fought and died for it, from the colonial era down to 1865 (a second volume will trace the struggle to the present).

For blacks, slave and free alike, God Himself was directing their long and continuous movement toward the Promised Land. Thus when the Civil War broke out, they saw it as the coming of Judgment Day. For them, Harding writes, "all the raucous, roaring guns of Charleston Harbor and Bull Run, of Antietam and Fort Pillow, of Shiloh and Murfreesboro and Richmond were the certain voice of God, announcing his judgment across the bloody stretches of the South, returning blood for blood to the black river." In the North, blacks surged forward to volunteer in Union armies, because they equated the cause of the free states with the cause of freedom. In the South, the war broadened the river of struggle, intensified "the self-liberating black movement" that had long gone on, as slaves escaped to Union lines by the thousands, running "toward a new history, a new life, a new beginning. . . . Their God was moving and they moved with him."

The villain of this story, of course, is Abraham Lincoln. He had not seen the visions of black people, Harding writes, "had not yet rightly measured 'the judgments of the Lord,' the movements of Providence." Like Bennett's Lincoln, Harding's is a dedicated white supremacist afflicted with tunnel vision. His obsession with saving the white Union "at all costs" blinds him to the spiritual and revolutionary nature of the conflict. He cares nothing for black people. For two years he will not let them serve in his armies, will not adopt an emancipation policy, lest that offend his "tender allies" in the "loyal" slave border. But the slaves could not care less. They swarm into Union lines in relentlessly increasing numbers, until Lincoln's armies find themselves "in the midst of a surging movement of black people" who in effect are "freeing themselves from slavery."

But then a harried Lincoln steps in and steals all their glory. Mainly to justify the use of the South's black "property" in his military forces, he issues an "ambiguous," restricted Emancipation Proclamation, which from "a certain legal view" sets free no slaves at all. Alas, though, the proclamation symbolizes all that blacks have "so deeply longed to experience," and it sends "a storm of long pent-up emotions surging through the churches and meeting halls."

Their rapture is understandable, Harding writes, "but like all ecstatic experiences, it carried its own enigmatic penalties." In his view, the Emancipation Proclamation was one of the worst things that ever happened to black people in this country. For the joy with which Civil War Negroes greeted the proclamation produced the myth of Lincoln as the Great Emancipator. It was an ugly irony. "While the concrete historical realities of the time testified to the costly, daring, courageous activities of hundreds of thousands of black people breaking loose from slavery and setting themselves free, the myth gave the credit for this freedom to a white Republican president" who never saw beyond the limitations of his own race, class, and time. "Yet thanks to the mythology of blacks and whites alike, it was the independent, radical action of the black movement toward freedom which was diminished, and the coerced, ambiguous role of a white deliverer which gained pre-eminence." For the development of black struggle and black radicalism, Harding says, the consequences of this myth were many and profound.

To emancipate today's Afro-Americans from the shackles of that myth, Harding has created an alternative myth, writing in a musical style that radiates the voice of soul. Here is how his message might be summarized: *Far from being the passive recipients of freedom, as white history has so long described them, our heroic, blood-stained forebears were gaining it for themselves dur-*

ing the Civil War. Yes, we were winning our own freedom, were forging a black radical consensus that could have liberated us from dependence on the white-man's Union. We didn't need Lincoln, didn't need the racist North, didn't need any white man. Had Lincoln not usurped our movement, misdirecting our river into waters he could control, we might have been freer, more independent, more radical and revolutionary, from then until now. Certainly this would not have been the country it became. For the sake of our liberation today, let us recapture what Lincoln took away from us in the Civil War. Let us carry on where our forefathers left off in the blood-red baptism of fire, and let us designate them, not Lincoln, as the instrument of our deliverance.

This is a potent myth, born of deep spiritual and psychological needs in black America that command our attention. Indeed, Harding is the black counterpart of Whitman and Sandburg. In Harding's mythic vision, Lincoln was not the poet hero of democracy. The true poet heroes were the immortal black masses who flung off their chains and seized their own freedom. A black radical and ideologue, Harding is offering today's Negro Americans his idea of a usable past, a way to feel as one with their slave forebears. "The river of black struggle is people," Harding writes, "but it is also the hope, the movement, the transformative power that humans create and that creates them, us, and makes them, us, new persons. So we black people are the river; the river is us. The river is in us, created by us, flowing out of us, surrounding us, re-creating us and this entire nation."

This vividly illustrates what critic Northrop Frye said of myth —that it is "the imitation of actions near or at the conceivable limits of desire." Yet it is a great pity, I think, that in order to build up his Civil War ancestors for the benefit of modern blacks, Harding felt obliged to tear down, not just the myth of the Great Emancipator, but the actual Lincoln of history.

But, some will say, are blacks not as entitled to their notions of Lincoln as white America is to the Man of the People? And is the Lincoln of Harding's *River* not preferable to the idea of the

saintly Emancipator, which obscures the heroic role that blacks
played in their own liberation?

That may be so, but the myth of the Great Emancipator and
the Man of the People does not defile the historical Lincoln.
Harding's portrait, like Bennett's, reduces him to a racist carica-
ture, stripping him of any complexity, any idealism, and any
humanity. And this is all the more regrettable because Harding,
a historian, really does believe that his glory-stealing white supremacist is the real Lincoln, and many blacks and whites are
certain to take this as historical gospel.

For the country at large, though, the scoundrelly Lincoln is in
no danger of replacing Sandburg's icon of democracy, for that
Lincoln still holds first place in the pantheon of American immortals. It is Sandburg's Lincoln who is quoted in the White House
and in Congress, that Lincoln who is produced on national television, that Lincoln who is held up as the unattainable standard for
anybody who undertakes a modern biography. Again, that Lincoln
has such staying power because he is a larger-than-life mirror of
ourselves, a god we have created in our idealized image of democratic man. As long as we believe in America, we will have towering Father Abraham as our greatest mythical hero. And as long
as he is that hero, he will remain a powerful presence to be
reckoned with.

Part Two

MANY-MOODED MAN

I made my song a coat
Covered with embroideries
Out of old mythologies
From heel to throat;
But the fools caught it,
Wore it in the world's eyes
As though they'd wrought it.
Song, let them take it,
For there's more enterprise
In walking naked.

WILLIAM BUTLER YEATS

1: RESURRECTING LIFE

I suggested that the myths of Lincoln reveal a great deal about our needs and longings as a people. But the real Lincoln, the actual man of history, can also have profound significance for us. For "history," as Michelet said, "is a reconstruction of life in its wholeness, not of the superficial aspects, but of the deeper, inner organic processes." By the historical Lincoln I do not mean some definitive portrait that will stand forever as the way he really was. Historical biography, after all, is an interpretative art, not an exact science. In fact, the very materials we rely on to forge biography —letters, diaries, journals, interviews, recollections, and the like —were all recorded by people who filtered things through their own senses and sensibilities. Because biographical materials are themselves imprecise and interpretative, it is impossible for anyone to produce a definitive biography—a fixed and final portrait —of Lincoln or any other figure.

As we strive for biographical truth, the best we can hope for is a careful approximation of what Lincoln was like in the days he lived. To arrive at that approximation, the Lincoln biographer must be painstaking in his pursuit of evidence—of Lincoln's own writings and all the other records germane to his life and times. Wary and skeptical of witnesses, the Lincoln biographer plays them off against one another, testing their reliability, until he can corroborate with some degree of accuracy. Then on the basis of authenticated detail, he begins to shape his portrait of the real-life man, striving to depict Lincoln in the context of *his* time, not according to the needs of the present. Moreover, since biographers are people, too, it is possible to offer several authentic approximations of the historical Lincoln, each portrait depending on the biographer's own inferences, insights, sense of importance, and conception of character.

In my own efforts to see the man as he was, I have tried to present an accurate and coherent characterization, one that draws from a vast array of reliable contemporary evidence and from a cornucopia of modern Lincoln scholarship. Not everyone will agree with my portrait. Many would paint Lincoln with different shades and hues, would stress this or that about him more or less than I. But perhaps we can agree that an effort to see Lincoln free of the mists of legend and counterlegend, to understand the man on his own terms and in the context of his age, is a beneficial enterprise. And the portrait that emerges contrasts sharply with the lofty Man of the People and the unswerving villain and racist sketched earlier.

2: A MATTER OF PROFOUND WONDER

Had we met Lincoln in his Springfield law office during the 1850s, we would have looked on a man in his forties, dressed well enough in a plain linen suit and boots. His feet were so large—size fourteen—that he had to have his boots specially made. He weighed 180 pounds and stood six feet four inches, an extraordinary height for those days, and it was all in his legs. When he was sitting, he was no taller than an average man; but when he stood, he kept rising until he towered over his friends as though he were standing on stilts. And he loomed taller still when he put on his stovepipe hat.

Parts of him did not seem to fit. His head appeared too small for his height, and his chest was narrow and thin in contrast to his long arms and legs, his huge hands and feet. His black hair was so coarse and unruly that it "lay floating where the fingers or the wind left it," Herndon said.

His gray eyes sparkled as he said "howdy" and shook hands with both of his. His hands were bony and rough—the hands of a man who had known hard physical toil in his youth. He had a dark leathery complexion, with a mole on his right cheek; large ears; and a scrawny neck with a conspicuous Adam's apple. His neck was too thin to fill the collar of his dress shirt, even when it was pulled tight with a black cravat.

We might have thought his face much more subtle and complex than his photographs reveal. "I have never seen a picture of him that does anything like justice to the original," said a young journalist. "He is a much better looking man than any of the pictures represent." A young southern woman agreed. "His face is certainly ugly, but not repulsive," she said; "on the contrary, the good humor, generosity and intellect beaming from it, make the eye love to linger there until you almost find him good-looking."

Had we talked at length with Lincoln, we might have thought he epitomized what a French philosopher once said: "No man is strongly marked unless he bears within his character antitheses strongly marked." Lincoln certainly had that. He was "a many mooded man," Herndon observed, "a man of opposites—of terrible contrasts"—now witty and outgoing, now sad, quiet, and remote. His mood changes could be startling. None of his friends and colleagues pretended to understand him. "He was, take him all in all, one of the most incomprehensible personages we have ever known," recalled a fellow lawyer. He did seem to enjoy people and companionship, and yet he hid his inner feelings behind a wall of stone. "Lincoln's nature was secretive," Herndon said. "He was the most reticent, secretive man I ever saw or expect to see," added Judge David Davis. Even Mary Lincoln found him that way. Despite his deep feelings, she remarked later, "he was *not,* a demonstrative man, when he felt most deeply, he expressed, the least."

One thing he felt "most deeply" was his log-cabin origins. The truth is that he felt embarrassed about his frontier past and never liked to talk about it. He seldom mentioned his parents either, particularly his real mother Nancy, who he feared was illegitimate. According to Herndon, Lincoln confessed that "my mother is a bastard" and admonished his partner to "keep it a secret while I live." True, Herndon is notoriously unreliable when reporting what others told him about Lincoln. But specialists agree that he is most authentic when relating things about Lincoln he personally witnessed. So Herndon is probably right that Lincoln had painful misgivings about his mother's legitimacy. Why else would he become profoundly silent about her and her past? In an 1860 autobiography, he dismissed Nancy with a single reference that she was born in Virginia. Yet in mood and appearance he resembled sad-eyed Nancy more than he did his father.

Thomas Lincoln, for his part, was not the shiftless oaf Herndon reported. If he was illiterate, as were most pioneers of his time and place, he was also a skilled carpenter who stayed sober, paid his taxes, accumulated land, and enjoyed the respect of his neighbors in Indiana and later in Illinois. Yet the important thing is how Lincoln viewed him. Here again, Herndon's opinion of Thomas was undoubtedly Lincoln's. In the son's eyes, the father did seem an unlettered, low-born product of the frontier, and Lincoln became permanently estranged from him. At age twenty-one, he escaped his father's world—a world of mindless physical toil—and never returned. What was more, Lincoln felt considerable contempt for his father's intellectual limitations, once remarking that Thomas "never did more in the way of writing than to bunglingly sign his own name." Lincoln did not invite his father to his wedding or take his family to visit him (Thomas never visited his son either). When his father died in a nearby Illinois county in 1851, Lincoln did not attend the funeral.

Lincoln became a literate and literary man, and he did so largely on his own. In all, he accumulated about a year of formal education in the "blab" schools of frontier Kentucky and Indiana. A gifted boy, he set about educating himself, borrowing whatever volumes he could find and reading the same one over and over. Contrary to legend, he did not study all night by the fireplace of the Lincolns' one-room cabin. Until young Lincoln got a loft, the entire family slept by the fireplace, and bedtime for hardworking farmers came early. Young Lincoln would take his book to the field and read at the end of each plow furrow while his lathered horse got its breath; and he would read again at the noon break.

In these delicious moments away from work, he would lose himself in romantic histories, in the adventures of *Robinson Crusoe* or the selected fables of *Dilworth's Spelling-Book*. He practically memorized the grammars he came across, which taught him rhetoric—that is, dramatic and oratorical effectiveness —as well as the mechanics of writing. Young Lincoln fell in love with language, with metaphors, with assonance and alliteration. His writings sparkle with such gems as "old and only," "a thousand thanks," and "high and beautiful terms." He delighted in creative expression, in the literary telling of a story. Even in a letter, as the critic Edmund Wilson pointed out, Lincoln could make a sentence sing with poetic eloquence. Another cause of his melancholy, he wrote at age thirty-three, was *"the absence of all business and conversation of friends,* which might divert your mind, and give it occasional rest from that *intensity* of thought, which will some times wear the sweetest idea thread-bare and turn it to the bitterness of death." Consider, too, the cadences and alliteration in a speech Lincoln read at the Springfield Young Men's Lyceum when he was twenty-eight. "Let reverence for the laws," Lincoln wrote, "be taught in schools, in seminaries, and in colleges;—let it be preached from the pulpit, proclaimed in legislative halls, and enforced in courts of justice. And, in short, let it become the *political religion* of the nation; and let the old and the young, the rich and the poor, the grave and the gay, of all sexes and tongues, and colors and conditions, sacrifice unceasingly upon its altars."

Lincoln's mature writings, Wilson says, "do not give the impression of a folksy and jocular countryman spinning yarns at the village store." Rather, they reveal a serious and literate Lincoln, "self-controlled" and "strong in intellect."

In truth, Lincoln had a talent for expression that in another time and place might have led him into a distinguished career in American letters. "By nature a literary artist," as one biographer described him, he fancied poetry and wrote verse himself. Here is a poem he composed at thirty-seven, about a visit to his boyhood home in Indiana. He hadn't seen the neighborhood in fourteen years, and nostalgia rose in him, easing his resentments for a region that held painful memories for him. Later, feeling pensive and poetic, he composed these lines:

> My childhood's home I see again,
>   And sadden with the view;
> And still, as memory crowds my brain,
>   There's pleasure in it too.
>
> O Memory! thou midway world
>   'Twixt earth and paradise,
> Where things decayed and loved ones lost
>   In dreamy shadows rise. . . .
>
> The friends I left that parting day
>   How changed, as time has sped!
> Young childhood grown, strong manhood gray,
>   And half of all are dead.
>
> I hear the loved survivors tell
>   How nought from death could save,
> Till every sound appears a knell,
>   And every spot a grave.
>
> I range the fields with pensive tread,
>   And pace the hollow rooms,
> And feel (companions of the dead)
>   I'm living in the tombs.

In his prose as in his verse, Lincoln strove to capture eighteenth-century rhythms without eighteenth-century pomposity. His public utterances, which he always wrote out himself, took on a lean, unembellished eloquence, gleaming with apt metaphors and precise allusions. We are all familiar with the brilliance of his best state papers during the war—with the Gettysburg Address, the ringing Second Inaugural. Novelist Harriet Beecher Stowe extolled Lincoln for his literary abilities. There were passages in his state papers, she declared, that ought "to be inscribed in letters of gold."

With his love for language, he studied Shakespeare, Byron, and Oliver Wendell Holmes, attracted especially to writings with tragic and melancholy themes. He examined the way celebrated orators turned a phrase or employed a figure of speech, looking for great truths greatly told. Though never much at impromptu oratory, he could hold an audience of fifteen thousand spellbound when reading from a written address, speaking out in a shrill, high-pitched voice of great power. On the platform, he often made a point by leaning his head to the side and leveling his finger. When he was "moved by some great & good feeling," Herndon observed, "by some idea of Liberty or Justice or Right then he seemed an inspired man" and "those little gray eyes . . . were lighted up by the inward soul on fires of emotion, defending the liberty of man or proclaiming the truths of the Declaration of Independence." On such occasions, reported a friend, "he was given to raising both arms high as if to embrace a spiritual presence."

Yet, in conversation, this literate and poetic man still showed the ineradicable influence of his Kentucky and Indiana background. All his life he said "sot" for *sat,* "thar" for *there,* "kin" for *can,* "airth" for *earth,* "heered" for *heard,* and "one of 'em" for *one of them.* He claimed that "I han't been caught lyin' yet, and I don't mean to be." He "pitched into" a difficult task "like a dog at root" until he had it "husked out." He pointed at "yonder" courthouse and addressed the head of a committee as

"Mr. Cheermun." And he "larned" about life and received an
"eddication" in the best school of all—the school of adversity.

One side of Lincoln was always supremely logical and analyti-
cal. He was fascinated by the clarity of mathematics and often
spoke and wrote with relentless logic and references to this or that
proposition. "Their ambition," he said of the Founding Fathers,
"aspired to display before an admiring world, a practical demon-
stration of the truth of a proposition, which had hitherto been
considered, at best no better, than problematical; namely, *the
capability of a people to govern themselves.*" This too came from
self-education, this time in Euclid's geometry. Law associates recalled how he used to ride the circuit with a copy of Euclid in his
saddlebags along with Blackstone and *The Revised Statutes of
Illinois.* More than one of them would wake up in the middle of
the night and spot Lincoln, his feet sticking over the footboard
of a bed, pondering Euclid in the flickering light of a candle,
impervious to the snoring of his colleagues in the crowded tavern
room.

Yet this same Lincoln was superstitious, believed in signs and
visions, contended that dreams were auguries of approaching triumph or doom. He even insisted that fat men were ideal jurors
because he thought them jolly by nature and easily swayed. He
was skeptical of organized religion and never joined a church; yet
he argued that an omnipotent God controlled all human destinies.

He was an intense, brooding man, plagued with chronic depression throughout his life. His friends did not know what to make
of his bouts of melancholia, or "hypochondria" or the "hypo" as
people called it then. In his earlier years, alienated from his parents, trying to escape their world and rise into the genteel middle
class, Lincoln tended to derive his sense of worth from the acceptance and approval of others. He said as much himself in his first
political platform, written in 1832. "I have no other [ambition]
so great as that of being truly esteemed of my fellow men, by
rendering myself worthy of their esteem." When his fellow men
rejected him at the polls, Lincoln could be devastated. Oh, he

would try to joke about political defeat. He would say, "Well, I feel just like the boy who stubbed his toe—too damned badly hurt to laugh and too damned proud to cry." But he still felt rejected and depressed.

The "hypo" could be worse when women and affairs of the heart were involved. In his youth, Lincoln was painfully shy around girls and covered it up by acting the neighborhood clown. In New Salem and later in Springfield, young Lincoln felt inadequate as a man, fearful of female rejection, doubtful that he could please or even care for a wife. As for Ann Rutledge, there is no evidence whatever that Lincoln and she ever had a romantic attachment. There is no evidence that theirs was anything more than a platonic relationship. In these years, in fact, his closest female relationships were with married women who posed no threat to him.

In 1836, he did become engaged to a Kentucky woman named Mary Owens, but in their notes and letters there is not a single mention of love or passion or even a kiss. In truth, Lincoln's communications to her reveal a confused and insecure young man as far as intimacy with a woman was concerned. He was very lonely, he wrote Mary in 1837, but he had thought over his agreement to wed her and decided to let her out if she wanted. He was so poor that if they married she would have to live in unaccustomed poverty. He wanted Mary to be happy. He would be happier with her than without her, but he asked her to think it over before throwing in with him. If she liked, they could still get married. But his honest opinion was that she "better not do it," because of the hardships this would impose on her.

A little later he wrote her again: "I want in all cases to do right, and most particularly so, in all cases with women. I want, at this particular time, more than anything else, to do right with you." If she wanted she could dismiss him from her thoughts, forget him. But she should not think that he wanted to cut off their "acquaintance," because he didn't. He would leave it up to her whether to stop or keep on seeing one another. If she felt bound

to him by any promise, he now released her from all obligations
—if that was what she wished. "On the other hand, I am willing,
and even anxious to bind you faster, if I can be convinced that
it will, in any considerable degree, add to your happiness. This,
indeed, is the whole question with me. Nothing would make me
more miserable than to believe you miserable—nothing more
happy, than to know you were so." But "if it suits you not to
answer this," then "farewell—a long life and a merry one attend
you."

Mary Owens never replied, later remarking that Lincoln "was
deficient in those little links which make up the chains of a
woman's happiness." For three years after that, Lincoln had no
romantic involvements, instead throwing himself into politics and
the law. Meanwhile he found acceptance and companionship
with Joshua Speed, a brooding, hefty Kentuckian who operated a
general store in Springfield. When Lincoln first came there looking for a place to stay, Speed gazed at him with amazement. "I
never saw so gloomy and melancholy a face in my life," he said.
Lincoln found him a warm and congenial companion: they slept
together in a bed upstairs, swapped jokes, and confided in one
another about their mutual troubles with women. In time, Speed
became Lincoln's "most intimate friend," the only friend to
whom he ever revealed his innermost thoughts and feelings.

By the summer of 1840, Lincoln felt a little more sure of
himself and began courting Mary Todd. They made a remarkable
couple—he tall, thin, and self-conscious, she five feet two, fashion-
ably plump, and the very creature of excitement, with radiant eyes
and a turned-up nose. Lincoln had a hard-won reputation as a
gifted young lawyer and a promising politician, and Mary considered him an excellent prospect for matrimony. She took a keen
interest in his political work, noted how ambitious he was, found
his "the most congenial mind she had ever met," and felt a
growing affection for this towering attorney who was unlike anybody she had ever known.

But as their relationship deepened, Lincoln had gnawing

doubts about his meager education and low-class background when compared to Mary's. After all, she came from a prominent Kentucky family—her father was a well-known banker and Whig politico in Lexington. And she had attended a stylish women's academy, where she had studied English literature and acquired a reading knowledge of French. Still, Mary fascinated him. She liked poetry and politics as much as he, and she was entirely free of snobbishness. She made it clear that she cared about him, not his family background. Encouraged, Lincoln talked with her about marriage, and in December, 1840, they became engaged.

But Mary's sister and brother-in-law—Elizabeth and Ninian Edwards—did not approve. Because Mary was living with them in their Springfield mansion, they felt responsible for her. And neither of them liked Lincoln. When he sat with Mary in the parlor, Elizabeth said, "he would listen and gaze on her as if drawn by some superior power. He never scarcely said a word," because he "could not hold a lengthy conversation with a lady—was not sufficiently educated and intelligent in the female line to do so." Yet here Mary was, wanting to marry this boorish man who came from "nowhere" and whose future was "nebulous." Well, Elizabeth and Ninian would not stand for it. They tried to break up the engagement and halt the courtship.

Their hostility inflamed Lincoln's anxieties about himself. In fact, he was annihilated. Then to compound his misery, Speed sold his store—he was moving back to Kentucky—and Lincoln had to find another room alone. His most intimate friend was leaving him, a friend he loved and needed now more than ever. It shattered whatever remained of his resolve. Plunging into the worst depression of his life, he broke off his engagement with Mary—this on the "fatal first" of January, 1841—and for a week lay in his room in acute despair. "I am now, the most miserable man living," he wrote a law associate. "If what I feel were equally distributed to the whole human family, there would not be one cheerful face on the earth." He added: "To remain as I am is impossible; I must die or be better."

Speed moved to Kentucky as planned, but Lincoln visited him there, and the two friends kept up an intense and intimate correspondence about their love lives. They openly discussed their self-doubts, their fears of premature death and "nervous debility" with women. Speed went ahead and married anyway and then wrote Lincoln that their anxieties were groundless. Lincoln could barely restrain his joy. "I tell you, Speed, our forebodings, for which you and I are rather peculiar, are all the worst sort of nonsense."

Encouraged by Speed's success, Lincoln started seeing Mary again, meeting her in secret lest the imperious Edwardses find out. Mary's continued affection for Lincoln helped restore some of his self-esteem. He wrote Speed again: "Are you now, in *feeling* as well as *judgment,* glad you are married as you are?" Speed replied that, yes, he was really glad. With that, Lincoln overcame his self-doubts enough to ask for Mary's hand a second time. He was thirty-three—a late age in those days for a first marriage. Mary was twenty-three.

Mary made it plain to her relatives that she intended to wed Lincoln whether they liked it or not, and their opposition gave way. On their wedding day, Lincoln gave her a wedding ring with the inscription "Love Is Eternal." A few days later, he wrote an acquaintance that nothing was new "except my marrying, which to me, is a matter of profound wonder."

Mary helped Lincoln immensely, gave him the tender support and understanding he needed, for they developed a strong physical and emotional love for one another. Yet Mary, so maligned in the Lincoln literature, has never received the credit she deserves for helping Lincoln resolve his fears of inadequacy with women.

Not that their marriage was a paragon of domestic bliss. The Lincolns had their spats and conflicts like any other married couple. Yet Mary was not the raging hellcat that Herndon and other detractors claimed. True, she was insecure, neurotic about money, given to headaches and outbursts of temper. Yet she was also a charming and graceful hostess, an affectionate mother to her sons, and a loyal wife who shared Lincoln's love for politics and was fiercely proud of him.

Those who denigrate Mary forget that Lincoln himself was hard to live with. If Mary liked a good argument now and then to clear the air, he often withdrew at the first sign of a confrontation, for he hated quarrels and tried to avoid them. He could be temperamental, introverted, and forlorn. And some of his daily habits irritated highborn Mary: he often answered the door in his stocking feet, and liked to lie in the hallway and read newspapers aloud. Yet he was proud of their sons and spoiled them as shamelessly as Mary did. Moreover, he understood her better than anyone else and could be tender to her, extremely tender. Because of all the ways he cared for her, Lincoln was everything to Mary: "lover—husband—father, *all.*"

Still, their intimacy suffered in later years. After the birth of Tad in 1853, Mary contracted a serious gynecological disease which, in the judgment of one specialist, "probably ended sexual intercourse between the Lincolns." After that, both became increasingly active outside their home, Mary in trips and shopping expeditions and Lincoln in politics. In 1858, the year Lincoln challenged Stephen A. Douglas for his seat in the United States Senate, he and Mary had separate bedrooms installed when they enlarged and remodeled their Springfield home.

3: ALL CONQUERING MIND

Even with marriage and a family, Lincoln remained a moody, melancholy man, given to long introspections about things like death and mortality. In truth, death was a lifelong obsession with him. His poetry, speeches, and letters are studded with allusions to it. He spoke of the transitory nature of human life, spoke of how all people of this world are destined to die in the end—all are destined to die. He saw himself as only a passing moment in a rushing river of time.

In a real sense, Lincoln had grown up with death, and the loss of those close to him caused incalculable pain in one so deeply sensitive as he. He lost his mother Nancy when he was nine, his only sister when he was eighteen, and his sons Eddie in 1850 and Willie in 1862. The deaths of his cherished boys proved to a grieving Lincoln how ephemeral were human dreams of happiness and lasting life.

When troubled by such thoughts, he would sink into depression again, lost in himself as he stared out the window of his law office, or looked blankly at a fireplace in some hostelry on the circuit. His friends worried about him when he got the "hypo" like that. He would become so dispirited, his eyes so full of pain, that it hurt to look at him. Then often as not he would start muttering the lines of his favorite poem, "Mortality," written by the Scotsman William Knox.

> So the multitude goes, like the flower or weed,
> That withers away to let others succeed;
> So the multitude comes, even those we behold,
> To repeat every tale that has often been told.
>
> For we are the same things our fathers have been;
> We see the same sights our fathers have seen;
> We drink the same stream, we feel the same sun,
> And run the same course our fathers have run. . . .
>
> They died—ah! they died;—we, things that are now,
> That walk on the turf that lies over their brow,
> And make in their dwellings a transient abode,
> Meet the changes they met on their pilgrimage road.
>
> Yea, hope and despondency, pleasure and pain,
> Are mingled together in sunshine and rain:

And the smile and the tear, the song and the dirge,
Still follow each other like surge upon surge.

'Tis the wink of an eye; 'tis the draught of a breath
From the blossom of health to the paleness of death,
From the gilded saloon to the bier and the shroud;
Oh, why should the spirit of mortal be proud?

Preoccupied with death, Lincoln was also afraid of insanity, afraid (as he phrased it) of "the pangs that kill the mind." In his late thirties, he wrote and rewrote a poem about a boyhood friend named Matthew Gentry, who became deranged and was locked "in mental night," condemned to a living death, spinning out of control in some inner void. Lincoln had a morbid fascination with Gentry's condition, writing about how Gentry was more an object of dread than death itself: "A human form with reason fled, while wretched life remains." Yes, Lincoln was fascinated with madness, troubled by it, afraid that what had happened to Matthew could also happen to him—his own reason destroyed, Lincoln spinning in mindless night without the power to know.

This also explains why Lincoln was a teetotaler. Liquor left him "flabby and undone," he said, blurring his mind and threatening his self-control. And he dreaded and avoided anything which threatened that. In one memorable speech, he heralded some great and distant day when all passions would be subdued, when reason would triumph and *"mind, all conquering mind"* would rule the earth.

It is true that Lincoln told folksy anecdotes to illustrate his points. But humor was also tremendous therapy for his depression —it was a device to "whistle down sadness," as Judge Davis put it. Said Lincoln himself: "I laugh because I must not weep—that's all, that's all." He remarked on another occasion: "I tell you the truth when I say that a funny story, if it has the element of genuine wit, has the same effect on me that I suppose a good square drink of whiskey has on an old toper; it puts new life into me."

An expert storyteller, Lincoln could work an audience with exquisite skill. As he related his yarns, fun danced in his eyes and grotesque expressions appeared on his face, until all his features appeared to take part in his performance. When telling a story, a friend said, mirth "seemed to diffuse itself all over him, like a spontaneous tickle."

On the political platform, Lincoln did like to spin tales that stressed some moral about human nature. But he also honed his humor into a potent political weapon. He was a master of ironic wit, of reducing a specious argument to its absurdity. "He can rake a sophism out of its hole better than all the trained logicians of all schools," chuckled a young admirer. Some examples: The claim that the Mexican War was not aggressive reminded Lincoln of the farmer who said, "I ain't greedy 'bout land, I only just wants what jines mine." On state sovereignty: "Advocates of that theory always reminded [me] of the fellow who contended that the proper place for the big kettle was inside of the little one." On the inconsistent politics of archrival Stephen A. Douglas: "Has it not got down as thin as the homeopathic soup that was made by boiling the shadow of a pigeon that had starved to death?" No wonder Douglas complained that "every one of his stories seems like a whack upon my back."

In his legal work, too, Lincoln found ample uses for his humor. As he and his colleagues walked around the little towns on the circuit, "he saw ludicrous elements in everything," one said, "and could either narrate some story from his storehouse of jokes, else he could improvise one." When some associates got to talking about constitutional construction, Lincoln said that "the strongest example of 'rigid government' and 'close construction' I ever knew, was that of Judge ——. It was once said of him that he would *hang* a man for blowing his nose in the street, but that he would *quash* the indictment if it failed to specify which *hand* he blew it with!"

In court, Lincoln could employ humor with devastating effect. An example was the indictment of a young U.S. Army officer, with Lincoln functioning as prosecuting attorney. Lincoln began, "This is an indictment against a soldier for assaulting an old man."

The defendant indignantly interrupted. "Sir, I am no soldier, I am an officer!"

"I beg your pardon," Lincoln said with a bland grin, "then gentlemen of the jury, this is an indictment against an *officer*, who is no *soldier*, for assaulting an old man."

In his law office, when friends and apprentices were gathered around, Lincoln often laid down his pen and treated them to "a burst of spontaneous storytelling," which left them "with their hands on their sides, their heads thrown back, their mouths open, and the tears coursing down their cheeks, laughing as if they would die." Some of Lincoln's private jokes were mindless one-liners like the ones he told in public. His own absentmindedness, he said, reminded him of "the story of an old Englishman who was so absent-minded that when he went to bed he put his clothes carefully into the bed and threw himself over the back of the chair."

In the company of his male friends, Lincoln did tell a Negro dialect joke from time to time. Offensive though these are, such jokes were commonplace among white men of Lincoln's generation, some of whom could boast an entire repertoire. By contrast, Lincoln is known to have related only three Negro tales. An example was the one about a black preacher named Mr. Johnson and a mathematical genius known as Pompey. Here it is in Lincoln's telling:

" 'Now, Pompey, spose dere am tree pigeons sittin' on a rail fence, and you fire a gun at 'em and shoot one, how many's left?'

" 'Two, ob coors,' replies Pompey after a little wool scratching.

" 'Ya-ya-ya,' laughs Mr. Johnson; 'I knowed you was a fool, Pompey; dere's *none* left—one's dead, and d'udder two's flown away.' "

Other tales Lincoln told in private were pungent rib-ticklers, like the one about his hard-drinking chum Leonard Swett. Said Lincoln: "I attended court many years ago at Mt. Pulaski, the first county seat of Logan County, and there was the jolliest set of rollicking young Lawyers there that you ever saw together. There was Bill F[ickli]n, Bill H[erndo]n, L[eonar]d S[wet]t, and a lot more, and they mixed law and Latin, water and whiskey, with equal success. It so fell out that the whiskey seemed to be possessed of the very spirit of Jonah. At any rate, S[wet]t went out to the hog-pen, and, leaning over, began to 'throw up Jonah.' The hogs evidently thought it feed time, for they rushed forward and began to squabble over the voided matter.

" 'Don't fight (hic),' said S[wet]t: 'there's enough (hic) for all.' "

Still other Lincoln stories were downright bawdy. His fondness for smut may not have been "akin to lunacy," as one old friend claimed. But Lincoln did like to regale his cronies with off-color jokes. One involved a youth who copulated with a female cat, another an old Virginia gentleman who stropped his razor "on a certain *member* of a young negro's body." Still another was the piece of foolery called "Bass-Ackwards" which Lincoln handed a bailiff in Springfield one day. "He said he was riding *bass-ackwards* on a *jass-ack*, through a *patton-cotch*, on a pair of *baddle-sags*, stuffed full of *binger gred*, when the animal *steered* at a *scump*, and the *lirrup-steather* broke, and throwed him in the *forner* of the *kence* and broke his *pishing-fole*. He said he would not have minded it much, but he fell right in a great *tow-curd*; in fact, he said it give him a right smart *sick* of *fitness*—he had the *molera-corbus* pretty bad. He said, about *bray dake* he come to himself, ran home, seized up a *stick* of *wood* and split the *axe* to make a light, rushed into the house, and found the *door* sick abed, and his *wife* standing open. But thank goodness she is getting right *hat* and *farty* again."

Some of Lincoln's best stories were those he told on himself. He liked to relate the time he was splitting rails with only a shirt and "breeches" on. A stranger passing by yelled at him, and Lincoln looked up. The stranger was aiming a gun his way. "What do you mean?" Lincoln sputtered. The stranger replied that he had promised to shoot the first man he met who was uglier than he. Lincoln peered at the stranger's face and then declared, "If I am uglier than you, then blaze away."

When he finished a joke, Lincoln would wrinkle his nose, show his front teeth with a high-pitched laugh, and fall to scratching his elbows.

4: MR. LINCOLN

Contrary to mythology, Lincoln was anything but a common man. In point of fact, he was one of the most ambitious human beings his friends had ever seen, with an aspiration for high station in life that burned in him like a furnace. Instead of reading with an accomplished attorney, as was customary in those days, he taught himself the law entirely on his own. He was literally a self-made lawyer. Moreover, he entered the Illinois legislature at the age of twenty-five and became a leader of the state Whig party, an indefatigable party campaigner, and a regular candidate for public office.

By the 1850s, Lincoln was one of the most sought-after attorneys in Illinois, with a reputation as a lawyer's lawyer—a knowledgeable jurist who argued appeal cases for other attorneys. He did his most influential legal work, not in the circuit courts as mythology claims, but in the Supreme Court of Illinois, where he participated in 243 cases and won most of them. He commanded the respect of his colleagues, all of whom called him "Mr. Lincoln" or just "Lincoln." He typically signed letters to his friends "Yours as ever, A. Lincoln." Even Mary referred to him as "Mr. Lincoln," or "Father." Nobody called him "Abe"—at least not to his face—because he loathed the nickname. It did not befit a

respected professional who had struggled hard to overcome the
limitations of his frontier background. In sum, Lincoln was an
outstanding attorney in a flourishing, populous western state that
had left its pioneer past behind, as he had.

Frankly Lincoln enjoyed his status as a prominent Illinois lawyer and politician. And he liked money, too, and used it to measure his worth. He was fair and reasonable when it came to legal
fees, but he did expect prompt remuneration for his services. "I
have news from Ottawa," he wrote an associate, "that we *win* our
Galatin & Saline county case. As the dutch Justice said, when he
married folks, 'Now, vere ish my hundred tollars.' " And if clients
refused to pay up, Lincoln sued them to get his money. By the
1850s, thanks to a combination of talent and sheer hard work,
Lincoln was a man of considerable wealth. He had an annual
income of $5,000 or more—the equivalent of many times that
today—and large financial and real-estate investments.

While Lincoln handled a remarkable variety of bread-and-but-
ter cases out on the circuit, he became known in the 1850s as a
railroad lawyer. And this was true to the extent that he and
Herndon regularly defended the Illinois Central and other railroad companies. After all, these were years of prodigious railroad
construction all over the Midwest, and this in turn created a whole
new area of law and legal practice in which Lincoln was anxious
to participate. Moreover, the coming of the Iron Horse marked
the end of steamboating's golden age and precipitated a titanic
struggle in the Midwest between rail and water interests for com-
mercial supremacy. And that struggle offered lucrative rewards for
attorneys like Lincoln who could command a mass of technical
data.

And he harvested the rewards, collecting fees of $400 to $5,000
for precedent-setting victories in both state and federal appeals
courts. Yet Lincoln never used the law for nefarious personal gain,
never used it to acquire cheap land and other property as did many
of his associates. No, Lincoln was as honest in real life as in the
legend. Even his enemies conceded that he was incorruptible.

"Resolve to be honest at all events," he urged potential attorneys; "and if in your judgment you cannot be an honest lawyer, resolve to be honest without being a lawyer."

Moreover, Lincoln had broad humanitarian views, some of them in advance of his time. Even though he was a teetotaler, he was extremely tolerant of alcoholics in a day when most temperance advocates branded them as criminals who ought to be locked up. Lincoln did not view them that way. In his opinion, alcoholics were unfortunates who deserved understanding, not vilification. He noted that some of the world's most gifted artists had succumbed to alcoholism, because they were too sensitive to cope with their insights into the human condition. When he said that, of course, church and temperance people accused Lincoln of favoring drunkenness.

When it came to religion, Lincoln was an open-minded man who regarded the entire subject as a matter of individual conscience. Personally he believed in God and was an avid student of the Scriptures. A religious fatalist like his mother Nancy, he maintained that nothing could hinder the designs of Providence, that whatever would be would be and people could do nothing about it. Yet, because he belonged to no church and read freethinkers like Voltaire and Thomas Paine, church folk often put Lincoln down as an atheist and opposed him in his political campaigns. For example, in Springfield—his home—twenty-one of twenty-four ministers voted against him in 1860, in large part because they considered him an infidel.

Lincoln also had a liberal mind in the matter of women's rights. This was not a leading issue in Illinois politics, so Lincoln's position cannot be attributed to political considerations. That position, as he publicly declared in 1836, was that women, like men, should have the right to vote so long as all paid taxes. "In this statement," as one specialist has stressed, "Lincoln was far ahead of most of his political contemporaries, and by no means behind even the crusading feminists and abolitionists of the day."

He stood out on another issue, too. His was an age of obstreper-

ous "Americanism," a xenophobic time when native-born white
Protestants campaigned and legislated against Catholics, Irish,
and immigrants. Yet Lincoln had no ethnic prejudices. His law
partner William Herndon, who raved against the Irish, reported
that Lincoln was not at all bigoted against "the foreign element,
tolerating—as I never could—even the Irish."

In the mid-1850s, nativism was so potent a force that it gave
rise to the American or Know-Nothing party, which set out to halt
immigration, suppress Catholics, and save the United States from
the menace of "Popery." Lincoln would have none of it. "Our
progress in degeneracy appears to me to be pretty rapid," he wrote
Joshua Speed. "As a nation, we began by declaring that *'all men
are created equal.'* We now practically read it 'all men are created
equal, *except negroes.'* When the Know-Nothings get control, it
will read 'all men are created equal, except negroes, *and foreigners,
and catholics.'* When it comes to this I should prefer emigrating
to some country where they make no pretence of loving liberty
—to Russia, for instance, where despotism can be taken pure, and
without the base alloy of hypocrisy."

Lincoln's letter affords considerable insight into his feelings
about prejudice and oppression, and his awareness of what was
going on in the world. But before turning to the political Lincoln,
let us summarize what we have seen of him in the prism of history.
Thus far, we have seen a complex, richly human Lincoln, a self-
made man who was witty and tolerant, proud of his achievements,
substantially wealthy, morbidly fascinated with madness, obsessed
with death, troubled with recurring bouts of melancholy, and
gifted with major talent for literary expression. This is a remark-
ably different Lincoln from the rumpled, simple, joke-cracking
commoner of mythology, or the villainous bigot of the counter-
myths. But there are other differences between the historical and
mythical Lincoln that are even more profound, particularly in the
combustible matter of slavery and Negro rights, the burning political issue of Lincoln's day.

Part Three

ADVOCATE
OF THE DREAM

❧❦❧

O my America! my new-found land.

John Donne

1: THE BEACON LIGHT OF LIBERTY

In presidential polls taken by *Life* Magazine in 1948, the *New York Times Magazine* in 1962, and the *Chicago Tribune Magazine* in 1982, historians and political scholars ranked Lincoln as the best chief executive in American history. They were not trying to mythologize the man, for they realized that errors, vacillations, and human flaws marred his record. Their rankings indicate, however, that the icon of mythology did rise out of a powerful historical figure, a man who learned from his mistakes and made a difference. Indeed, Lincoln led the lists because he had a moral vision of where his country must go to preserve and enlarge the rights of all her people. He led the lists because he had an acute sense of history—an ability to identify himself with a historical turning point in his time and to articulate the promise that held for the liberation of oppressed humanity the world over. He led the lists because he perceived the truth of his age and embodied it in his words and deeds. He led the lists because, in his interaction with the spirit and events of his day, he made momentous *moral* decisions that affected the course of humankind.

It cannot be stressed enough how much Lincoln responded to the spirit of his age. From the 1820s to the 1840s, while Lincoln was growing to manhood and learning the art and technique of politics, the Western world seethed with revolutionary ferment. In the 1820s, revolutions broke out not only in Poland, Turkey, Greece, Italy, Spain, and France, but blazed across Spain's ramshackle South American empire as well, resulting in new republics whose capitals rang with the rhetoric of freedom and independence. The Republic of Mexico even produced laws and promulgations that abolished slavery throughout the nation, including Mexico's subprovince of Texas. In that same decade, insurrection panics rocked the Deep South, especially the South Carolina tidewater, as America's disinherited Africans reflected the revolutionary turbulence sweeping the New World. In 1831, in an effort to liberate his people, a visionary slave preacher named Nat Turner incited the most violent slave rebellion in American history, a revolt that shook the South to its foundations and cleared the way for the Great Southern Reaction against the human-rights upheavals of the time. In the 1830s, a vociferous abolitionist movement sprang up in the free states; Great Britain eradicated slavery in the Empire; and impassioned English emancipators came to crusade in America as well. In distant Russia, Czar Nicholas I established an autonomous communal structure for Russia's millions of serfs—the first step in their eventual emancipation two decades later. In the 1840s, while Lincoln practiced law and ran for Congress, reformist impulses again swept Europe. Every major country there had liberal parties that clamored for representative government, self-rule, civil liberties, and social and economic reform. In 1848, the year Congressman Lincoln denounced "Mr. Polk's War" against Mexico, defended the right of revolution, and voted against slavery expansion, revolutions again blazed across Europe, flaring up first in France against the July Monarchy, then raging through Italy and central Europe. These were revolutions against monarchy, despotism, exploitation by the few, revolutions that tried to liberate individuals, classes, and nationalities alike from the shackles of the past. In sum, it was an age of revolution, a turbulent time when people throughout the Western world were searching for definitions of liberty, fighting and dying for liberty, against reactionary forces out to preserve the status quo.

Out in Illinois, Lincoln identified himself with the liberating forces of his day. In fact, he became the foremost political spokesman for those impulses in the United States, a man with a world view of the meaning and mission of his young country in that historic time.

From earliest manhood, Lincoln was a fervent nationalist in an age when a great many Americans, especially in Dixie, were aggressive localists. His broad outlook began when he was an Indiana farm boy tilling his father's mundane wheatfield. During lunch breaks, when he was not studying grammar and rhetoric, Lincoln would peruse Parson Weems's eulogistic biography of George Washington, and he would daydream about the Revolution and the origins of the Republic, daydream about Washington, Jefferson, and Madison as great national statesmen who shaped the course of history. By the time he became a politician in the 1830s, Lincoln idolized the Founding Fathers as apostles of liberty (never mind for now that many of those apostles were also southern slaveowners). Young Lincoln extolled the Fathers for beginning a noble experiment in popular government on these shores, to demonstrate to the world that a free people could govern themselves without hereditary monarchs and aristocracies. And the foundation of the American experiment was the Declaration of Independence, which in Lincoln's view proclaimed the highest political truths in history: that all men were created equal and entitled to liberty and the pursuit of happiness. This meant that men like Lincoln were not chained to the conditions of their births, that they could better their station in life and realize the rewards of their own talent and toil.

A good example, Lincoln believed, was his political idol, Whig national leader Henry Clay of Kentucky. Born into a poor farm family, Clay lifted himself all the way to the United States Senate and national and international fame. For Lincoln, this taught a "profitable lesson"—"it teaches that in this country, one can scarcely be so poor, but that, if he *will*, he *can* acquire sufficient education to get through the world respectably." Thanks to the Declaration, which guaranteed Americans "the right to rise," Lincoln himself had acquired enough education to "get through the world respectably." Thus he had a deep, personal reverence for the Declaration and insisted that all his political sentiments flowed from that document.

All his economic beliefs derived from that document, too. Indeed, Lincoln's economics were as nationalistic and deeply principled as his politics. Schooled in the Whig doctrine of order and national unity, Lincoln advocated a strong federal government to maintain a prosperous, stable economy for the benefit of all Americans—"the old and the young, the rich and the poor, the grave and the gay, of all sexes and tongues, and colors and conditions," as he would say. Thus he championed a national bank, internal improvements financed by the federal government, federal subsidies to help the states build their own canals, turnpikes, and railroads, and state banks whose task was to ensure financial growth and stability. "The legitimate object of government," Lincoln asserted later, "is to do for the people what needs to be done, but which they can not, by individual effort, do at all, or do so well, for themselves."

Lincoln's national economic program was part of his large vision of the American experiment in popular government. By promoting national prosperity, stability, and unity, his economics would help guarantee his "American dream"—the right of all Americans to rise, to harvest the full fruits of their labors, and so to better themselves as their own talent and industry allowed. Thus the American experiment ensured two things essential to liberty: the right of self-government and the right of self-improvement.

Nor was the promise of America limited to the native-born. Her frontier, Lincoln said, should function as an outlet for people the world over who wanted to find new homes, a place to "better their conditions in life." For Lincoln, the American experiment was the way of the future for nations across the globe. A child of the Enlightenment, the American system stood as a beacon of hope for "the liberty party throughout the world."

Yet this beacon of hope harbored a monstrous thing, a relic of despotism in the form of Negro slavery. In Lincoln's view, bondage was the one retrograde institution that disfigured the American experiment, and he maintained that he had always hated it, as much as any abolitionist. His family had opposed slavery, and he had grown up and entered politics thinking it wrong. In 1837, in his first public statement on slavery, Lincoln contended that it was "founded both on injustice and bad policy," and he never changed his mind. But before 1854 (and the significance of this date will become clear), Lincoln generally kept his own counsel about slavery and abolition. After all, slavery was the most inflammable issue of his generation, and Lincoln observed early on what violent passions Negro bondage—and the question of race that underlay it—could arouse in white Americans. In his day, slavery was a tried and tested means of race control in a South dedicated to white supremacy. Moreover, the North was also a white supremacist region, where the vast majority of whites opposed emancipation lest it result in a flood of southern "Africans" into the free states. And Illinois was no exception, as most whites there were anti-Negro and anti-abolition to the core. Lincoln, who had elected to work within the American system, was not going to ruin his career by trumpeting an unpopular cause. To be branded as an abolitionist in central Illinois—his constituency as a legislator and a U.S. congressman—would have been certain political suicide.

Still, slavery distressed him. He realized that it should never have existed in a self-proclaimed free and enlightened Republic. He who cherished the Declaration of Independence understood only too well how bondage mocked and contradicted that noble document. Yes, he detested slavery. It was a blight on the American experiment in popular government, the one institution that robbed the Republic of its just example in the world, robbed the United States of the hope it should hold out to oppressed people everywhere.

He opposed slavery, too, because he had witnessed some of its evils firsthand. In 1841, on a steamboat journey down the Ohio

River, he saw a group of manacled slaves on their way to the cruel cotton plantations of the Deep South. Lincoln was appalled at the sight of those chained Negroes. Fourteen years later he wrote that the spectacle "was a continual torment to me" and that he saw something like it every time he touched a slave border. Slavery, he said, "had the power of making me miserable."

Again, while serving in Congress from 1847 to 1849, he passed slave auction blocks in Washington, D.C. In fact, from the windows of the Capitol, he could observe the infamous "Georgia pen"—"a sort of Negro livery stable," as he described it, "where droves of negroes were collected, temporarily kept, and finally taken to southern markets, precisely like droves of horses." The spectacle offended him. He agreed with a Whig colleague that the buying and selling of human beings in the United States capital was a national disgrace. Accordingly Lincoln drafted a gradual abolition bill for the District of Columbia. But powerful southern politicians howled in protest, and his own Whig support fell away. At that, Lincoln dropped the bill and sat in gloomy silence as Congress rocked with debates—with drunken fights and rumbles of disunion—over the status of slavery in the territories. Shocked at the behavior of his colleagues, Lincoln confessed that slavery was the one issue that threatened the stability of the Union.

Yet Attorney Lincoln had to concede that bondage was a thoroughly entrenched institution in the southern states, one protected by the U.S. Constitution and a web of national and state laws. This in turn created a painful dilemma for Lincoln: a system he deeply loved had institutionalized a thing he abominated. What could be done? Lincoln admitted that the federal government had no legal authority in peacetime to harm a state institution like slavery. And yet it should not remain in what he considered "the noblest political system the world ever saw."

Caught in an impossible predicament, Lincoln persuaded himself that if slavery were confined to the South and left alone there, time would somehow solve the problem and slavery would ultimately die out. Once it was no longer workable, he believed, southern whites would gradually liberate the blacks on their own. They would do so voluntarily.

And he told himself that the Founding Fathers—that Washington, Jefferson, and Madison—had felt the same way, that they too had expected slavery to perish some day. In Lincoln's interpretation, the Fathers had tolerated slavery as a necessary evil, one that could not be removed where it already existed without causing wide-scale chaos and destruction, But, Lincoln contended, they had taken steps to restrict the growth of bondage (had prohibited it in the old Northwest Territories, had outlawed the international slave trade) and thus to place the institution on the road to extinction. And he decided that this was why the Fathers had not included the words *slave* or *slavery* in the Constitution. When bondage did disappear, "there should be nothing on the face of the great charter of liberty suggesting that such a thing as negro slavery had ever existed among us."

So went Lincoln's argument before 1854. Thanks to the Founding Fathers, slavery was on its way to its ultimate doom. And he believed that southerners and northerners alike accepted this as axiomatic. The task of his generation, Lincoln thought, was to keep the Republic firmly on the course charted by the Fathers, guiding America toward that ultimate day when slavery would finally be removed, the nation righted at last with her own ideals, and popular government preserved for all humankind. It was this vision—this sense of America's historic mission in the progress of human liberty—that shaped Lincoln's beliefs and actions throughout his mature years.

Still, despite his passionate convictions about popular government and human liberty, Lincoln before the Civil War did not envision black people as permanent participants in the great American experiment. On the contrary, he feared that white Americans were too prejudiced to let Negroes live among them as equals. If it was impossible for blacks to be completely free in America, then he preferred that they be free somewhere else. Once slavery died out in Dixie, he insisted that the federal government should colonize all blacks in Africa, an idea he got from Henry Clay.

Of course, emancipation and colonization would depend entirely on the willingness of southerners to cooperate. Lincoln hoped and assumed that they would. Before the Civil War, he always sympathized with the mass of southern whites and thought them inherently humane and patriotic. After all, Lincoln himself was a native Kentuckian, and *he* loved the American experiment and tried to be a fair-minded man. He said of southern whites and slavery, "They are just what we would be in their situation. When it is said that the institution exists, and that it is very difficult to get rid of . . . I can understand and appreciate the saying." Yet he thought the great majority of southern whites "have human sympathies, of which they can no more divest themselves than they can of their sensibility to physical pain." Because of their human sympathies, he assumed that they would abolish slavery when it became necessary to do so.

Assumptions aside, though, Lincoln had no evidence that southerners would ever voluntarily surrender their slaves, voluntarily give up their status symbols and transform their cherished way of life founded on the peculiar institution. In 1832, the year Lincoln entered politics, Virginia had actually considered emancipation and colonization (in the aftermath of Nat Turner's insurrection), but had rejected colonization as too costly and complicated to carry out. And neither they nor their fellow southerners were about to emancipate their blacks and leave them as free people in a white man's country. As a consequence, they became adamantly determined that slavery should remain on a permanent basis, not just as a labor device, but as a means of race control in a region brimming with Negroes.

Yet Lincoln clung to the notion that slavery would eventually perish in Dixie, that southerners were rational men who would gradually liberate their blacks when the time came. And he clung to the belief that somehow, when the time did come, the Republic would pay out all the millions of dollars necessary to compensate slaveowners for their losses and ship more than three million blacks out of the country. And he assumed, too, that southerners would consent to the deportation of their entire labor force.

Students often ask me, "Was Lincoln serious? How could a logical and reasonable man like him embrace such fantastic notions?" I can only guess at the answer. Given the tenacious existence of slavery in Dixie and the white supremacist attitudes that prevailed all over his country, what other choices did Lincoln have? His whole idea of southern-initiated emancipation and federal colonization may seem chimerical to us. But in his view it appeared to be the only course short of war that had the slightest chance of working. And he *had* to believe in something. He could not accept the monstrous possibility that southern slavery might continue indefinitely. No, he told himself, it must and would die out as he figured. And so he said in 1852: if the Republic could remove the danger of slavery and restore "a captive people to their long-lost father-land," and do both so gradually "that neither races nor individuals shall have suffered by the change," then "it will indeed be a glorious consummation."

2: THIS VAST MORAL EVIL

Then came 1854 and the momentous Kansas-Nebraska Act, brainchild of Senator Stephen A. Douglas of Illinois. Douglas's measure overturned the old Missouri Compromise line, which excluded slavery from the vast northern area of the old Louisiana Purchase territory. The act then established a new formula for dealing with slavery in the national lands: now Congress would stay out of the matter, and the people of each territory would decide whether to retain or outlaw the institution. Until such time as the citizens of a territory voted on the issue, southerners were free to take slavery into most western territories, including the new ones of Kansas and Nebraska. These were carved out of the northern section of the old Louisiana Purchase territory. Thanks to the Kansas-Nebraska Act, a northern domain once preserved for freedom now seemed open to a proslavery invasion.

At once a storm of free-soil protest broke across the North, and scores of political leaders branded the Kansas-Nebraska Act as part of a sinister southern plot to extend slave territory and augment southern political power in the national capital. Had not the pro-southern Pierce administration and powerful southern politicians like Senator David R. Atchison of Missouri helped Douglas ram the measure through Congress? Had not every southern senator but two voted in favor of it? Were not Missouri border captains vowing to make Kansas a gateway for proslavery expansion to the Pacific?

There followed a series of political upheavals. The old Whig party disintegrated, and in its place emerged the all-northern Republican party, dedicated to blocking slavery extension, saving the cherished frontier for free white labor, and dismantling southern power in Washington. At the same time, a civil war blazed up in Kansas, as proslavery and free-soil pioneers came into bloody collisions on the prairie there—proof that slavery was far too volatile ever to be solved as a purely local matter.

No one was more upset about Kansas-Nebraska than Lincoln. In his view, the southern-controlled Democratic party—the party that dominated the presidency, the Senate, and the Supreme Court—had launched a revolt against the Founding Fathers and the entire course of the Republic as far as slavery was concerned. Now bondage was not going to die out in the South. It was going to grow and expand and continue indefinitely, as slaveholders dragged manacled black people across the West, adapting slave labor to mines and farms and whatever conditions they found there. Now southern leaders would create new slave states on the frontier and make bondage powerful and permanent in America. Now the Republic would never remove the cancer that afflicted its political system—would never remove a "cruel wrong" that marred her global image and made a mockery of the Declaration.

Lincoln plunged into the antiextension fight. He campaigned for the national Senate. He joined the Republicans and became head of the new party in Illinois. He inveighed against the "Slave Power" and its insidious "new designs" to place bondage on the road to expansion and perpetuity. He spoke with an urgent sense of mission that gave his speeches a searching eloquence—a mission to save the American experiment, turn back the tide of slavery expansion, restrict the peculiar institution once again to the South, and place it back on the road to extinction, as Lincoln believed the Founding Fathers had so placed it.

Still, he could not believe that the southern people were involved in the new slave policy. No, they were beguiled by scheming Democratic politicians—by Douglas and southern leaders in Washington and back in Dixie, who were out to enlarge slave territory under the guise of popular sovereignty, under the pretext that it was all "a sacred right of self-government." On the stump in Illinois, Lincoln engaged in a rhetorical dialogue with the southern people, speaking as though they were in his audiences. He did not fault them for the origin of slavery; he bore them no ill-will of any kind. He still believed in their intrinsic decency and sense of justice, still believed that they too regarded slavery as wrong—that they too felt there was humanity in the Negro. Do you deny this? he asked them at Peoria in 1854. Then why thirty-four years ago did you join the North in branding the African slave trade as an act of piracy punishable by death? "Again," Lincoln went on, "you have amongst you, a sneaking individual, of the class of native tyrants, known as the 'SLAVEDEALER.' He watches your necessities, and crawls up to buy your slave, at a speculating price. If you cannot help it, you sell to him; but if you can help it, you drive him from your door. You despise him utterly. You do not recognize him as a friend, or even as an honest man. Your children must not play with his; they may rollick freely with the little negroes, but not with the 'slave-dealers' children. If you are obliged to deal with him, you try to get through the job without so much as touching him. It is common with you to join hands with the men you meet; but with the slave dealer you avoid the ceremony—instinctively shrinking from the snaky contact."

Now why is this? Lincoln asked southern whites. Is it not because your human sympathy tells you "that the poor negro has some natural right to himself—that those who deny it, and make mere merchandise of him, deserve kickings, contempt and death?" He beseeched southerners not to deny their true feelings about slavery. He beseeched them to regard bondage strictly as a necessity, as the Fathers had so regarded it, and to contain its spread as those "old-time men" had done.

"Fellow countrymen—Americans south, as well as north," Lincoln cried, let us prevent the spirit of Kansas-Nebraska from displacing the spirit of the Revolution. "Let us turn slavery from its claims of 'moral right,' back upon its existing legal rights . . . and there let it rest in peace. Let us re-adopt the Declaration of Independence, and with it, the practices, and policy, which harmonize with it. Let north and south—let all Americans—let all lovers of liberty everywhere—join the great and good work. If we do this, we shall not only have saved the Union; but we shall have so saved it, as to make, and to keep it, forever worthy of the saving."

But Lincoln's entreaties fell on deaf ears in Dixie. Across the region, in an age of revolutionary agitation, proslavery apologists disparaged the Declaration of Independence and the idea of human equality as "a self-evident lie." They trumpeted Negro bondage as a great and glorious good, sanctioned by the Bible and ordained by God throughout eternity. They contended that Negroes were subhuman and belonged in chains as naturally as cattle in pens. Cranky George Fitzhugh even exhorted southerners to destroy free society (or capitalism), revive the halcyon days of feudalism, and enslave all workers—white as well as black. And he ranted at abolitionists for allying themselves with the "uncouth, dirty, naked little cannibals of Africa." Because "free society" was "unnatural, immoral, unchristian," the proslavery argument went, "it must fall and give way to a slave society—a system as old as the world." For "two opposite and conflicting forms of society cannot, among civilized men, co-exist and endure. The one must give way and cease to exist—the other become universal." "Free society!" shrieked one Alabama paper. "We sicken of the name! What is it but a conglomeration of greasy mechanics, filthy operatives, small-fisted farmers, and moonstruck theorists?"

Such pronouncements made Lincoln grimace. They convinced him that a contemptible breed of men had taken over in the South and "debauched" the public mind there about the moral right of slavery. "The slave-breeders and slave-traders, are a small, odious and detested class, among you," he wrote a southern friend; "and yet in politics, they dictate the course of all of you, and are as completely your masters, as you are the masters of your own negroes." But to Lincoln's despair, proslavery, anti-northern declarations continued to roar out of Dixie. Worse still, in 1857 the pro-southern Supreme Court handed down the infamous Dred Scott decision, which sent Republicans reeling. In it, the court decreed that Negroes were inferior beings who were not and never had been United States citizens and that the Constitution and Declaration were whites-only charters that did not apply to them. What was more, the court ruled that neither Congress nor a territorial government could outlaw slavery in the national lands, because that would violate southern property rights as guaranteed by the Fifth Amendment. As Lincoln and other Republicans observed, the net effect of the decision was to legalize slavery in all federal territories from Canada to Mexico.

The ominous train of events from Kansas-Nebraska to Dred Scott shook Lincoln to his foundations. By 1858, he and a lot of other Republicans began to see a treacherous conspiracy at work in the United States—a plot on the part of southern leaders and their northern Democratic allies to reverse the whole course of modern history, to halt the progress of human liberty as other reactionary forces in the world were attempting to do. As Lincoln and his colleagues saw it, the first stage of the conspiracy was to betray the Fathers and expand bondage across the West, ringing the free North with satellite slave states. At the same time, pro-slavery theorists were out to discredit the Declaration and replace the idea of the equality of men with the principles of inequality and human servitude. The next step, Lincoln feared, would be to nationalize slavery. The Supreme Court would hand down another decision, one declaring that states could not exclude slavery either because that too violated the Fifth Amendment. Then the institution would sweep into Illinois, sweep into Indiana and Ohio, sweep into Pennsylvania and New York, sweep into Massachusetts and New England, sweep all over the northern states, until at last slavery would be nationalized and America would end up a slave house. At that, as Fitzhugh advocated, the conspirators would enslave all American workers regardless of color. The northern free-labor system would be expunged, the Declaration of Independence overthrown, self-government abolished, and the conspirators would restore despotism with class rule, an entrenched aristocracy, and serfdom. All the work since the Revolution of 1776 would be annihilated. The world's best hope—America's experiment in popular government—would be destroyed, and humankind would spin backward into feudalism.

For Lincoln, the Union had reached a monumental crisis in its history. If the future of a free America was to be saved, it was imperative that Lincoln and his party block the conspiracy in its initial stage—the expansion of slavery onto the frontier. To do that, they demanded that slavery be excluded from the territories by federal law and once again placed on the road to its ultimate doom. In 1858 Lincoln set out after Douglas's Senate seat, inveighing against the Little Giant for his part in the proslavery plot and warning Illinois—and all northerners beyond—that only the

Republicans could save their free-labor system and their free government.

Now Lincoln openly and fiercely declaimed his antislavery sentiments. He hated the institution. Slavery was "a vast moral evil" he could not but hate. He hated it because it degraded blacks and whites alike. He hated it because it violated America's *"central idea"*—the idea of equality and the right to rise. He hated it because it was cruelly unjust to the Negro, prevented him from eating "the bread that his own hands have earned," reduced him to "stripes, and unrewarded toils." He hated slavery because it imperiled white Americans, too. For if one man could be enslaved because of the color of his skin, Lincoln realized, then any man could be enslaved because of skin color. Yet, while branding slavery an evil and doing all they could to contain it in Dixie, Lincoln and his Republican colleagues would not, legally could not, molest the institution in those states where it already existed.

Douglas, fighting for his political life in free-soil Illinois, lashed back at Lincoln with unadulterated race baiting. Throughout the Great Debates of 1858, Douglas smeared Lincoln and his party as Black Republicans, as a gang of radical abolitionists out to liberate southern slaves and bring them stampeding into Illinois and the rest of the North, where they would take away white jobs and copulate with white daughters. Douglas had made such accusations before, but never to the extent that he did in 1858. Again and again, he accused Lincoln of desiring intermarriage and racial mongrelization.

Lincoln did not want to discuss such matters. He complained bitterly that race was not the issue between him and Douglas. The issue was whether slavery would ultimately triumph or ultimately perish in the United States. But Douglas understood the depth of anti-Negro feeling in Illinois, and he hoped to whip Lincoln by playing on white racial fears. And so he kept warning white crowds: Do you want Negroes to flood into Illinois, cover the prairies with black settlements, and eat, sleep, and marry with white people? If you do, then vote for Lincoln and the "Black Republicans." But *I* am against Negro citizenship, Douglas cried. I want citizenship for whites only. I believe that this government "was made by the white man, for the benefit of the white man, to be administered by white men." "I do not question Mr. Lincoln's conscientious belief that the negro was made his equal, and hence his brother"—great laughter at that—"but for my own part, I do not regard the negro as my equal, and positively deny that he is my brother or any kin to me whatever."

Such allegations forced Lincoln to take a stand. It was either that or risk political ruin in white-supremacist Illinois. What he said carefully endorsed the kind of racial discrimination then enforced by Illinois law. Had he not done so, as one scholar has reminded us, "the Lincoln of history simply would not exist." At Charleston, Illinois, Lincoln conceded that he was not and never had been in favor "of making voters or jurors of Negroes, nor of qualifying them to hold office, nor to intermarry with white people." There was, he said at Ottawa, "a physical difference" between the black and white races that would "probably" always prevent them from living together in perfect equality. And Lincoln wanted the white race to have the superior position so long as there must be a difference. Therefore any attempt to twist his views into a call for perfect political and social equality was "but a specious and fantastic arrangement of words by which a man can prove a horse chestnut to be a chestnut horse."

We shall probably never know whether Lincoln was voicing his own personal convictions in speeches like these, given in the heat of political debate before all-white audiences. To be sure, this is one of the most hotly disputed areas of Lincoln scholarship, with several white historians siding with Bennett and Harding and labeling Lincoln a white supremacist. Certainly in the 1850s he had ambivalent feelings about what specific social and political rights black people ought to enjoy. But so did a good many principled and dedicated white abolitionists. When compared to the white-supremacist, anti-Negro attitudes of Douglas and most other whites of that time, Lincoln was an enlightened man in the matter of race relations. In those same 1858 debates, he consistently argued that if Negroes were not the equal of Lincoln and Douglas in moral or intellectual endowment, they *were* equal to Lincoln, Douglas, and "every living man" in their right to liberty, equality of opportunity, and the fruits of their own labor. (Later he insisted that it was bondage that had "clouded" the slaves' intellects and that Negroes were capable of thinking like whites.) Moreover, Lincoln rejected "the counterfeit argument" that just because he did not want a black woman for a slave, he therefore wanted her for a wife. He could just let her alone. He could let her alone so that she could also enjoy her freedom and "her natural right to eat the bread she earns with her own hands."

While Douglas (like the Supreme Court) emphatically denied that the Declaration of Independence applied to Negroes, Lincoln's position held that it did. The Negro was a man; Lincoln's "ancient faith" taught him that all men were created equal; therefore there could be no "moral right" in one man's enslaving another. As historian Richard N. Current has said, Lincoln left unstated the conclusion of his logic: that there was no moral right in one man's making a political and social inferior of another on grounds of race.

In the debate at Alton, Lincoln took his reasoning even further as far as the Declaration was concerned. "I think the authors of that notable document intended to include *all* men," Lincoln said, "but they did not intend to declare all men equal in *all* respects. They did not mean to say all were equal in color, size, intellect, moral development, or social capacity." What they meant was that all men, black as well as white, were equal in their inalienable rights to life, liberty, and the pursuit of happiness. When they drafted the Declaration, they realized that blacks did not then have full equality with whites, and that whites did not at that time have full equality with one another. The Founding Fathers did not pretend to describe America as it was in 1776. "They meant to set up a standard maxim for free society," Lincoln said, "which should be familiar to all, and revered by all; constantly looked to, constantly labored for, and even though never perfectly attained, constantly approximated, and thereby constantly spreading and deepening its influence, and augmenting the happiness and value of life to all people of all colors everywhere."

By stressing "to all people of all colors everywhere," Lincoln reminded his countrymen that the American experiment remained an inspiration for the entire world. But he reminded them, too, as historian Current has noted, that "it could be an effective inspiration for others only to the extent that Americans lived up to it themselves." No wonder Lincoln said he hated Douglas's indifference toward slavery expansion. "I hate it because of the monstrous injustice of slavery itself," Lincoln explained at Ottawa. "I hate it because it . . . enables the enemies of free institutions, with plausibility, to taunt us as hypocrites."

Exasperated with Douglas and white Negrophobia in general, Lincoln begged American whites "to discard all this quibbling about this man and the other man—this race and that race and the other race as being inferior," begged them to unite as one people and defend the ideal of the Declaration of Independence and its promise of liberty and equality for all humankind.

Lincoln's remarks, however, aggravated a lot of common people in Illinois; they voted for Douglas candidates in 1858 and helped return Lincoln's rival to the Senate.* The historical Lincoln even lost Springfield and Sangamon County, because his controversial views on slavery and the Negro, as one historian has argued, were too advanced for his neighbors. If we are to understand Lincoln's

*In those days, state legislatures chose U.S. Senators. Lincoln hoped to win by persuading Illinois voters to elect Republican rather than Democratic candidates to the legislature.

attitudes on slavery and race, it is imperative that we weigh them in proper historical context. We can learn nothing, nothing at all, if his words are lifted from their historical setting and judged only by the standards of another time.

3: My Dissatisfied Fellow Countrymen

We return to why Lincoln still ranks as the best President Americans have had. In large measure, it was because of his sense of history and his ability to act on that. It was because he saw the slavery problem and the future of his country in a world dimension. He saw that what menaced Americans of his day affected the destinies of people everywhere. On the stump in Illinois, Ohio, and New York, he continued to warn free men of the heinous efforts to make bondage permanent in the United States. He would not let up on his countrymen about the *moral* issue of slavery. *"If slavery is not wrong,"* he warned them, *"nothing is wrong."* He would not let up on "the miners and sappers" of returning despotism, as he called proslavery spokesmen and their northern allies, and on the historical crisis threatening his generation, a crisis that would determine whether slavery or freedom—despotism or popular government, the past or the future—would triumph in his impassioned time.

Yet in the late 1850s Lincoln's goal was not the presidency. One of the more popular misconceptions about him was that he had his eye on the White House even in the Great Debates. Yet there is not a scintilla of reliable evidence to support this. What Lincoln wanted, and wanted fervently, was a seat in the national Senate, because in the antebellum years it was the Senate that featured the great orators of the day—men like Daniel Webster, John C. Calhoun, and especially Lincoln's idol, Henry Clay. The presidency, by contrast, was a mundane administrative job that offered little to a man of Lincoln's oratorical abilities. No, he preferred the national Senate, because in that august body he could defend the containment of slavery, defend free labor, defend popular government and the American experiment, in speeches that would be widely read and preserved for posterity in the *Congressional Globe.* As a loyal Republican, he would take any respectable national office that would simultaneously "advance our cause" and give him personal fulfillment. But throughout 1859 and early 1860, he kept his eye on Douglas's Senate seat in 1864.

So it was that Lincoln kept assailing Douglas for his role in the proslavery plot Lincoln saw at work in his country. And he reminded northerners of the Republican vision of a future America —a better America than now existed—an America of thriving farms and bustling villages and towns, an America of self-made agrarians, merchants, and shopkeepers who set examples and provided jobs for self-improving free workers—an America, however, that would never come about if slavery, class rule, and despotism triumphed in Lincoln's time.

Meanwhile, he kept trying to reach the southern people, to reason with them about slavery and the future of the Union, to woo them away from their reactionary leaders. He observed how ironic it was that the Democrats had abandoned their Jeffersonian heritage and that the Republicans—supposedly the descendants of the old Federalists—now defended Jeffersonian ideals. He warned southerners that "This is a world of compensations; and he who would *be* no slave, must consent to *have* no slave. Those who deny freedom to others, deserve it not for themselves."

"I think Slavery is wrong, morally, and politically," he told southern whites at Cincinnati in 1859, still speaking to them as though they were in his audience. "I desire that it should gradually terminate in the whole Union." But "I understand you differ radically with me upon this proposition." You believe that "Slavery is a good thing; that Slavery is right; that it ought to be extended and perpetuated in this Union." But we Republicans not only disagree with you; we are going to "stand by our guns" and beat you in a fair election. Yet we will not hurt you. We will treat you as Washington, Jefferson, and Madison treated you, and will leave slavery alone where it already exists among you. "We mean to remember that you are as good as we are; that there is no difference between us other than the difference of circumstances. We mean to recognize and bear in mind always that you have as good hearts in your bosoms as other people, or as we claim to have, and treat you accordingly. We mean to marry your girls when we have a chance—the white ones I mean—[laughter] and I have the honor to inform you that I once did have a chance that way."

But he cautioned southerners about their threats to disrupt the Union should the Republicans win the government in 1860. How will disunion help you? Lincoln demanded. If you secede, you will no longer enjoy the protection of the Constitution, and we will no longer be forced to return your fugitive slaves. What will you do—build a wall between us? Make war on us? You are brave and gallant, "but man for man, you are not better than we are, and there are not so many of you as there are of us." Because you are inferior in numbers, "you will make nothing by attempting to master us."

Despite Lincoln's reassurances, southern spokesmen derided the Republicans as warmongering abolitionists out to destroy the southern way of life based on slavery. In October, 1859, they got all the evidence they needed that this was so. Old John Brown and a handful of revolutionaries—most of them young, five of them black—invaded Harpers Ferry in an attempt to incite a full-scale slave rebellion. Though the raid failed and Brown was captured and hanged, the South convulsed in hysteria, as rumors of slave uprisings and abolitionist invasions pummeled the region. For their part, southern politicians pronounced the raid a Republican conspiracy, a mad and monstrous scheme to drown the South in rivers of blood. During a tour of the embattled Kansas Territory, Lincoln denied such accusations and argued that hanging

Brown was just. But he warned southerners that "if constitutionally we elect a President, and therefore you undertake to destroy the Union, it will be our duty to deal with you as old John Brown has been dealt with."

At Cooper Union the following year, Lincoln responded to continued southern imputations about the Republicans and John Brown. "You charge that we stir up insurrections among your slaves," Lincoln said. "We deny it; and what is your proof? Harper's Ferry! John Brown!! John Brown was no Republican; and you have failed to implicate a single Republican in his Harper's Ferry enterprise." But he saved his most eloquent remarks for his fellow Republicans. Since they intended southerners no harm and promised over and over to leave their slaves alone, what then was the dispute about? "The precise fact upon which depends the whole controversy" was that southerners thought slavery right and Republicans thought it wrong. "Thinking it right, as they do, they are not to blame for desiring its full recognition, as being right; but, thinking it wrong, as we do, can we yield to them? Can we cast our votes with their view, and against our own? In view of our moral, social, and political responsibilities, can we do this?" No, the Republicans' sense of duty would not let them yield to southern demands about slavery. Nor would Republicans be frightened from their duty by threats of disunion and destruction to the government. "LET US HAVE FAITH THAT RIGHT MAKES MIGHT, AND IN THAT FAITH, LET US, TO THE END, DARE TO DO OUR DUTY AS WE UNDERSTAND IT."

Impressed by his impassioned oratory and firm commitment to party principles, and impressed too by his availability, the Republicans chose Lincoln to be their standard bearer in 1860, to run for President on their free-soil, free-labor platform. In the countdown to the Republican nomination, Lincoln insisted that he preferred the Senate to the White House. But as his chances for the nomination brightened he confessed that "the taste *is* in my mouth a little," and he let a cadre of zealous lieutenants work to secure his nomination. Contrary to a persistent popular misconception, they did not do so simply by making bargains with Republicans from other states, promising Cabinet positions and other offices if they would throw their delegations to Lincoln. Modern scholarship has thoroughly demolished this claim. While Lincoln's managers may have made conditional overtures (as any manager would do), they followed Lincoln's own instructions and did not bind him to any convention deals. Moreover, supporters of William H. Seward, the front-running candidate before the convention, had as many offices to disseminate as Lincoln's men. What won Lincoln the nomination was not the peddling of spoils but a hard decision on the part of the Republican delegates that Seward "could not win and must give way to someone who could," as one historian has phrased it. And that someone was Abraham Lincoln, who was available, who was a loyal party man, who came from a crucial state, and who was more likely than any other candidate to carry the populous lower North, which was indispensable for a Republican victory.

Lincoln, for his part, accepted the nomination because he was as ambitious as he was deeply principled. While he preferred to serve the Republican cause on Capitol Hill, he would work for it wherever the party wanted to put him so long as it was a meaningful national office. And in 1860 that was the White House. In Lincoln, as it turned out, the Republicans chose a candidate more unbending in his commitment to Republican principles than anybody else they might have selected. As the Republican standard bearer, Lincoln was inflexible in his determination to prohibit slavery in the territories by national law and to save the Republic (as he put it) from returning "class," "caste," and "despotism." He exhorted his fellow Republicans to stand firm in their duty: to brand slavery as an evil, contain it in the South, look to the future for slavery to die a gradual death, and promise colonization to solve the question of race. Someday, somehow, the American house must be free of slavery. That was the Republican vision, the distant horizon Lincoln saw.

Yet, for the benefit of southerners, he repeated that he and his party would not interfere with slavery in Dixie. The federal government had no constitutional authority in peacetime to tamper with a state institution like slavery.

But southerners in 1860 were in no mood to believe anything Lincoln said. In their eyes, he was a "horrid looking wretch," another John Brown, "a black-hearted abolitionist fanatic" who lusted for Negro equality. There were, of course, a number of loyal Unionists in the South who pleaded for reason and restraint, who beseeched their fellow southerners to wait for an overt Republican act against them before they did anything rash. For most, though, Brown's Harpers Ferry invasion was all the overt action they intended to tolerate. For all classes in Dixie, from poor whites in South Carolina to rich cotton planters in Mississippi, Lincoln personified the feared and hated *Yankee*—the rapacious entrepreneur, the greasy mechanic, the mongrel immigrant, the frothing abolitionist, the entire "free-love, free-nigger" element, all of whom in southern eyes had combined in Lincoln's party. In him, southerners saw a monster who would send a Republican army into Dixie to free the slaves by gunpoint and whip up a racial storm that would consume their farms and plantations, their investments, their wives and daughters. Even if the South had to drench the Union in blood, exclaimed an Alabama paper, "the South, the loyal South, the Constitutional South, would never submit to such humiliation and degradation as the inauguration of Abraham Lincoln."

For Lincoln, the slavedealers had indeed assumed leadership in Dixie, and he would never compromise with them over a single plank in the Republican platform. Anyway, he still refused to believe that the South's blustery spokesmen truly reflected popular sentiment there. "The people of the South," he remarked during the obstreperous 1860 campaign, "have too much good sense, and good temper, to attempt the ruin of the government." He agreed with his advisers that southern Unionism was too powerful for secession to triumph. Surely, he reasoned, the southern people shared his own sentiments about the future of the American experiment. Surely, like the powerful southerners who helped found the country, like Washington, Jefferson, and Madison, the southern people of his day believed in the Declaration of Independence, which was their charter of liberty as much as his own and that of the Republicans. Surely the southern people would reject the forces of reaction in the world and come around to Lincoln's view, to stand with those who sought the liberation and uplift of the human spirit.

On election day, November 6, telegraph dispatches across the country carried the crucial news: Lincoln had defeated his three leading opponents—John Breckinridge of the southern Democrats, Douglas of the northern Democrats, and John Bell of the Constitutional Union ticket—and was to be the sixteenth President. Lincoln had won, not because his foes were split, but because he carried California and Oregon and every northern state except New Jersey, which divided its electoral votes between him and Douglas. In the electoral college, where Lincoln gained his triumph, his total vote exceeded that of his combined opponents by a margin of 187 to 123. In popular votes, though, Lincoln was a minority President, with 1,866,452 ballots compared to 2,815,-617 for his combined foes. Many factors were involved in this confusing and raucous contest, but the fact remains that the majority of Americans in 1860 regarded Lincoln as too radical and dangerous to occupy the White House. Of course, you don't learn about this in the story of Lincoln as Man of the People.

In the Deep South, newspapers screamed with headlines about Lincoln, and people thronged the streets of southern cities with talk of secession everywhere. "Now that the black radical Republicans have the power," asserted a South Carolinian, "I suppose they will [John] Brown us all." Of course, Lincoln and his party did not have the power. They had only won the presidency. The Democrats, though divided, still controlled the Supreme Court and both houses of Congress, and would have demolished any abolition bill the Republicans might have introduced there. But for southerners that stormy winter, the nation had reached a profound turning point: an all-northern party avowedly hostile to slavery had gained control of the executive branch of the government. In the Deep South, a white man reading his newspaper could rehearse what was bound to follow. With the North's supremacy in population and drift toward abolition and revolutionary violence, that party was certain to win the rest of the government one day and then attack slavery in Dixie. Better, then, to strike for southern independence now than to await the Republican blow. Thus, even before Lincoln could be inaugurated, the seven states of the Deep South—with their heavy slave concentrations—left the Union and established the slave-based Confederacy. As a South Carolina resident explained to President Buchanan: "Slavery with us is no abstraction—but a *great* and *vital fact*. Without it our every comfort would be taken from us. Our wives, our children, made unhappy—education, the light of knowledge—all *all* lost and our *people ruined for ever. Nothing short of separation from the Union can save us.*" The editor of the Montgomery *Mail* agreed. "To remain in the Union is to lose all that white men hold dear in government. We vote to get out."

In Springfield, President-elect Lincoln admitted that there were "some loud threats and much muttering in the cotton states," but insisted that the best way to avoid disaster was through calmness and forbearance. What reason did southerners have to be so incensed? What had the Republicans done to them? What southern rights had they violated? Did not southerners still have the fugitive slave law? Did they not have the same Constitution they had lived under for seventy-odd years? "Why all this excitement?" Lincoln asked. "Why all these complaints?"

With the border states also threatening to secede, Lincoln seemed confused, incredulous, at what was happening to his country. He seemed not to understand how he appeared in southern eyes. He kept telling himself that his advisers were right, that southern Unionism would somehow bring the errant states back. He could not accept the possibility that *his* election to the presidency might cause the collapse of the very system which had enabled him to get there. The irony of that was too distressing to contemplate.

In his Inaugural Address of March 4, 1861, Lincoln pleaded for southern whites to understand the Republican position on slavery. He assured them once again that he would not molest slavery in Dixie, that he had no legal right to molest it there. He even approved the original Thirteenth Amendment, just passed by Congress, that would have explicitly guaranteed slavery in the southern states. Lincoln endorsed the amendment because he deemed it consistent with Republican ideology. And in his conclusion he spoke personally to the southern people, as he had done so often since 1854: "In *your* hands, my dissatisfied fellow countrymen, and not in *mine,* is the momentous issue of civil war. The government will not assail *you.* You can have no conflict, without being yourselves the aggressors. *You* have no oath registered in Heaven to destroy the government, while *I* shall have the most solemn one to 'preserve, protect and defend' it."

"I am loth to close. We are not enemies, but friends. We must not be enemies. Though passion may have strained, it must not break our bonds of affection. The mystic chords of memory, stretching from every battlefield, and patriot grave, to every living heart and hearthstone, all over this broad land, will yet swell the chorus of the Union, when again touched, as surely they will be, by the better angels of our nature."

In Dixie, excitement was so great that men read in Lincoln's words, not conciliation, but provocation. The feverish Charleston *Mercury* even blasted it as a declaration of war. At that very moment, in fact, war threatened to break out in Charleston harbor, where hostile rebel cannon ringed Fort Sumter and its lonely Union flag. The Confederates had already seized every U.S. fort in Dixie except for Sumter and one other in the Florida Gulf. Now Sumter became a symbol for both sides, as the rebels demanded that Lincoln surrender it and angry Union men exhorted him to hold.

In the ensuing crisis, Lincoln clung to the belief that the southern people would overthrow the secessionists and restore the southern states to the Union. But he had little time to wait, for the Sumter garrison was rapidly running out of provisions. Should he send a relief expedition? But what if that betrayed southern Unionists and detonated a civil war? In "great anxiety" about what to do, Lincoln consulted repeatedly with his Cabinet and with high-ranking officers of the army and navy, but they gave him conflicting advice. Far from being an aggressive tyrant who forced the innocent South to start the war, the historical Lincoln vacillated over Sumter, postponed a decision, suffered terribly. He told an old Illinois friend that "all the troubles and anxieties" of his life could not equal those that beset him during the Sumter nightmare. They were so great, Lincoln said, that he did not think it possible to survive them.

Then a report from an emissary he had sent to Charleston smashed his hope that the crisis could be peacefully resolved. The emissary reported that South Carolinians had "no attachment to the Union," and that some wanted a clash with Washington to unite the Confederacy. Moreover, Unionism was equally dead everywhere else in Dixie, and the seceded states were "irrevocably gone." There was no conceivable way that Lincoln could avoid an armed collision with southern rebels: if he did not hold Sumter, he would have to stand somewhere else or see the government collapse.

It was a rude awakening for Lincoln, who had placed great faith in the potency of southern Unionism, who had always thought that southern white people loved the country as much as he and shared his faith in the American promise. Well, he had been wrong. Out of that sobering realization, out of everything he held dear about the Union, out of all his suffering, came a decision to stand firm. After all, he had won the presidency in a fair and legal contest. He would not compromise his election mandate. He would preserve the Union and the principle of self-government on which the Union was based: the right of a free people to choose their leaders and expect the losers to acquiesce in that decision. If southerners disliked him, they could try to vote him out of office in 1864. But he was not going to let them separate from the Union, because that would set a catastrophic precedent that any unhappy state could leave the Union at any time. For Lincoln, the philosophy of secession was "an ingenious sophism" southerners had contrived to vindicate their rebellion. This sophism held that each state possessed "some omnipotent, and sacred supremacy," and that any state could lawfully and peacefully leave the Union without its consent. "With rebellion thus sugar coated," Lincoln complained, southern leaders "have been drugging the public mind of their section for more than thirty years." Yet it was a preposterous argument. The Constitution specifically stated that the Constitution and the national laws made under it were the supreme law of the land. Therefore the states could not be supreme as the secessionists claimed; the Union was paramount and permanent, and could not be legally wrecked by a disaffected minority. The principle of secession was disintegration, Lincoln said. And no government based on that principle could possibly endure.

Yes, he would hold Fort Sumter. In that imperiled little garrison in Charleston Harbor, surrounded by rebel batteries and a hostile population, Lincoln saw the fate of popular government hanging in the balance. He would send a relief expedition to Sumter, and if the Confederates opened fire, the momentous issue of civil war was indeed in their hands.

And so the fateful events raced by: the firing on the fort, Lincoln's call for 75,000 troops, the secession of four border states, and the beginning of war. Deeply embittered, Lincoln grumbled about all the *professed* Union men" in Dixie who had gone over to the rebellion. And he looked on in distress as one supposedly loyal southerner after another resigned from the United States Army and headed south to enlist in the rebel forces. It depressed him immeasurably. He referred to Robert E. Lee, Joseph E. Johnston, John Bankhead Magruder, and all like them as traitors.

And in his public utterances he never again addressed the southern people as though they were in his audiences. Instead he spoke of them in the third person, calling them rebels and insurrectionaries—a domestic enemy engaged in treason against his government.

And so the Civil War had come—a war that no reasonable man in North or South had wanted. What began as a ninety-day skirmish on both sides swelled instead into a vast inferno of destruction with consequences beyond calculation for those swept up in its flames. For Lincoln, the country was out of control, threatening to annihilate everyone and everything, all promise and all hope, and he did not think he could bear the pain he felt. His election had provoked this madness, and he took it personally. Falling into a depression that would plague him throughout his embattled presidency, he remarked that the war was the supreme irony of his life: that he who sickened at the sight of blood, who abhorred stridency and physical violence, who dreamed that "mind, all conquering *mind,*" would rule the world someday, was caught in a national holocaust, a tornado of blood and wreckage with Lincoln himself whirling in its center.

Part Four

WARRIOR
FOR THE DREAM

❦

We shall nobly save, or meanly lose,
the last best, hope of earth.

ABRAHAM LINCOLN

1: THE CENTRAL IDEA

In the flames of civil war, Lincoln underwent seemingly endless crises that might have shattered a weaker man. Here he was —a President who lacked administrative experience, suffered from chronic depression, hated to fire inept subordinates and bungling generals (he had never liked personal confrontations anyway)—thrust into the center of a fratricidal conflict. Here he was, forced to make awesome decisions in a war that had no precedent in all American history, a war without constitutional or political guidelines for him to follow. At the same time, Lincoln had to live with the knowledge that he was the most unpopular President the Republic had known up to that time. His hate mail from the public was voluminous and grotesque, as for instance the letter that came to him in 1861: "You are nothing but a goddamned Black nigger." On his desk, too, fell a southern newspaper clipping that offered $100,000 for his "miserable traitorous head." Some Man of the People, this Lincoln of history! Through that first year of the war, Lincoln was a deeply troubled President, caught in a vortex of problems and pressures. One can picture him standing as he often did at a White House window, a haunted, harried man who did not know whether he could quell this "clear, flagrant, gigantic case of Rebellion" against him and his government.

When an old friend visited him early in the war, Lincoln confessed that he was depressed and "not at all hopeful" about his or his country's future. And the ravages of war—the wrecked homes, broken families, mounting casualties—took a terrible toll on one who was obsessed with death anyway, who had written lugubrious verse about it and still recited the mournful refrains of the poem "Mortality." *Oh, why should the spirit of mortal be proud,* when so many already lay dead and gone: Elmer Ellsworth, a close friend of the Lincoln family, shot in Alexandria after taking down a rebel flag . . . 460 Union soldiers slain and 2,430 wounded or missing in the swamps and woods of Bull Run (a distraught Lincoln watching from the White House as the remnants of the Union army staggered into Washington, moving like phantoms in the fog and rain) . . . Edward Baker, Lincoln's old friend from Whig days in Sangamon County, blown to eternity at Ball's Bluff. And who knew how many more would follow.

And the country! From all directions came cries that Lincoln was unfit to be President, that he was too inexperienced, too inept, too stupid and imbecilic, to reunite the country. Even some of his Cabinet secretaries, even some of his friends, feared that the war was too much for him.

Melancholy and inexperienced though he was, unsure of himself and savagely criticized though he was, Lincoln managed nevertheless to see this huge and confusing conflict in a world dimension. He defined and fought it according to his core of unshakable convictions about America's experiment and historic mission in the progress of human liberty. The central issue of the war, he told Congress on Independence Day, 1861, was whether a constitutional republic—a system of popular government—could preserve itself. There were Europeans who argued that anarchy and rebellion were inherent weaknesses of a republic and that a monarchy was the more stable form of government. Now, in the Civil War, popular government was going through a fiery trial for its very survival. If it failed in America, if it succumbed to the forces of reaction represented by the slave-based Confederacy, it might indeed perish from the earth. The beacon of hope for oppressed humanity the world over would be destroyed.

To prevent that, Lincoln said, the government must meet force with force. It must teach southern dissidents "the folly of being the beginners of a war." It must show the world "that those who can fairly carry an election, can also suppress a rebellion," and that popular government was a viable system. "This is essentially a People's contest," the President said. "On the side of the Union, it is a struggle for maintaining in the world, that form, and substance of government, whose leading object is, to elevate the condition of men—to lift artificial weights from all shoulders— to clear the paths of laudable pursuit for all—to afford all, an unfettered start, and a fair chance, in the race of life."

Yes, this was the central idea of the war. This was what Lincoln had in mind when he said, "I shall do nothing in malice. What I deal with is too vast for malicious dealing." And in various ways he repeated that central idea in the difficult days ahead. They were fighting, he told crowds and visitors at the White House, to preserve something that lay at the heart of the American promise, something he had cherished and defended almost all his political life. "I happen temporarily to occupy this big White House," he said to an Ohio regiment. "I am a living witness that one of your children may look to come here as my father's child has. It is in order that each of you may have through this free government which we have enjoyed, an open field and a fair chance for your industry, enterprise and intelligence; that you may all have equal privileges in the race of life, with all its desirable human aspirations. It is for this the struggle should be maintained, that we may not lose our birthright."

Fighting for that idea, keeping it uppermost in his mind, Lincoln found the inner strength to surmount his multitude of woes— the vituperation he suffered throughout his presidency, the devastating loss of his cherished son Willie, the ensuing breakdown of his wife Mary, and above all the endless, endless war. The war consumed him, demanding almost all his energy from dawn until late into the night. He had almost no time for his family, for recreation beyond a daily carriage ride, for meals and leisurely jokes and laughter with old friends, for government matters unrelated to the conflict. He seldom initiated legislation on Capitol Hill and used his veto less than any other important American President. Beyond signing his name, he had little connection with the homestead, railroad, and banking bills flowing out of the wartime capitol. Not that he lacked interest in such measures. No, they implemented his own national economic outlook—they promoted the "material growth of the nation" and the rise of the "many," and so were related to the central idea. Yet he was too preoccupied with the war to initiate economic legislation in Congress.

Every day, whenever he could spare a moment, Lincoln hurried to the telegraph office of the War Department to get the latest war news. He was there during almost all the crucial campaigns, pacing back and forth with his hands clasped behind him, sending out anxious telegraphic messages to some southern battlefront: *What news now? What from Hooker? What goes?* He even brought documents to the telegraph office and worked on them at a borrowed desk. It was here, as he awaited military developments, that he wrote an early draft of his preliminary Emancipation Proclamation.

In short, the war and Lincoln's response to it defined him as a President. Here is a classic illustration of how the interaction of people and events shapes the course of history. As the war grew and changed, so Lincoln grew and changed. At first, he warned that the conflict must not turn into a "remorseless revolutionary struggle," lest that cause wide-scale social and political wreckage. As a consequence, his initial war strategies were cautious and limited. But when the conflict ground on with no end in sight, Lincoln resorted to one harsh war measure after another to subdue the rebellion and save popular government: he embraced martial law, property confiscation, emancipation, Negro troops, conscription, and scorched-earth warfare. These turned the war into the very thing he had cautioned against: a remorseless revolutionary struggle whose concussions are still being felt.

And it became such a struggle because of Lincoln's unswerving commitment to the war's central idea.

2: DEATH WARRANT FOR SLAVERY

Nowhere was the struggle more evident than in the nagging problem of slavery. How Lincoln approached that problem—and what he did about it—is one of the most written about and least understood facets of his presidency. As we examine this dramatic and complicated story, recall that what guided Lincoln in the matter of emancipation was his commitment, not just to the Union, but to what it represented and symbolized. Here, as in all war-related issues, Lincoln's devotion to the war's central idea— to preserving a system that guaranteed to all the right of self-government—dictated his course of action.

At the outset of the conflict, Lincoln strove to be consistent with everything he and his party had said about slavery: his purpose was to save the old Union as it was and not to uproot bondage in the South. He intended to crush the rebellion with his armies and restore the national authority in Dixie with slavery intact. Then Lincoln and his party would resume and implement their policy of slave containment, putting bondage once again on the road to extinction.

There were other reasons for Lincoln's hands-off policy about slavery in the South. Four slave states—Delaware, Maryland, Kentucky, and Missouri—remained in the Union. Should he try to free the slaves, Lincoln feared it would drive the crucial border into the Confederacy, which would have been a calamity for the Union. A rebel Maryland would create an impossible situation for Washington, D.C. And a Confederate Missouri and Kentucky would give the insurrectionists potential bases from which to invade Illinois, Indiana, and Ohio. As a popular witticism went, "Lincoln would like to have God on his side, but he must have Kentucky." So Lincoln rejected emancipation in part to appease the loyal border.

He was also waging a bipartisan war effort, with northern Democrats and Republicans alike enlisting in his armies to save the Union and its experiment in popular government. Lincoln encouraged this because he insisted that the North must be united if it was to win the war. An emancipation policy, he feared, would alienate northern Democrats, ignite a racial powder keg in the northern states, and possibly cause a civil war in the rear. Then the Union cause really would be lost.

But in little more than a year the pressures and problems of civil war caused Lincoln to change his mind, caused him to abandon his hands-off policy and strike at slavery in the rebel states, thus making emancipation a Union war objective. There was no single reason why he did so—certainly the reason was not political expediency. On the contrary, the pressures operating on Lincoln were varied and complex.

First, from the summer of 1861 on, several Republican senators —chief among them Charles Sumner of Massachusetts, Benjamin F. Wade of Ohio, and Zachariah Chandler of Michigan—met frequently with Lincoln and implored him to alter his slave policy. Perhaps no other group prodded and pushed the President so much as they.

Sumner was a tall, elegant bachelor, with rich brown hair, a massive forehead, blue eyes, and a rather sad smile. He had traveled widely in England, where his friends included some of the most eminent political and literary figures. A humorless, erudite Bostonian, educated at Harvard, Sumner had a fondness for tailored coats, checkered trousers, and English gaiters. He was so conscious of manners, said a contemporary, "that he never allowed himself, even in the privacy of his own chamber, to fall into a position which he would not take in his chair in the Senate." He spoke out with great courage against racial inequality. Back in

1856, Representative Preston Brooks of South Carolina had beaten him almost to death in the Senate chamber for his "Crime Against Kansas" speech, and Sumner still carried physical and psychological scars from that attack. The senator now served as one of Lincoln's chief foreign policy advisers, often accompanied him on his carriage rides, and became the President's warm personal friend and a close companion of his wife.

Zachariah Chandler was a Detroit businessman who had amassed a fortune in real estate and dry goods. Profane, hard-drinking, and eternally grim, Chandler had been one of the founders of the national Republican party and had served on the Republican National Committee in 1856 and 1860. Elected to the Senate in 1857, he had plunged into the acrimonious debates over slavery on the frontier, exhorting his colleagues not to surrender another inch of territory to slaveholders. When southerners threatened to murder Republicans, brandishing pistols and bowie knives in the Senate itself, Chandler took up calisthenics and improved his marksmanship in case he had to fight. Once civil war commenced, he demanded that the government suppress the "armed traitors" of the South with all-out warfare.

New serving his second term as Senator from Ohio, Benjamin Franklin Wade was short and thick-chested, with iron-gray hair, sunken black eyes, and a square and beardless face. He was blunt and irascible, known as "Bluff Ben" for his readiness to duel with slaveowners, and he told more ribald jokes than any other man in the Senate. Yet he also had a charitable side: once when he spotted a destitute neighbor robbing his corncrib, Wade moved out of sight in order not to humiliate the man. Once the war began, he was determined that Congress should have an equal voice with Lincoln in shaping Union war policies. According to a foreign diplomat, Wade was "perhaps the most energetic personality in the entire Congress." "That queer, rough, but intelligent-looking man," said one Washington observer, "is old Senator Wade of Ohio, who doesn't care a pinch of snuff whether people like what he says or not." Wade hated slavery as Sumner and

Chandler did, and promised southern secessionists that "the first blast of civil war is the death warrant of your institution."

But, like most whites of his generation, Wade was prejudiced against blacks: he complained about their "odor," growled about all the "Nigger" cooks in Washington, and insisted that he had eaten food "cooked by Niggers until I can smell and taste the Nigger . . . all over." Like most Republicans, he thought the best solution to America's race problem was to ship all Negroes back to Africa.

As far as the Republican party was concerned, the three Senators belonged to a loose faction inaccurately categorized as "radicals," a misnomer that has persisted through the years. These "more advanced Republicans," as the Detroit *Post and Tribune* called them, were really progressive, nineteenth-century liberals who felt a powerful kinship with English liberals like John Bright and Richard Cobden. What advanced Republicans wanted was to reform the American system—to bring their nation into line with the Declaration's premise—by ridding it of slavery and the South's ruling planter class. But, while the advanced Republicans supported other social reforms, spoke out forthrightly against the crime and anachronism of slavery, and refused to compromise with the "Slave Power," they desired no radical break with American ideals and liberal institutions. Moreover, they were often at odds with one another on such issues as currency, the tariff, and precisely what rights black people should exercise in American white society.

Before secession, the advanced Republicans had endorsed the party's hands-off policy about slavery in the South: they all agreed that Congress had no constitutional authority to menace slavery as a state institution; all agreed, too, that the federal government could only abolish slavery in the national capital and outlaw it in the national territories, thus confining the institution to the South where they hoped it would perish, as Lincoln did. But civil war had removed their constitutional scruples about slavery in the southern states, thereby bringing about the first significant difference between them and the more "moderate" and "conservative" members of the party. While the latter insisted that the Union must be restored with slavery undamaged, the advanced Republicans argued that the national government could now remove the peculiar institution by the war power, and they wanted the President to do it in his capacity as Commander-in-Chief.

This was what Sumner, Wade, and Chandler came to talk about with Lincoln. They respected the President, had applauded his nomination, campaigned indefatigably in his behalf, and cheered his firm stand at Fort Sumter. Now they urged him to destroy slavery as a war measure, pointing out that this would maim and cripple the Confederacy and hasten an end to the rebellion. Sumner flatly asserted that slavery and the rebellion were "mated" and would stand or fall together.

Second, they reminded Lincoln that slavery had caused the war, was the reason the southern states had seceded, and was now the cornerstone of the Confederacy. It was absurd, the senators contended, to fight a war without removing the thing that had brought it about. Should the South return to the Union with slavery intact, as Lincoln desired, southerners would just start another war over slavery, whenever they thought it threatened again, so that the current struggle would have accomplished nothing. If Lincoln really wanted to save the Union, he must tear slavery out root and branch and smash the South's planter class —that mischievous class the senators thought had masterminded secession and fomented war.

Sumner, as a major Lincoln adviser on foreign affairs, also linked emancipation to foreign policy. There was a strong possibility that Britain would recognize the Confederacy as an independent nation —something that could be disastrous for the Union. As a member of the family of nations, the Confederacy could form alliances and seek mediation and perhaps armed intervention in the American conflict. But, Sumner argued, if Lincoln made the destruction of slavery a Union war aim, Britain would balk at recognition and intervention. Why so? Because she was proud of her antislavery tradition, Sumner said, and would refrain from helping the South protect human bondage from Lincoln's armies. And whatever powerful Britain did the rest of Europe was sure to follow.

Also, as Sumner kept reminding everyone, emancipation would break the chains of several million oppressed human beings and right America at last with her own ideals. Lincoln and the Republican party could no longer wait for time to remove slavery. The President must do it by the war power. The rebellion, monstrous and terrible though it was, had given him the opportunity to do it.

The abolitionists belabored that point too. They wrote Lincoln, petitioned him, addressed him from the stump and in their newspapers, descended on the White House one after another —right-minded men and women, black people and white, who battled slavery in Dixie and racial discrimination in the North, come now to convert the President himself. Foremost in that effort was Frederick Douglass, the most eminent Negro of his generation, a handsome, eloquent man who had escaped slavery in Maryland and become a self-made man like Lincoln, raising himself to prominence as an editor and reformer. From the outset, Douglass saw the end of slavery in this war, and he mounted a one-man crusade to win Lincoln to that idea. In his newspaper and on the platform, Douglass thundered at the man in the White House, playing on his personal feelings about slavery, rehearsing the same arguments that Sumner and his colleagues were giving Lincoln in person. You fight the rebels with only one hand, Douglass said. The mission of this war is the destruction of bondage as well as the salvation of the Union. "The very stomach of this rebellion is the negro in the condition of a slave. Arrest that hoe in the hands in the negro, and you smite rebellion in the very seat of its life," he said. "The Negro is the key of the situation—the pivot upon which the whole rebellion turns," he said. "Teach the rebels and traitors that the price they are to pay for the attempt to abolish this Government must be the abolition of slavery," he said. "Hence forth let the war cry be down with treason, and down with slavery, the cause of treason."

The pressure on Lincoln to strike at slavery was unrelenting. In between abolitionist delegations came Sumner and his stern colleagues again, with Vice-President Hannibal Hamlin and Congressman Owen Lovejoy, also advanced Republicans, often with them. As the war progressed, they raised still another argument for emancipation, an argument Douglass and members of Lincoln's own Cabinet were also making. In 1862, his armies suffered from manpower shortages on every front. Thanks to repeated Union military failures and to a growing war weariness across the North, volunteering had fallen off sharply; and Union generals bombarded Washington with shrill complaints, insisting that they faced an overwhelming southern foe and must have reinforcements before they could win battles or even fight. While Union commanders often exaggerated rebel strength, Union forces did need reinforcements to carry out a successful offensive war. As Sumner reminded Lincoln, the slaves were an untapped reservoir of strength. "You need more men," Sumner said, "not only at the North, but at the South. You need the slaves." If Lincoln freed them, he could recruit black men into his armed forces, thus helping to solve his manpower woes.

On that score, the slaves themselves were contributing to the pressures on Lincoln to emancipate them. Far from being passive recipients of freedom, as Vincent Harding has rightly reminded us, the slaves *were* engaged in self-liberation, abandoning rebel farms and plantations and escaping to Union lines by the thousands. This in turn created a tangled legal problem that bedeviled the Lincoln administration. What was the status of such "contraband of war," as Union General Benjamin F. Butler designated them? Were they still slaves? Were they free? Were they somewhere in between? The administration tended to follow a look-the-other-way policy, allowing field commanders to solve the contraband problem any way they wished. Some officers sent the fugitives back to the Confederacy, others turned them over to refugee camps, where benevolent organizations attempted to care for them. But with more and more slaves streaming into Union lines, Sumner, several of Lincoln's Cabinet members, Douglass, and many others urged him to grant them freedom and enlist the able-bodied men in the army. "Let the slaves and free colored people be called into service and formed into a liberating army," Douglass exhorted the President, "to march into the South and raise the banner of Emancipation among the slaves."

At first, Lincoln rejected a presidential move against slavery. "I think Sumner and the rest of you would upset our applecart altogether if you had your way," he told some advanced Republicans one day. "We didn't go into the war to put down slavery, but to put the flag back; and to act differently at this moment would, I have no doubt, not only weaken our cause, but smack of bad faith. . . . This thunderbolt will keep."

In short, as President he was accountable to the entire country, or what remained of it in the North and West, and the vast majority of whites there remained adamantly opposed to emancipation.

Still, Lincoln was sympathetic to the entire range of arguments Sumner and his associates rehearsed for him. Personally, Lincoln hated slavery as much as they did, and many of their points had already occurred to him. On certain days he could be seen like them in the lecture hall of the Smithsonian Institution, listening quietly and intently as antislavery orators damned slavery for the evil that it was. Under the combined and incessant demands that he act, Lincoln began wavering in his hands-off policy about slavery; as early as November and December, 1861, he began searching about for some compromise—something short of a sweeping emancipation decree, which he still regarded as "too big a lick." Again he seemed caught in an impossible dilemma: how to remove the cause of the war, keep Britain out of the conflict, solve the refugee problem, cripple the Confederacy, and suppress the rebellion, and yet retain the allegiance of northern Democrats and the critical border.

In March, 1862, he proposed a plan to Congress he thought might work: a gradual, compensated emancipation program to commence in the loyal border states. According to Lincoln's plan, the border states would gradually abolish slavery themselves over the next thirty years, and the federal government would compensate slaveowners for their loss. The whole program was to be voluntary; the states would adopt their own emancipation laws without federal coercion. This was consistent with Lincoln's old hope that when slavery was no longer workable southerners would get rid of it themselves. That moment had arrived.

At the same time, the federal government would sponsor a colonization program, which was also to be entirely voluntary. Lincoln was not going to make Negroes leave America anymore than he was going to coerce the states into liberating them. The idea of forcing people out of the country violated his very conception of what it was about.

Lincoln had good reason to attach colonization to his federal-state emancipation plan. Without a promise of colonization, he understood only too well, most northern whites would never accept emancipation, even if it was carried out by the states. From now on, every time he contemplated some new antislavery move, he made a great fuss about colonization: he embarked on a resettlement project in central America and another in Haiti, and he held an interview about colonization with Washington's black leaders, an interview he published in the press. In part, the ritual of colonization was designed to calm white racial fears.

If his gradual, state-guided plan was adopted, Lincoln contended that a presidential decree—federally enforced emancipation—would never be necessary. Abolition would begin on the local level in the loyal border and then be extended into the rebel states as they were conquered. Thus by a slow and salubrious process would the cause of the rebellion be removed and the future of the American experiment guaranteed.

On Capitol Hill, Congressman Thaddeus Stevens of Pennsylvania belittled Lincoln's scheme as "diluted milk-and-water gruel." But Sumner and other advanced Republicans, noting that Lincoln's was the first emancipation proposal ever offered by an American President, acclaimed it as an excellent step. On April 10, 1862, the Republican-controlled Congress endorsed Lincoln's plan.* But the border-state representatives, for whom it was intended, rejected the scheme emphatically. "I utterly spit at it and despise it," said one Kentucky congressman. "Emancipation in the cotton States is simply an absurdity. . . . There is not enough power in the world to compel it to be done."

As Lincoln promoted his gradual, compensated scheme, advanced Republicans on Capitol Hill launched a furious antislavery attack of their own. By now, they had won over many Republican moderates to forge a new congressional majority on the slavery issue. As the war raged into its second year, moderate Republicans came to agree with their advanced colleagues that it was senseless to pretend that the Union could be restored without removing the cause of the rebellion.

In the House, the leader of the advanced Republican offensive was sixty-nine-year-old Thaddeus Stevens, who controlled the nation's purse strings as chairman of the powerful Committee on Ways and Means. Stevens was a grim, sardonic bachelor with a cutting wit ("I now yield to Mr. B.," he once said, "who will make a few feeble remarks") and a fondness for gambling that took him almost nightly to Washington's casinos. To the delight of his colleagues, he indulged in witticisms so indecorous that they had to be deleted from the *Congressional Globe.* A wealthy ironmaster with a Jekyll-and-Hyde personality, as one biographer described him, he had contributed generously to charities and causes, crusaded for public schools in Pennsylvania, and defended fugitive slaves there. Afflicted with a club foot, Stevens spoke of bondage "in terms of shackled limbs and a longing for freedom to dance." He lived with his mulatto housekeeper, Lydia Smith,

---

*Because so many southerners had resigned their congressional seats and joined the Confederacy, the Republicans had gained control of both houses on Capitol Hill. Thereupon they had voted to expel the secessionists as traitors.

and there is strong evidence that they were lovers. Anti-mis-cegenation laws made marriage impossible, and their liaison not only generated malicious gossip but probably kept Stevens from becoming what he most wanted to be—a United States senator. He liked to quote the Bible that "He hath made of one blood all nations of men," yet he never championed complete equality for blacks—"not equality in all things," he once asserted, "simply before the laws, nothing else." Serving a fourth term as congress-man, this bitter, intimidating, high-minded man ruled the Civil War House and was "the master-spirit," said Republican journal-ist Alexander McClure, "of every aggressive movement in Con-gress to overthrow the rebellion and slavery."

Over howling Democratic opposition, Stevens, Sumner, and their Republican cohorts rammed a procession of antislavery mea-sures through Congress. One forbade the return of fugitive slaves to the rebels; another abolished slavery in Washington, D.C., and compensated owners for their loss; still another outlawed human bondage in all federal territories, thus reversing the hated Dred Scott decision. Lincoln signed all these bills into law, and joined with Congress in recognizing the black republics of Haiti and Liberia, a move that would facilitate colonization efforts in those lands.

The flood of antislavery legislation delighted Frederick Doug-lass. "I trust I am not dreaming," he wrote Sumner, "but the events taking place seem like a dream." But he was grievously disappointed in Lincoln's colonization moves, which he did not fully understand. Hurt and perplexed by them, Douglass damned the President for "his pride of race and blood, his contempt for Negroes and his canting hypocrisy." And he warned that the Union cause "would never prosper till the war assumed an anti-slavery attitude, and the Negro was enlisted on the loyal side."

Lincoln meanwhile had run into trouble with his gradual, state-guided emancipation plan. He couldn't even persuade Delaware, with its small and relatively harmless slave population, to adopt it. In desperation, Lincoln on three different occasions—in the spring and summer of 1862—pleaded with border-state congress-men to endorse his program. In their third meeting, held in the White House on July 12, Lincoln warned the border representa-tives that it was impossible now to restore the Union with slavery preserved. Slavery was doomed. They could not be blind to the signs, blind to the fact that his plan was the only alternative to a more drastic move against slavery, one that would cause tremen-dous destruction in the South. Please, he said, commend my gradual plan to your people.

But most of the border men turned him down. They thought his plan would cost too much, would only whip the flames of rebellion, would cause dangerous discontent in their own states. Their intransigence was a sober lesson to Lincoln. It was proof indeed that slaveowners—even loyal slaveowners—were too tied up in the slave system ever to free their own Negroes and voluntar-ily transform their way of life. If abolition must come, it must begin in the rebel South and then be extended into the loyal border later on. Which meant that the President must eradicate slavery himself. He could no longer avoid the responsibility. By mid-July, 1862, the pressures of the war had forced him to aban-don his hands-off policy and lay a "strong hand on the colored element."

On July 13, the day after his last talk with the border men, Lincoln took a carriage ride with a couple of his Cabinet secretar-ies. His conversation, when recounted in full, reveals a tougher Lincoln than the middle-of-the-road President of Sandburg's myth-building biography. Lincoln said he was convinced that the war could no longer be won through forbearance toward southern rebels, that it was "a duty on our part to liberate the slaves." The time had come to take a bold new path and hurl Union armies at "the heart of the rebellion," using the military to destroy the very institution that caused and now sustained the insurrection. Southerners could not throw off the Constitution and at the same time invoke it to protect slavery. They had started the war and must now face its consequences.

He had given this a lot of grave and painful thought, he said, and had concluded that a presidential declaration of emancipation was the last alternative, that it was "a military necessity absolutely essential to the preservation of the Union." Because the slaves were a tremendous source of strength for the rebellion, Lincoln must invite them to desert and "come to us and uniting with us they must be made free from rebel authority and rebel masters." His interview with the border men yesterday, he said, "had forced him slowly but he believed correctly to this conclusion."

On July 22, 1862, Lincoln summoned his Cabinet members and read them a draft of a preliminary Emancipation Proclamation. Come January 1, 1863, in his capacity as Commander-in-Chief of the armed forces in time of war, Lincoln would free all the slaves everywhere in the rebel states. He would thus make it a Union objective to annihilate slavery as an institution in the Confederate South.

Contrary to what many historians have said, Lincoln's projected Proclamation went further than anything Congress had done. True, Congress had just enacted (and Lincoln had just signed) the second confiscation act, which provided for the seizure and liberation of all slaves of people who supported or participated in the rebellion. Still, most slaves would be freed only after protracted case-by-case litigation in the federal courts. Another section of the act did liberate certain categories of slaves without court action, but the bill exempted loyal slaveowners in the rebel South, allowing them to keep their slaves and other property. Far short of a genuine emancipation measure, the act was about as far as Congress could go in attacking slavery, for most Republicans still acknowledged that Congress had no constitutional authority to remove bondage as a state institution. Only the President with his war powers—or a constitutional amendment—could do that. Nevertheless, the measure seemed a clear invitation for the President to exercise his constitutional powers and abolish slavery in the rebellious states. And Stevens, Sumner, and others repeatedly told Lincoln that most congressional Republicans now favored this.

In contrast to the confiscation act, Lincoln's Proclamation was a sweeping blow against slavery as an institution in the rebel states, a blow that would free *all* slaves there—those of secessionists and loyalists alike. Thus Lincoln would handle emancipation himself (as congressional Republicans wanted him to do), avoid judicial red tape, and use the military to vanquish the cornerstone of the Confederacy. Again, he justified this as a military necessity to save the Union—and with it America's experiment in popular government.

But William H. Seward and other Cabinet secretaries dissuaded Lincoln from issuing his Proclamation in July. Seward argued that the Union had won no clear military victories, particularly in the showcase eastern theater. As a consequence, Europe would misconstrue the Proclamation as "our last shriek on the retreat," as a wild and reckless attempt to compensate for Union military ineptitude by provoking a slave insurrection behind rebel lines. If Lincoln must give an emancipation order, Seward warned, he must wait until the Union won a military victory.

Lincoln finally agreed to wait, but he was not happy about it: the way George B. McClellan and his other generals had been fighting in the eastern theater, Lincoln had no idea when he would ever have a victory.

While he waited, he published his famous "open" letter to Horace Greeley of the New York *Tribune,* a letter that has been persistently misunderstood and misrepresented. "My paramount object in this struggle *is* to save the Union," Lincoln told Greeley (and the nation beyond), "and is *not* either to save or to destroy slavery. If I could save the Union without freeing *any* slave I would do it, and if I could save it by freeing *all* the slaves I would do it; and if I could save it by freeing some and leaving others alone I would also do that. What I do about slavery, and the colored race, I do because I believe it helps to save the Union." He noted in closing, "I have here stated my purpose according to my view of *official* duty; and I intend no modification of my oft-expressed *personal* wish that all men every where could be free."

As I tried to explain in *With Malice Toward None,* Lincoln had little choice but to speak of slavery strictly in terms of preserving the Union: they were the only terms the white public was likely to accept. In truth, his letter to Greeley was a calculated statement, part of several efforts on Lincoln's part to prepare northern whites for the Proclamation he intended to foist on them. You see, he was suggesting, I am keeping my personal hatred of slavery out of this. If I free some or all the slaves (and for the first time in public he claimed the authority to free them), I do so only to save our Union, our cause, our cherished experiment in popular government.

One of the great ironies of the war was that George McClellan presented Lincoln with the military triumph he needed to issue his Proclamation. A Democrat who sympathized with southern slavery and opposed wartime emancipation with a passion, McClellan outfought Robert E. Lee at Antietam Creek in September, 1862, forcing the rebel army to leave the battlefield. Thereupon Lincoln promulgated his preliminary Proclamation, with its warning that if the rebellion did not cease by January 1, 1863, the executive branch, including the army and the navy, would destroy slavery in the rebel states. Lincoln had no illusions that the rebels would now throw down their arms and rush back to the Union before the ninety-day deadline. But at least it would signal the white North that he was proceeding with extreme caution in this inflammable area.

Let him be cautious. Frederick Douglass, for one, could not restrain his ecstasy that Lincoln had come around at last. "We shout for joy that we live to record this righteous decree," he recorded in his journal. And his attitude toward Lincoln now underwent a total transformation. He assured his readers that "Abraham Lincoln will take no step backward. His word has gone out over the country and the world, giving joy and gladness to the friends of freedom and progress wherever these words are read, and he will stand by them and carry them out to the letter." He told his friends in Great Britain that "the hopes of millions, long trodden down, now rise with every advancing hour."

The advanced Republicans were also delighted. "Hurrah for Old Abe and the proclamation," Wade exulted. Stevens extolled Lincoln for his patriotism and said his Proclamation "contained precisely the principles which I had advocated." "Thank God that I live to enjoy this day!" Sumner exclaimed in Boston. "Freedom is practically secured to all who find shelter within our lines, and the glorious flag of the Union, wherever it floats, becomes the flag of Freedom." A few days later, Sumner announced that "the Emancipation Proclamation . . . is now the corner-stone of our national policy."

As it turned out, though, the preliminary Proclamation helped lead to a Republican disaster in the fall by-elections of 1862. Already northern Democrats were upset with Lincoln's harsh war measures, especially his use of martial law and military arrests. But Negro emancipation was more than they could stand, and they stumped the northern states that fall, beating the drums of Negrophobia, warning of massive influxes of southern blacks into the North once emancipation came. Sullen, war weary, and racially aroused, northern voters dealt the Republicans a smashing blow, as the North's five most populous states—all of which had gone for Lincoln in 1860—now returned Democratic majorities to Capitol Hill. While the Republicans narrowly retained control of Congress, the future looked bleak indeed for 1864.

Republican analysts—and Lincoln himself—conceded that the preliminary Proclamation was a major factor in the Republican defeat. But Lincoln told a delegation from Kentucky that he would rather die than retract a single word in his Proclamation.

In December, in the midst of rising racial protest against him, Lincoln asked Congress—and northern whites beyond—for their support in his moves against slavery. "The dogmas of the quiet past," he reminded them, "are inadequate to the stormy present. The occasion is piled high with difficulty, and we must rise with the occasion. As our case is new, so we must think anew, and act anew. We must disenthrall our selves, and then we shall save our country.

"Fellow-citizens, *we* cannot escape history. . . . The fiery trial through which we pass, will light us down, in honor or dishonor, to the latest generation. . . . In *giving* freedom to the slave, we *assure* freedom for the *free*—honorable alike in what we give, and what we preserve. We shall nobly save, or meanly lose, the last best, hope of earth."

That message provoked a fusillade of abuse from congressional Democrats, who blasted Lincoln's projected Proclamation as blatantly unconstitutional and warned that any attempt to overthrow state institutions would be "a high crime"—that is, an impeachable offense. Lincoln's "thunderbolt," raged one Democrat, left them all "mute in amazement. Its suddenness, its utter contempt for the Constitution, its imperial pretension, the thorough upheaving of the whole social organization which it decreed, and the perspective of crime, and blood, and ruin, which it opened to the vision, filled every patriotic heart with astonishment, terror and indignation."

Said Frederick Douglass: "From the genuine abolition view, Mr. Lincoln seemed tardy, cold, dull, and indifferent, but measuring him by the sentiment of his country—a sentiment he was bound as a statesman to consult—he was swift, zealous, radical, and determined."

As the New Year approached, conservative Republicans begged Lincoln to abandon his "reckless" emancipation scheme lest he shatter their demoralized party and wreck what remained of their country. At the same time, Sumner and Wade admonished Lincoln to stand firm, and he promised that he would. On New Year's Day, 1863, he officially signed the final Emancipation Proclamation in the White House. His hand trembled badly, not because he was nervous, but because he had shaken hands all morning in a White House reception. He assured everyone present that he was never more certain of what he was doing. "If my name ever goes into history," he said, "it will be for this act."

In the final Proclamation, Lincoln said nothing about colonization or compensation to slaveowners. He did temporarily exempt occupied Tennessee and certain occupied places in Louisiana and Virginia. But later, in reconstructing those states, he withdrew the exemptions and made emancipation a mandatory part of his reconstruction program. His Proclamation also excluded the loyal slave states because they were not in rebellion and he lacked the legal authority to uproot slavery there. He would, however, keep goading them to obliterate slavery themselves—and would later push a constitutional amendment that liberated their slaves as well. With the exception of the loyal border and certain occupied areas, the final Proclamation declared that as of this day, all slaves in the rebellious states were "forever free." The document also asserted that black men—southern and northern alike—would now be enlisted in Union military forces.

All in all, advanced and moderate Republicans were pleased. In fact, Sumner, Wade, Chandler, and their colleagues took a lot of credit for prodding Lincoln at last to act. Perhaps the President should not have exempted Tennessee and southern Louisiana, Horace Greeley said, "but let us not cavil." Lincoln had now "played his grand part" in the destruction of slavery, said another Republican, and some thought how ironic it was that the Proclamation had now made Lincoln and all of them abolitionists.

In Boston, abolitionist Wendell Phillips observed that to white Americans the Proclamation was a step in the progress of humanity, but to Negroes it was "the sunlight scattering the despair of centuries." A Negro preacher named Henry M. Turner summed up what Lincoln's decree meant to that whole generation of black Americans. "The time has come in the history of this nation,"

Turner said, "when the downtrodden and abject black man can assert his rights, and feel his manhood. . . . The first day of January, 1863, is destined to form one of the most memorable epochs in the history of the world."

3: THE MAN OF OUR REDEMPTION

Lincoln's Proclamation was not "of minor importance," as one historian maintained several years ago. On the contrary, it was the most revolutionary measure ever to come from an American President up to that time. This "momentous decree," as Martin Luther King, Jr., later described it, was an unprecedented use of federal military power against a state institution. It was an unprecedented federal assault against the very foundation of the South's ruling planter class and economic and social order. As Union armies punched into rebel territory, they would tear slavery out root and branch, automatically freeing all slaves in the areas and states they conquered. In this respect (as Lincoln said), the war brought on changes more fundamental and profound than either side had expected when the conflict began. Now slavery would perish as the Confederacy perished, would die by degrees with every Union advance, every Union victory.

Moreover, word of the Proclamation hummed across the slave grapevine in the Confederacy; and as Union armies drew near, more slaves than ever abandoned rebel farms and plantations and (as one said) "demonstrated with their feet" their desire for freedom. In short, slaves like these did not sit back and wait for their liberty: they went out and got it for themselves.

The Proclamation was not some anemic document that in

effect freed no slaves. By November, 1864, the Philadelphia *North American* estimated that more than 1,300,000 Negroes had been liberated by Lincoln's Proclamation or "the events of the war." By war's end, all three and a half million slaves in the defeated Confederacy could claim freedom under Lincoln's Proclamation and the victorious Union flag.

What is more, the Proclamation did something for Lincoln personally that has never been stressed enough. In truth, the story of emancipation could well be called the liberation of Abraham Lincoln. For in the process of granting freedom to the slaves, Lincoln also emancipated himself from his old dilemma. His Proclamation now brought the private and the public Lincoln together: now the public statesman could obliterate a wicked thing the private citizen had always hated, a thing that had long had "the power of making me miserable." Now the public statesman could destroy what he regarded as "a cruel wrong" that had always besmirched America's experiment in popular government, had always impeded her historic mission in the progress of human liberty in the world.

The Proclamation also opened the army to black volunteers, and northern free Negroes and southern ex-slaves now enlisted as Union soldiers. As Lincoln said, "the colored population is the great *available* and yet unavailed of, force for restoring the Union." And he now availed himself of that force. In occupied northern Alabama, a Union recruiter "of salty temper" put up a large poster with the legend: **"ALL SLAVES WERE MADE FREEMEN BY ABRAHAM LINCOLN, PRESIDENT OF THE UNITED STATES.** Come, then, able-bodied **COLORED MEN,** to the nearest United States Camp, and fight for the **STARS AND STRIPES."** And fight they did. In all, some 186,000 Negro troops—most of them emancipated slaves— served in Union forces on every major battle front, helping to liberate their brothers and sisters in bondage and to save the American experiment. As Lincoln observed, the blacks added enormous and indispensable strength to the Union war machine. Without them, it is doubtful that he could have won the war.

Unhappily, the blacks fought in segregated units under white officers, and until late in the war received less pay than whites did. In 1863 Lincoln told Frederick Douglass that he disliked the practice of unequal pay, but that the government had to make some concessions to white prejudices, noting that a great many northern whites opposed the use of black soldiers altogether. But he promised that they would eventually get equal pay—and they did. Moreover, Lincoln was proud of the performance of his black soldiers: he publicly praised them for fighting "with clenched teeth, and steady eye, and well poised bayonet" to save the Union, while certain whites strove "with malignant heart" to hinder it.

As one historian has noted, the use of black troops had potent social and psychological overtones. A black soldier, dressed in Union blue and armed with a rifle and bayonet, posed a radically different picture from the obsequious "Sambo" image cultivated and cherished by southern whites. Fighting as soldiers not only gave black men a new sense of manhood, as the Reverend Turner had predicted, but undermined the whole nineteenth-century notion of innate Negro inferiority.

With blacks now fighting in his armies, Lincoln abandoned colonization as a solution to racial adjustment in Dixie. His colonization schemes had all floundered, and in any case black people adamantly refused to participate in the President's voluntary program. Across the North, free Negroes denounced Lincoln's highly publicized colonization efforts—this was their country too!—and they petitioned him to deport slaveholders instead. And Lincoln seemed in sympathy with that. Later, as the war drew to a close, he told his Cabinet that he would like to frighten rebel leaders out of the country. He waved his arms as though he were shooing chickens.

After he issued the Emancipation Proclamation, Lincoln never again urged colonization in public—an eloquent silence, indicating that he had concluded that Dixie's whites and liberated Negroes must somehow learn to live together. How, then, could Lerone Bennett and others maintain that Lincoln to the end of his life was a champion of colonization? That argument rests exclusively on the 1892 autobiography of Union political general Benjamin F. Butler. In it, Butler claimed that in April, 1865, Lincoln feared a race war in the South and still wanted to ship the blacks abroad. Not only is Butler a highly dubious witness, but there is not a scintilla of corroborative evidence to support his story, which one Lincoln scholar has recently exposed as "entirely a fantasy." There is not a single other source that quotes the President, in public or in private, as stating that he still favored colonization.

In any case, such a stance would have been glaringly inconsistent with Lincoln's Gettysburg Address, which called for a new birth of freedom in America for blacks and whites alike (here, in fact, is the eloquent defense of liberty that critics have found lacking in the Proclamation itself). And a colonization stance would have been inconsistent, too, with Lincoln's appreciation of the indispensable role his black soldiers played in subduing the rebellion. No man of Lincoln's honesty and sense of fair play would enlist 186,000 black troops to save the Union and then advocate throwing them out of the country. He simply did not advocate that.

Still, he needed some device during the war, some program that would pacify white northerners and convince them that southern freedmen would not flock into their communities, but would remain in the South instead. What Lincoln worked out was a refugee system, installed by his adjutant general in occupied Dixie, which utilized blacks there in a variety of military and civilian pursuits. Then Republican propaganda went to work selling northern whites on the system and the Emancipation Proclamation: *See, liberated Negroes will not invade the North, but will stay in Dixie as free wage earners, learning to help themselves and our Union cause.*

Even so, emancipation remained the most explosive and unpopular act of Lincoln's presidency. By mid-1863, thousands of
Democrats were in open revolt against his administration, de-
nouncing Lincoln as an abolitionist dictator who had surrendered
to radicalism. In the Midwest, dissident Democrats launched a
peace movement to throw "the shrieking abolitionist faction" out
of office and negotiate a peace with the Confederacy that would
somehow restore the Union with slavery unmolested. There were
large antiwar rallies against Lincoln's war for slave liberation. Race
and draft riots flared in several northern cities.

With all the public unrest behind the lines, conservative
Republicans beseeched Lincoln to abandon emancipation and
rescue his country "from the brink of ruin." But Lincoln seemed
intractable. He had made up his mind to smash the slave society
of the rebel South and eliminate the moral wrong of Negro bondage, and no amount of public discontent, he indicated, was going
to change his mind. He had deemed his Proclamation "an act of
justice" and contended in any case that blacks who had tasted
freedom would never consent to be slaves again. "To use a coarse,
but an expressive figure," he wrote an aggravated Democrat, "broken eggs cannot be mended. I have issued the Proclamation, and
I cannot retract it."

On Capitol Hill, the advanced Republicans were overjoyed.
"He is stubborn as a mule when he gets his back up," Chandler
said of Lincoln, "*& it is up* now on the Proclamation." "His mind
acts slowly," said Owen Lovejoy, "but when he moves, it is *forward.*"

He wavered once—in August, 1864, a time of unrelenting
gloom for Lincoln, when his popularity had sunk to an all-time low
and it seemed he could not be reelected. He confessed that maybe
the country would no longer sustain a war for slave emancipation,
that maybe he shouldn't pull the nation down a road it did not
want to travel. On August 24 he decided to offer Jefferson Davis
peace terms that excluded emancipation as a condition, vaguely
suggesting that slavery would be adjusted later "by peaceful

means." But the next day Lincoln changed his mind. With awakened resolution, he vowed to fight the war through to uncondi-
tional surrender and to stick by emancipation come what may. He
had made his promise of freedom to the slaves, and he meant to
keep it as long as he was in office.

When he won the election of 1864, Lincoln interpreted it as
a popular mandate for him and his emancipation policy. But in
reality the election provided no clear referendum on slavery, since
Republican campaigners had played down emancipation and con-
centrated on the folly of the Democrats in running General
George McClellan on a peace plank in the midst of civil war.
Nevertheless, Lincoln used his reelection to promote a constitutional amendment that would guarantee the freedom of all slaves,
those in the loyal border states as well as those in the rebel South.
Even before issuing his Proclamation, Lincoln had worried that
it might be nullified in the courts or thrown out by a later Congress or a subsequent administration. Consequently he wanted a
constitutional amendment that would safeguard his Proclamation
and prevent emancipation from ever being overturned.

Back in December, 1862, Lincoln himself had called on Congress to adopt an emancipation amendment, and advanced
Republicans had introduced one in the Senate and guided it
through, reminding their colleagues that nobody could deny that
all the death and destruction of the war stemmed from slavery and
that it was their duty to support this amendment. In April, 1864,
the Senate adopted it by a vote of thirty-eight to six, but it failed
to muster the required two-thirds majority in the House.

After that Lincoln had insisted that the Republican platform
endorse the measure. And now, over the winter of 1864 and 1865,
he put tremendous pressure on the House to approve the amendment, using all his powers of persuasion and patronage to get it
through. He buttonholed conservative Republicans and opposition Democrats and exhorted them to support the amendment.
He singled out "sinners" among the Democrats who were "on
praying ground," and informed them that they had a lot better
chance for the federal jobs they desired if they voted for the

measure. Soon two Democrats swung over in favor of it. In the House debates, meanwhile, Republican James Ashley quoted Lincoln himself that *"if slavery is not wrong, nothing is wrong,"* and Thaddeus Stevens, still tall and imposing at seventy-two, asserted that he had never hesitated, even when threatened with violence, "to stand here and denounce this infamous institution." With the outcome much in doubt, Lincoln and congressional Republicans participated in secret negotiations never made public—negotiations that allegedly involved patronage, a New Jersey railroad monopoly, and the release of rebels related to congressional Democrats—to bring wavering opponents into line. "The greatest measure of the nineteenth century," Stevens claimed, "was passed by corruption, aided and abetted by the purest man in America."

On January 31, 1865, the House adopted the present Thirteenth Amendment by just three votes more than the required two-thirds majority. At once a storm of cheers broke over House Republicans, who danced around, embraced one another, and waved their hats and canes. "It seemed to me I had been born into a new life," recalled one advanced Republican, "and that the world was overflowing with beauty and joy."

Lincoln, too, pronounced the amendment "a great moral victory" and "a King's cure" for the evils of slavery. When ratified by the states, the amendment would end human bondage everywhere in America.* Lincoln pointed across the Potomac. "If the people over the river had behaved themselves, I could not have done what I have."

Lincoln conceded, though, that he had not controlled the events of the war, but that events had controlled him instead, that God had controlled him. He thought about this a good deal, especially at night when he couldn't sleep, trying to understand the meaning of the war, to understand why it had begun and grown into such a massive revolutionary struggle, consuming hundreds of thousands of lives (the final casualties would come to

---

*The amendment was finally ratified in December, 1865. Until then, the freedom of most southern blacks rested on Lincoln's Proclamation.

620,000 on both sides). By his second inaugural, he had reached an apocalyptic conclusion about the nature of the war—had come to see it as divine punishment for the "great offense" of slavery, as a terrible retribution God had visited on a guilty people, in North as well as South. Lincoln's vision was close to that of old John Brown, who had prophesied on the day he was hanged, on that balmy December day back in 1859, that the crime of slavery could not be purged from this guilty land except by blood. Lincoln's vision was close to that of the deeply religious slaves, to the self-liberating forebears of historian Vincent Harding, who saw the hand of God in this terrible war and the inexorable approach of Judgment Day. Now, in his Second Inaugural Address, Lincoln too contended that God perhaps had willed this "mighty scourge of War" on the United States, "until all the wealth piled by the bondman's two hundred and fifty years of unrequited toil shall be sunk, and until every drop of blood drawn with the lash, shall be paid by another drawn from the sword."

He had come a long distance from the harassed political candidate of 1858, opposed to emancipation lest his political career be jeopardized, convinced that only the distant future could remove slavery from his troubled land, certain that only colonization could solve the ensuing problem of racial adjustment. He had also come a long way in the matter of Negro social and political rights, as we shall see. The Proclamation had indeed liberated Abraham Lincoln, enabling him to act more consistently with his moral convictions.

He had none of the racial prejudice that infected so many whites of that time, even advanced Republicans like Benjamin Wade. Frederick Douglass, who interviewed Lincoln in 1863, said he was "the first great man that I talked with in the United States freely who in no single instance reminded me of the difference between himself and myself, of the difference of color." Other blacks also testified that the President treated them as they wanted to be treated—as human beings with feelings. He did not tell dialect jokes in their presence, did not condescend to them, did not spell out his thoughts in imbecilic one-syllable language, as did many other whites when speaking to Negroes. He opened the White House doors to black visitors as no other President had ever done before and as few would do after. At his New Year's reception in 1865, he shook hands with a parade of Negro men and women, some in their Sunday finest, others in patched overalls, who had come to pay their respects to the man who signed "the Freedom bill."

During his inaugural reception that March, the President learned that Frederick Douglass was at the front door of the executive mansion, but was having trouble getting past the police because he was a Negro. Lincoln had him shown in at once, hailed him as "my friend Douglass," and asked what he thought of the Inaugural Address. "There is no man in the country whose opinion I value more than yours," Lincoln said. Douglass replied that he was impressed, that he thought it "a sacred effort." "I am glad you liked it!" Lincoln said. In truth, he strongly identified with this proud black man, referring to "the similarity with which I had fought my way up, we both starting off at the lowest round of the ladder."

Douglass, reflecting back on Lincoln's presidency, recalled how in the first year and a half of the war, Lincoln "was ready and willing" to sacrifice black people for the benefit and welfare of whites. But since the preliminary Emancipation Proclamation, Douglass said, American blacks had taken Lincoln's measure and had come to admire and some to love this complicated man. Though Lincoln had taxed Negroes to the limit, they had decided, in the roll and tumble of events, that "the how and the man of our redemption had somehow met in the person of Abraham Lincoln."

4: NECESSITY KNOWS NO LAW

Lincoln became a tough wartime President, flexing his executive muscles and expanding his war powers whenever necessity demanded. "Necessity," he argued, "knows no law." In the exigency of domestic insurrection, he would do whatever he thought imperative to save the country and all it represented. Yet he did not intend to establish a precedent for an "imperial presidency," one that would allow subsequent chief executives to meddle in the internal affairs of other nations, under the pretext of saving the world. In short, we cannot blame Lincoln for Lyndon Johnson's disastrous policy in Vietnam. Except for emancipation, Lincoln regarded all of his severe war measures as temporary necessities to end the rebellion and preserve the American experiment, the central idea of the war.

Consider his emergency measures during the eighty days between the outbreak of war and the convening of Congress on Independence Day, 1861. Since rebel forces were threatening to occupy Washington and the nation was on the brink of disintegration, Lincoln met with his Cabinet, and they all decided that they must assume broad emergency powers or let the government fall. Accordingly, Lincoln directed that Secretary of the Navy Gideon Welles empower several individuals—among them his own brother-in-law—to forward troops and supplies to embattled Washington. The President allowed his Secretary of War to authorize the governor of New York and one Alexander Cummings to transport troops and acquire supplies for the public defense. Since Lincoln believed that government departments brimmed with traitors, he himself chose private citizens known for "their ability, loyalty, and patriotism" to spend public money for arms and military preparations. Perhaps these emergency measures were "without authority of law," Lincoln told Congress later, but he deemed them absolutely necessary to save popular government itself. And his Cabinet unanimously agreed.

With Cabinet approval, Lincoln also declared a blockade of the southern coast, added 22,000 men to the regular army and 18,000 to the navy, called for 42,000 three-year volunteers, and put national armories into full production. As Lincoln subsequently informed Congress, "These measures, whether strictly legal or not, were ventured upon, under what appeared to be a popular demand, and public necessity; trusting, then as now, that Congress would readily ratify them." When Congress convened in July, it did indeed ratify "all the acts, proclamations, and orders of the President" relating to the army and navy and the volunteers, "as if they had been issued and done under the previous express authority and direction of Congress." In short, if Lincoln went beyond the letter of the law to save the government, Congress sanctioned his actions.

Generally Congress did the same in the area of martial law and military arrests. From the outset, Lincoln dealt harshly with "the enemy in the rear"—with what he called "a most efficient corps of spies, informers, suppliers, and aiders and abettors" of the rebellion who took advantage of "Liberty of speech, Liberty of the press and *Habeas corpus*" to disrupt the Union war effort. Consequently, he suspended the writ of habeas corpus—which required that a citizen be told why he was being held—and authorized army commanders to declare martial law in various areas behind the lines and to try civilians in military courts without juries. Lincoln openly defended such an invasion of civil liberties, contending that strict measures were essential if the laws of the Union —and liberty itself—were to survive the war.

Lincoln's suspension of the writ of habeas corpus infuriated Roger B. Taney, Chief Justice of the U.S. Supreme Court, who accused the President of usurping power. Taney argued that only Congress could legally suspend the writ, and he admonished Lincoln not to violate the very laws he had sworn to defend. "Are all the laws, but one, to go unexecuted," Lincoln asked Congress, in reference to habeas corpus, "and the government itself go to pieces lest that one be violated?" Moreover, the Constitution did not specify which branch of the government could suspend the writ, so that Lincoln did not think he had broken any laws or violated his oath of office.

Still, he invoked his presidential powers in heretofore undreamed-of ways, as we have seen in the matter of emancipation. Recall, though, the novelty of the war. Nothing like this had ever occurred in America, and there were no guidelines in dealing with dissent and national security in the midst of a giant domestic insurrection that imperiled the nation itself. As in most war matters, Lincoln and his Cabinet found themselves in uncharted legal territory.

In 1862 the President centralized jurisdiction over internal-security matters in the War Department. To deal with such matters, the department created a corps of civilian provost marshals, but allowed them too much independence in policing and jailing alleged disloyalists. Their zealous, far-ranging operations led to widespread criticism of the Lincoln administration. At the same time, Lincoln's War Department empowered army officers to apprehend anybody who discouraged volunteering or otherwise helped the enemy. And the department got up dragnets in which state militia, home guards, police chiefs, and vigilantes all participated. In all, they seized and imprisoned at least 14,000 people—many of them antiwar Democrats—under Lincoln's authority. The outcry against arbitrary arrests became so strident that Lincoln tried to restrain excessive use of power whenever he could. He speedily ordered the release of people unwarrantedly arrested, especially political prisoners. Also, when General Ambrose E. Burnside suspended the Chicago *Times* for virulent outbursts against the administration, Lincoln promptly revoked the order.

The most controversial military arrest was that of Clement L. Vallandigham, an Ohio congressman and a leading antiwar Democrat. "Valiant Val," as his friends called him, accused Lincoln of dishonoring the Constitution with his "tyrannical" measures, of abandoning the war for the Union in favor of a crusade for Negroes in which the white people were to be enslaved. "I see nothing before us," he warned war-weary northerners, "but universal political and social revolution, anarchy and bloodshed, compared with which the Reign of Terror in the French Revolution was a merciful visitation." For Vallandigham, the solution was clear: stop the fighting and negotiate a peace with the rebels that would somehow restore the old Union and the old certitudes. Stumping Ohio in the spring of 1863, he denounced abolition, the war, and the despotism of "King Lincoln" and demanded a truce with the Confederacy. During one of his orations, an officer in civilian dress, detailed from General Burnside's headquarters, leaned against the platform taking notes. Three days later an infantry column broke into his Dayton home at midnight, found him in his underwear, gave him time to dress, and hauled him off to prison in Cincinnati. Dayton citizens rioted in protest, but to no avail. A military commission convicted Vallandigham of undermining government efforts "to suppress an unlawful rebellion" and sentenced him to imprisonment for the duration of the war.

Across the North, Democrats demanded Vallandigham's release and castigated Lincoln for exercising "arbitrary power" at the expense of liberty. In an open letter to them, Lincoln spoke bluntly in his own defense. Because he had "a reverence for the guaranteed rights of individuals," Lincoln said, he had been "slow to adopt the strong measures, which by degrees I have been forced to regard as being within the exceptions of the constitution, and as indispensable to the public Safety." He pointed out that military arrests of civilians had been made to *prevent* injury to the Union war effort; his government could not always wait for overt acts of treason before it moved. Had he promptly arrested traitors like Robert E. Lee, Lincoln said, it would almost certainly have weakened the rebellion and shortened the war. In truth, he argued, "the time [is] not unlikely to come when I shall be blamed for having made too few arrests rather than too many."

As for Vallandigham, the army had seized him because he was "laboring, with some effect, to prevent the raising of troops, to encourage desertions from the army, and to leave the rebellion without an adequate military force to suppress it." In short, he was "warring upon the military," on which the very life of the nation depended. Long experience, Lincoln went on, demonstrated that armies could not be maintained unless desertion was punished by the death penalty. "Must I shoot a simple-minded soldier boy who deserts," Lincoln asked, "while I must not touch a hair of a wiley agitator who induces him to desert? This is none the less injurious when effected by getting a father, a brother, or friend, into a public meeting, and there working upon his feelings, till he is persuaded to write the soldier boy, that he is fighting in a bad cause, for a wicked administration of a contemptible government, too weak to arrest and punish him if he shall desert. I think that in such a case, to silence the agitator, and save the boy, is not only constitutional, but, withal, a great mercy." Though he may actually have regretted Vallandigham's arrest, Lincoln refused to pardon him, instead ordering Vallandigham banished to the Confederacy.

Lincoln admitted that internal security in the midst of civil war was a complex problem and that errors and excesses had occurred. It pained him that government agents often confused antiwar rhetoric with disloyal designs and that innocent people suffered. That was why he tempered military arrests with generous pardons and refused to suppress popular assemblies and antiwar newspapers. Yet throughout the conflict he maintained a severe line on disloyalty; and most Republicans supported him. Without military law, they all feared, the rebellion would rage into the North and consume the government from within.

Lincoln was a tough warrior in other ways, too. He fully endorsed military conscription—which Congress authorized in April, 1863—and saw to it that the War Department rigorously enforced the measure. No matter what some historians have claimed, the President also enforced the confiscation of enemy property, believing as he did that "the traitor against the general government" should forfeit his farms, plantations, and other property as just punishment for the crime of insurrection.

Still, Lincoln was no dictator—the very idea appalled him, for it violated everything he held sacred in government. In fact, one of the major reasons he remains our best President is that he shunned a dictatorship, even when some Americans thought it the only way to save the country. But what kind of country would remain if popular government itself were sacrificed? Was it not for this that the war was being fought? Consider Lincoln's stand on the presidential election of 1864. With Union fortunes still uncertain, some men urged Lincoln to cancel the contest lest it result in the victory of antiwar Democrats who would sell out the Union cause. Lincoln refused. "The election," he said later, "was a necessity." "We can not have free government without elections; and if the rebellion could force us to forego, or postpone a national election, it might fairly claim to have already conquered us." So he ran against George B. McClellan and the peace plank of the Democratic party, and he won in a fair and open contest.

Later he told a group of White House serenaders what this meant to him. Above all, it meant that the American system still worked, that the people could still choose their leaders even in the middle of domestic rebellion. By holding the contest, Lincoln and the northern people had preserved their popular government and demonstrated how strong they were. And Lincoln was glad, he told the serenaders, that most voters had gone for him, the candidate most devoted to the Union and opposed to treason.

Harriet Beecher Stowe, who interviewed Lincoln in 1864, thought him the most trusted leader the country could have in war. "Surrounded by all sorts of conflicting claims," she wrote, "by traitors, by half-hearted, timid men, by Border States men, and Free States men, by radical Abolitionists and Conservatives, he has listened to all, weighed the words of all, waited, observed, yielded now here and now there, but in the main kept one inflexible, honest purpose, and drawn the national ship through." Had he been "a reckless, bold, theorizing, dashing man of genius," she said, he "might have wrecked our Constitution and ended us in a splendid military despotism."

5: THE WARRIOR

He was, then, a warrior for the American dream, prepared to do whatever was necessary to save it short of abandoning the dream itself. This ends-justifies-the-means philosophy was blazingly clear in Lincoln's approach to military strategy. Here he faced some perplexing questions: How could he utilize the Union's vast superiority in manpower and war matériel to stamp out the rebellion? Should he battle only the armies of the insurrectionists, or their institutions and resources as well?

At first, Lincoln elected to fight only the rebel military forces, a decision that would alter drastically as the war roared on and necessity demanded a harsher strategy. But almost from the start Lincoln had the whole military picture in mind, which was to be expected of a man who saw the struggle itself in a world dimension. Before any of his generals or advisers, Lincoln understood that the only way to whip the hard-fighting Confederates was to hit them with coordinated attacks in all theaters. Only that way could the Union bring to bear its tremendous advantage in manpower and war resources.

Yet it took Lincoln a long time to translate his strategic insights into action. He made mistakes. He gave too many important commands to "political" generals or to incompetent professionals who impressed him simply because they were generals. Who was he, a mere civilian, to question their military expertise? When his chosen commanders failed to fight as he wanted, he could lose his temper and cry "damn" or "hell" and even throw his stovepipe hat on the floor, as he did on one battlefront visit in 1862. Too many of his early generals, as he put it himself, had the "slows" when it came to fighting. Yet it was Lincoln who had chosen them.

Let us examine the cases of George B. McClellan and Don Carlos Buell. McClellan was a bright and brash young general with red hair, a red mustache, and irresistible military good looks. He had an air of cocky arrogance and called himself "the Little Napoleon." But he was a superb organizer. And so was aloof, irascible Buell. In 1861, after the Union reversal at Bull Run, Lincoln put McClellan in command of the showpiece Army of the Potomac and Buell in charge of the Department of the Ohio, with headquarters in Louisville, Kentucky. The President intended for them to operate in concert, for McClellan to attack rebel forces in northern Virginia while Buell smashed into east Tennessee, liberated its pro-Union population, severed the East Tennessee and Georgia Railroad, put his forces between the rebels and their "hog and hominy" (as Lincoln phrased it), and then menaced the flank of the Confederates in Virginia.

It was a fine idea. The only trouble was with McClellan and Buell, both of whom bogged down in endless delays, organizing and reorganizing their armies, drilling and drilling their men. Unsure of how to deal with professional soldiers, the President recommended that they move. With rising anxiety, he asked them why they did not move. With both generals it was always the same: they faced insuperable problems with preparation and supply. Worse still, both insisted that the rebels overwhelmingly outnumbered them and both cried for reinforcements. McClellan, for his part, was almost paranoid about the Confederate army in front of him. In the enemy entrenchments around Manassas Junction, he saw the Russian hordes massed at Sevastapol during the Crimean War. He insisted that the rebels then numbered 220,000 (actual size: about 36,000) and that it would be suicidal for him to attack with only 120,000 men. He needed 273,000. Only then could he attack Manassas, seize Richmond, and win the war. In the meantime, he had to train his army, train and train it. Give him credit for whipping the Potomac Army into a potent fighting force. He pleaded with Lincoln not to force him into a premature advance, pleaded for time and understanding. Lincoln gave him plenty of both. But in January, 1862, with the public clamoring for McClellan to move, clamoring for a decisive victory that would end the rebellion, Lincoln started losing his patience. He said if McClellan was not going to use the army, he would like to borrow it. He wasn't joking. "I am thinking of taking the field myself," he told an old Illinois friend.

But he didn't take the field himself. McClellan, after all, was a professional soldier, second in his class at West Point, author of a text on the art of war. Lincoln, by contrast, had never commanded anything beyond a company of unruly volunteers back in the Black Hawk Indian War of 1832. And even then he had not come close to real combat. With no Indians to shoot, his hard-bitten boys had "made war" on nearby farms, liberating pigs and chickens for their evening fires. Lincoln's singular claim to military glory, he liked to say, had been "a good many bloody struggles with the musquetoes."

Still, he had sound military concepts, and he wanted them adopted. In mid-January, he wrote down his "general idea of the war" and how it ought to be fought, a strategic plan that grew out of his own military studies (he had been reading books on warfare borrowed from the Library of Congress) and his notions about concerted action. Lincoln noted that the Union had the superior forces, but the rebels, by shifting their troops across interior lines, had the greater ability to concentrate their manpower "upon points of collision." To defeat them, Union armies must worry the enemy simultaneously at various points. If the rebels made no change in their forces, the Union could launch coordinated attacks all across the front. Or, if they weakened one spot to reinforce another, the Union could hit the weakened point and smash through to victory. How did this apply to the current military situation? His armies in the West could threaten the rebels in Kentucky and eastern Tennessee while McClellan attacked them at Manassas: at some point the rebels would have to weaken—and when they did, Union forces could drive through the lines and rout them.

Lincoln's generals were slow to implement his plan. Buell, coming alive in eastern Kentucky, did move out and win a battle there. At the same time, Brigadier General Ulysses S. Grant drove into northwestern Tennessee and captured Fort Henry on the Tennessee River and Fort Donelson on the Cumberland. The two forces were not cooperating as Lincoln desired, but he was so desperate for a victory that he personally nominated Grant for promotion to Major General.

In the East, though, McClellan's inaction had become chronic. Lincoln and cavalcades of angry Republicans called on the general and exhorted him to move. McClellan lashed back at them all. Who were they—who was the President—to interfere with a professional soldier? He refused to take his Commander-in-Chief into his confidence and discuss frankly and fully what he planned to do. Finally, Lincoln simply ordered him to advance and engage the enemy. But the President did not order McClellan to embrace his plan of operation. In place of that, McClellan offered his own, a brilliant plan in McClellan's judgment: his army would sail down Chesapeake Bay, land at the sandy peninsula between the York and James rivers, and dash boldly northwest into Richmond, the capture of which would virtually end the rebellion in a master-stroke.

While Lincoln had serious reservations about the plan, he told McClellan to go ahead. At all events, he must fight the enemy somewhere. Again, Lincoln's self-doubts overrode his better judgment, and he authorized a campaign he disliked, sent forth a general whose fighting abilities he questioned. No wonder he was beset with anxiety.

A first-rate organizer, McClellan was simply inept in the field.

He consumed an entire month besieging lightly defended York-town when he could have taken it with a single offensive thrust. Then McClellan inched up the peninsula toward Richmond, only to halt, entrench, and howl for reinforcements, convinced that the rebels outnumbered him two to one. This was sheer hallucina-tion. Throughout the peninsula operation, McClellan had a larger army than the Confederates.

Lincoln and McClellan haggled over the size of his army, hag-gled over reinforcements, haggled over McDowell's corps and the defense of Washington—all in the middle of a campaign. No wonder it went nowhere. Before McClellan had set out for Vir-ginia, Lincoln had ordered him to secure the capital with 40,000 men. It was the beginning of a fateful misunderstanding. There were 40,000 men in Washington and northern Virginia, and McClellan assumed that this met the President's stipulation. But Lincoln meant that number in the capital itself. When he and his advisers discovered that only 19,000 troops manned the forts and redoubts around Washington, they concluded that McClellan had arrogantly disobeyed orders. Therefore the President detained McDowell's corps of 38,000 intended for McClellan's army and had it guard the capital. McClellan, of course, cried out in protest. He still had about 100,000 men, but in his mind this was not nearly enough to battle the rebel masses he envisioned in his front. In righteous indignation, he blasted the government for refusing to send him additional troops and warned that it would shoulder full responsibility for any disaster that befell him.

It was Lincoln's turn to fume. Your complaints "pain me very much," he informed McClellan. "I give you all I can." By now, Lincoln realized that he should never have let McClellan take his army down to the peninsula on the other side of Richmond. He should have made McClellan launch his big strike at Manassas while the rebel army was still there. Now that army was en-trenched in front of Richmond, McClellan was belligerently inert, Union forces in Virginia badly divided, Buell again im-mobilized in the West, and the chances of victory increasingly

dim. Then McClellan did an astonishing thing. Instead of attacking Richmond, he retreated from it, switching his base of supply
down to the James River and squalling for reinforcements as he
went.

The peninsula campaign was a fiasco, and Lincoln in approving
it had to shoulder the consequences, as cries of outrage pummeled
him from all corners of the Union. With Buell and McClellan
bogged down again, Lincoln decided that he needed a general at
his side, a military man to direct and coordinate his armies and
translate his ideas into language his field commanders could understand. He therefore made Henry Halleck General-in-Chief,
thus relieving Lincoln of the harrowing responsibilities of that job,
and installed Halleck in Washington. Lincoln liked "Old Brains,"
a stout officer with watery eyes and a Phi Beta Kappa key from
Union College, and told him it was his job to make his field
commanders fight. For Lincoln agreed with his congressional
colleagues that "fighting, and *only* fighting," would ever end the
rebellion.

He realized something else, too. The war could never be won
simply by seizing the rebel capital. What Lincoln perceived from
his White House windows was that only the complete annihila-
tion of the enemy armies could win this war. Only when they had
no armies left would the tenacious insurrectionists give up the
fight.

And now Halleck must communicate that to his field commanders, make them understand in their own language what
Lincoln saw. Through Halleck, Lincoln ordered Buell to advance
against East Tennessee or *else*. When he still did not budge,
Lincoln twice intended to sack him, and twice let Halleck talk him
out of it, because Lincoln trusted the general's judgment more
than his own.

Alas, Lincoln's new command set-up brought no victories. In
despair, the President summoned a griping McClellan back to
Washington and waited in mounting distress as a new army under
blustering John Pope engaged the rebels in the battle of second

Bull Run, near Manassas. It was another Union debacle, as Robert E. Lee smashed up Pope's army and sent it reeling back to Washington. Lincoln was so depressed that he said "we may as well stop fighting."

With awakened resolution, though, he fired Pope and put McClellan in command of a reorganized Potomac Army that included the remnants of Pope's force. The Cabinet strenuously objected—not McClellan again! But who else did he have? Lincoln said. Who else was better at regrouping dispirited and defeated men? When Lee invaded Maryland in the autumn of 1862, McClellan led his army out to do battle, vowing to give Bobbie Lee the drubbing of his life. McClellan fought Lee at Antietam Creek, but was so obsessed with the possibility of retreat that he held an entire corps in reserve. Had he thrown that into the battle, he might have crippled Lee seriously. As it was, he forced Lee to withdraw from the battlefield, thus halting his invasion. McClellan was so excited that he wired Washington that his victory was "complete." Lincoln, of course, interpreted this to mean that Lee's army had been eliminated as a fighting force. When he found out that this was not the case, that Lee in fact had escaped to fight again, Lincoln was thoroughly disgusted with McClellan. Yet Antietam did give him a triumph of sorts, enough for him to issue the preliminary Emancipation Proclamation, as we have seen.

Almost a month later, McClellan was still encamped on the Antietam battlefield. Lincoln hectored him until he moved, hounded him southward into Virginia, and finally removed him from command—something he should have done long before. "He is an admirable engineer," Lincoln said of McClellan, "but he seems to have a special talent for a stationary engine."

Lincoln's relationship with McClellan is a measure of his own self-doubts and vacillations as Commander-in-Chief: he had appointed McClellan field general of the Potomac Army, promoted him to General-in-Chief, demoted him to field commander again, allowed him to undertake a campaign Lincoln seriously questioned, interfered with it because McClellan was not a fighter, recalled him from Virginia when his operation was plainly a disaster, put him back in charge of a reorganized army, and then fired him after Antietam because he moved with all the speed of a glacier. Still, Lincoln learned from his mistakes. Never again would he leave a balking general so long in command.

Lincoln lowered the ax on Buell too—Buell who after ten months of campaigning was no closer to eastern Tennessee than when he had begun. Why, Lincoln groaned, can't we march as the enemy marches, fight as he fights? In a desperate search for aggressive generals, Lincoln put William S. Rosecrans in command of Buell's force (now called the Army of the Cumberland) and Ambrose E. Burnside in charge of the Army of the Potomac. But Lincoln's armies continued to function with cheerful disregard for one another. In central Tennessee, "Old Rosey" did repel a Confederate attack at Murfreesboro, only to sit on his haunches and rail at the government for not supporting him. In the East, Burnside sputtered that he was not fit to command a whole *army*—and then proved it in the terrible Union reversal at Fredericksburg. Looking about in his grab bag of eastern generals, Lincoln next produced Joseph Hooker of Massachusetts to head the Army of the Potomac, whose brave men deserved better than that handsome incompetent. "Beware of rashness," Lincoln admonished Hooker, "but with energy, and sleepless vigilance, go forward, and give us victories." When Hooker promised to go forward, talking grandiosely about what he would do once he captured Richmond, Lincoln became apprehensive again.

In April, 1863, Hooker launched his Chancellorsville campaign, boasting that "the rebel army is now the legitimate property of the Army of the Potomac." Alas, "Fighting Joe" Hooker could not live up to his nickname. He lost his nerve at Chancellorsville and led the luckless Army of the Potomac to yet another defeat, sustaining 17,000 casualties in the process. Lincoln was in such a state of tension that he raced to Virginia to make certain the army was still intact. The army, of course, rocked with recriminations, and the country put up a howl that made Lincoln shudder. Yet he left Hooker in command until June, when Lee unleashed his second invasion of the North. Finally Lincoln turned to snappish George Gordon Meade to lead the Potomac Army—the fifth general to do so.*

Meade was an excellent battlefield general, as he demonstrated at Gettysburg, the biggest and bloodiest engagement of the war, where he shattered Lee's army and forced him to retire. Like McClellan, though, Meade had no comprehension of what it meant to pursue and destroy an enemy army, and he let Lee escape. For Meade, it was enough that he had driven the invader from Union soil. "My God!" Lincoln exclaimed. "Is that all?" When he learned that Lee was safe in Virginia, Lincoln's "grief and anger," said a friend, "were something sorrowful to behold."

Lincoln did take heart when Grant captured Vicksburg after a protracted siege. Here, the President rejoiced, was a total victory, the conquest of a powerful rebel garrison on the Mississippi—and the elimination of its defenders as a fighting force. Lincoln loved Grant. He was the President's kind of general: a fighting, innovative officer who went after the insurrectionists with fierce determination and never once begged for reinforcements.

During the summer and autumn of 1863, Lincoln kept prodding his generals to fight in concert, to move against Confederate forces with coordinated attacks. He wanted to "hurt this enemy," to "whip these people." But it took Lincoln until 1864 before he found in Grant and William Tecumseh Sherman the right combination to implement his big-picture strategy. In the spring of that year, Lincoln made Sherman overall commander in the West and called Grant to the East as General-in-Chief of all Union armies. Now Lincoln had a command set-up that he hoped would produce victories. With Grant as General-in-Chief, Halleck functioned officially as chief of staff, integrating information and giving out advice. Grant, electing to travel with Meade and the Army of the Potomac, would coordinate its movements with those of armies in other theaters.

*Irvin McDowell had been the army's first commander; McClellan had replaced him.

A terse, slight man who chewed cigars and walked with a lurch, Grant worked out with Lincoln a Grand Plan that called for simultaneous offensive movements on all battlefronts. In the East, Grant and Meade would attempt to obliterate Lee's force while Sherman's powerful army would punch into Georgia, seize Atlanta and its crucial railway nexus, and destroy rebel resources in the Atlanta area. In sum, the Union war machine would now utilize its vastly superior manpower and smash the Confederacy with concerted blows in all theaters.

Lincoln was delighted. The Grand Plan entailed exactly the kind of concerted action he had advocated since 1861. And though it was basically Grant's design, Lincoln helped forge it in weekly strategy sessions in the White House. So in May, 1864, Union armies on all fronts moved forward in the mightiest offensive of the war, battering the Confederacy from all directions and thrusting toward "a common center." Alas, in East and West alike, the offensive mired down and Union casualties, especially in Virginia, were staggering. Yet Lincoln never lost hope. Even when Lee escaped to the redoubts of Petersburg and Grant settled in for a protracted siege, Lincoln urged him to "hold on with bull-dog grip, and chew & choke, as much as possible."

The Grand Plan worked better in the western theater, where Sherman captured and burned Atlanta, and General George "Old Pap" Thomas smashed the Confederate Army of Tennessee, destroying it so completely that it could never fight again. What Lincoln had long desired had finally been accomplished.

In the late fall of 1864 red-haired Bill Sherman, a tall, lean man who spoke in picturesque phrases, proposed to take Lincoln's strategic notions a step further. Even more than Grant, Sherman realized that modern wars were won not simply by fighting enemy armies, but by destroying the very ability of the enemy to wage war—that is, by wrecking railroads, burning fields, and eradicating other economic resources. "We are not only fighting hostile armies," Sherman reasoned, "but a hostile people, and must make old and young, rich and poor, feel the hard hand of war." "There is many a boy here who looks on war as all glory," Sherman later told his veterans, "but, boys, it is all hell."

Those were Lincoln's sentiments exactly. And since war was hell, it should be ended as swiftly as possible, by whatever means were necessary. Thus, when Sherman proposed to visit total war on the people of the Deep South, Lincoln approved. With ruthless efficiency, Sherman's army stormed through Georgia and the Carolinas, tearing up railroads, pulverizing corn and cotton fields, assassinating cows and chickens, wiping out all and anything that might sustain Lee's army and all other rebel forces. At the same time, Union cavalry in Virginia's Shenandoah Valley burned a broad path of destruction clear to the Rapidan River. The Union's scorched-earth warfare earned Lincoln and Sherman undying hatred in Dixie, but it paid off: within five months after Sherman started his march through Georgia, the war was over.

It cannot be stressed enough that Lincoln, then deeply involved in matters of reconstruction, fully endorsed Sherman's scorched-earth policy. If Sherman was "a total warrior," so was his Commander-in-Chief. Putting aside his own aversion to bloodshed and violence, Lincoln ended up pounding all his southern foes into submission—civilians and soldiers alike. And he did so because that was the surest way he knew to shorten the conflict, end the killing, and salvage his American dream.

6: TOWARD A NEW BIRTH OF FREEDOM

When it came to reconstruction, the historical Lincoln was no saintly Father Abraham extending the conquered South a tender and forgiving hand. He was not locked in a feud with "vindictive radicals" like Sumner and Stevens, who wanted to carve Dixie up in an ecstasy of revenge. This is a potent myth, *à la* Carl Sandburg, which most Americans still regard as historically accurate. Yet it scarcely fits with the President who sanctioned total war against southern insurrectionaries. In fact, a body of modern scholarship has persuasively demonstrated that Lincoln became a pretty tough reconstructionist, too. Not only did the historical Lincoln side with Sumner and Stevens on most crucial reconstruction issues; by 1865 he was prepared to reform and reshape the South's shattered society with the help of military force. Again, as in his harsh war measures, Lincoln's evolving approach to reconstruction became inextricably linked to his vision of what this conflict was about: on the Union side, as he said, it was a struggle to preserve for all humanity a system of government whose mission was to elevate the conditions of all its people, to afford all equal privileges in the race of life.

During the course of the war, Lincoln went through three phases in his efforts to reconstruct the rebel South, that is, to restore federal authority and establish loyal state regimes in captured Confederate territory. In phase one, which began with the start of the fighting, Lincoln relied on pro-Union elements within a state to create loyal governments. But, as he should have remembered from the Sumter crisis, Unionist sentiment was too weak for such a policy to work. So in the spring and summer of 1862, the President initiated a second phase of reconstruction and installed military governors in the occupied portions of Tennessee, North Carolina, Louisiana, and Arkansas, instructing them to restore those states to their former places in the Union. As in his plan of voluntary, state-guided emancipation, which he was promoting at this time, Lincoln sought merely to advise his military governors and not interfere directly in their efforts to establish loyal state regimes. But even so, as one scholar has observed, Lincoln's use of military governors was "a radical extension of federal authority into the internal affairs of the states"—and a harbinger of what was to come in the President's evolving reconstruction policy.

Phase two of that policy proved a failure, because the military governors floundered in their attempts to harmonize conflicting Unionist sentiment and woo back disaffected rebels. The lesson here became as clear to Lincoln as that about slavery: he had to reconstruct Dixie himself. The impetus, direction, and purpose of southern restoration had to come from above, from the chief executive. As he had assumed control of emancipation, so he must take direct charge of restoring conquered rebel states to their "proper practical relation with the Union."

In his Gettysburg Address of November, 1863, Lincoln signaled the nation that something new was afoot, that something more was needed to win this historic war between the forces of liberty and the forces of reaction in the world. With emancipation now under way in occupied areas of Dixie, with 100,000 former slaves now serving the Union war effort, and with a new plan of reconstruction taking shape in his mind, Lincoln stood on Cemetery Hill south of Gettysburg and called for a national rededication to the proposition that all men are created equal, a new resolve to fight for that proposition and salvage America's experiment in popular government for all humankind. Let Union people of all colors and conditions come together in a new commitment to freedom and a new national crusade. Let them cease their petty quarrels, put aside their differences, and vow that "these honored dead" had not died in vain.

Two and a half weeks later, in his Proclamation of Amnesty and Reconstruction, Lincoln promulgated a new plan for constructing loyal, slaveless regimes in occupied Dixie, thus inaugurating phase three of his approach to that difficult problem. First, Lincoln made it clear that he intended to control the reorganization of civilian government in conquered Dixie, that he regarded this as chiefly an executive responsibility to be carried out by the army. In fact, Lincoln was adamant about the role of the army in the reconstruction process, contending that it was indispensable in safeguarding the freedom of the very slaves it liberated. It was also necessary in protecting the loyal southern minority—harried little bands of Unionist Whigs and antisecessionists on whom Lincoln's entire efforts depended. In sum, Lincoln would employ the army to oversee the task of building free-state governments in the occupied South, designating generals there as the "masters" of reconstruction.

Second, Lincoln offered a solution to one of the most perplexing difficulties of southern restoration: "how to keep the rebellious populations from over-whelming and outvoting the loyal minority," as he put it, and returning the old southern ruling class to power. For now, the President's solution was to guard the loyal minority with the army, offer an oath that separated "the opposing elements, so as to build from the sound," and virtually outlaw the old and current leaders in rebel Dixie. To accomplish the latter, Lincoln refused to pardon the following classes, thus preventing them from voting or holding political office in the occupied South: all men who had held Confederate civilian and diplomatic posts, all who had served as rebel officers above the rank of colonel in the army and lieutenant in the navy, all who had resigned from the U.S. armed forces or left Congress or judicial positions to help the rebellion, and all who had treated Union soldiers other than as prisoners of war. Apart from these, he fully pardoned all other southerners who had engaged in rebellion so long as they took an oath of allegiance to the Union, swearing "henceforth" to support it. Lincoln considered this a fair and liberal test "which accepts as sound whoever will make a sworn recantation of his former unsoundness." Once a number of people equal to ten percent of those who had voted in 1860 had taken the oath, these people could establish a loyal civilian government and elect U.S. representatives, and their state would be restored to the Union with full federal protection.

Third, all reconstructed regimes must accept and obey the emancipation proclamation and all congressional laws bearing on slavery. "To now abandon them would be not only to relinquish a lever of power," Lincoln said, "but would also be a cruel and an astounding breach of faith." Far from being a lenient plan as many have claimed, Lincoln's Proclamation made emancipation the very basis of reconstruction, thus placing him again on the side of Sumner and the advanced and moderate members of his party (conservative Republicans and Democrats, recall, still wanted to restore the rebel South with slavery preserved). Moreover, the President indicated that he intended to control the affairs of emancipated blacks in conquered Dixie.

As for the old southern ruling class, Lincoln agreed with Sumner that it should be eradicated, and the President's emancipation and reconstruction policies were calculated to do just that. Emancipation, as we have seen, would obliterate the very institution on which the southern master class depended for its existence. And Lincoln's Proclamation of Amnesty and Reconstruction excluded nearly all rebellious southern leaders from participating in his reconstructed governments. True, Lincoln said he might modify his classes of pardons if that seemed warranted, and he did let disqualified individuals apply to him for clemency. But in his Message to Congress in December, 1864, he warned that the time might come—probably would come—when "public duty" would force him to "close the door" on all pardons and adopt "more rigorous measures." At all events, Lincoln had no intention of allowing prewar southern leaders—a class he had once castigated as slavedealers in politics—to regain power in postwar Dixie.

Apart from eliminating slavery and the southern ruling class, Lincoln made it plain that he would be flexible in reconstructing the rebel South, that the ten percent plan was only one formula and that he would gladly consider others. As he set about restoring Louisiana and Arkansas by the ten percent plan, he indicated that his approach as to the mode of reconstruction would be empirical: what plan he adopted for other conquered areas would depend on the circumstances and exigencies of each place and moment. The ten percent plan above all was a wartime measure, designed to weaken the Confederacy and to create loyal state governments in occupied areas brimming with hostile rebel sympathizers.

In his reconstruction efforts, Lincoln sought Congress's approval and cooperation, for he acknowledged that Capitol Hill had a powerful voice in the reconstruction process, since both houses would decide whether to accept representatives from the states he restored. He did clash with advanced Republicans like Sumner, Stevens, and Wade, who argued that reconstruction was a congressional and not a presidential responsibility. Sumner also opposed Lincoln's military approach because he did not understand how the army could produce an American state. But, despite their differences, Lincoln and the advanced and moderate Republicans on Capitol Hill stood together on most crucial reconstruction issues. They agreed that the South must be remade. They meant to abolish slavery there forever, and they worked closely, as we have seen, in guiding the present Thirteenth Amendment through Congress. They were concerned about the welfare of the freedmen. And they intended for southern Unionists to rule in postwar Dixie. Above all, they wanted to prevent ex-Confederate leaders from taking over the postwar South and forming a coalition with northern Democrats that might imperil the gains of the war. Lincoln and his congressional associates often differed on how to implement their goals—nearly all congressional Republicans, for instance, demanded a tougher loyalty oath than that required by the President's ten percent plan. And they disagreed, too, on the issue of Negro voting rights, as I shall discuss in a moment. But even so, the President and congressional Republicans retained a close and mutually respectful relationship, so much so that many contemporaries thought they would remain as united in working out reconstruction problems as they had in prosecuting the war.

One more thing about Sumner and Lincoln. While the President had his differences with the high-minded Senator, he always felt closest to Sumner's wing of the party. He remarked that men like the senator were the conscience of the party, and during the course of the war, as we have seen, Lincoln moved over to Sumner's position on emancipation, Negro troops, and other

harsh war measures. Moreover, the two men remained warm
personal friends. Mary Lincoln recalled how the President welcomed Sumner's visits and how they talked and laughed together
"like *two* schoolboys." While their disagreements over reconstruction were sometimes rancorous, Lincoln and Sumner knew
they needed one another in the hard days ahead, and they maintained close personal and political ties.

Inevitably bound up with any reconstruction program were
pressing questions about the welfare of the freedmen. How were
they to provide for themselves? Should they be given the right to
vote, to run for political office? Lincoln's solution to the first question was the refugee system, which the army was already setting up
in occupied Dixie. Through that system, officers enlisted liberated
slaves as soldiers, employed others as military laborers, and hired
still others to work in agricultural pursuits under government
supervision. For a time in 1863, Lincoln vacillated as to whether
the freed people should work for wages by contract, or whether
they should first labor for whites as temporary apprentices. On
several occasions he said he had no objection if white authorities
assumed control of former slaves "as a laboring, landless, and homeless class" and adopted some temporary arrangement by which the
two races in Dixie "could gradually live themselves out of their old
relation to each other, and both come out better prepared for the
new." But when congressional Republicans steadfastly opposed
any such arrangement, Lincoln dropped the apprenticeship idea
and ordered those involved in the refugee system to employ contract labor for southern blacks, so that they could receive wages set
by the government and become self-supporting. And he insisted
that the government contracts be fair to them. Moreover, he happily approved when his ten percent government in Louisiana rejected apprenticeship and granted economic independence to
Louisiana Negroes. In this respect, Lincoln doubtless expected
Louisiana to serve as a model for other rehabilitated states.

While there were many faults with Lincoln's refugee system,

it was based on sound Republican dogma: it kept southern blacks out of the North, and it secured them jobs as wage earners on captured farms and plantations. The system thus helped southern blacks to help themselves and prepared them for life in a free society in postwar Dixie.

When it came to Negro suffrage, Lincoln displayed the same capacity for growth and change that had characterized his approach to emancipation. By 1864, with tens of thousands of black men fighting for the Union cause, Lincoln endorsed limited suffrage for Louisiana Negroes. He wrote Governor Michael Hahn that he wished "the very intelligent" blacks and especially those "who have fought gallantly in our ranks" could be enfranchised. Yet Lincoln would not force Negro suffrage on Louisiana—certainly not in a presidential election year—because he knew what a combustible issue it was in both the North and the South. What is more, he feared that mandatory Negro suffrage would alienate white Unionists in Louisiana and ruin all his reconstruction efforts there.

Nevertheless, when the Louisiana constitutional convention refused to give black men the vote, Lincoln helped persuade the lawmakers to reconsider their decision and forge a compromise: while the Louisiana constitution did not enfranchise Negroes, it did empower the legislature to do so. At the same time, the constitution not only outlawed slavery (as Lincoln insisted it must), but opened the courts to all persons regardless of color and established free public education for both races. For his part, Lincoln accepted this as the best that could be done in the Louisiana of 1864 and 1865, and he commented—with a touch of irony—that Louisiana's new constitution was "better for the poor black man than we have in Illinois." Maybe Louisiana's all-white government was imperfect, but Lincoln thought it better than no government at all. While he wished it had provided limited Negro suffrage, he believed this could be accomplished faster "by saving the already advanced steps toward it, than by running backward over them." In sum, the Louisiana government was a foundation to build on for the future—for blacks as well as whites.

Yet, characteristically, Lincoln left himself room to maneuver on the Louisiana question. He publicly asserted that he would not be bound by an outmoded policy: he had promised to support Hahn's all-white government in occupied Louisiana, "but, as bad promises are better broken than kept, I shall treat this as a bad promise, and break it, whenever I shall be convinced that keeping it is adverse to the public interest."

Contrary to what some have claimed, Lincoln's interest in Negro suffrage was not confined to Louisiana, with its relatively well-educated and outspoken black community in New Orleans. Over the winter of 1864–65, in fact, Lincoln approved some form of Negro suffrage for other rebel states if Congress would accept his Louisiana regime. This was part of a compromise he made with Sumner and a few other advanced Republicans, who demanded universal male suffrage for southern blacks so that they could protect their liberty. But the compromise fell apart because most congressional Republicans opposed even limited Negro suffrage as too radical. In the matter of black political rights, Lincoln was ahead of most members of his party—and far ahead of the vast majority of northern whites at that time.

So far, Lincoln had supported limited Negro suffrage only in his correspondence and private negotiations. But in his last speech, on April 11, 1865, the President addressed reconstruction in Louisiana and publicly endorsed enfranchising "the very intelligent" blacks there and "those who serve our cause as soldiers." In fact, he went further than that. In a telling line toward the end of his speech, Lincoln all but granted that the black man deserved the elective franchise. Though he was speaking in the context of Louisiana, he asserted that "what has been said of Louisiana will apply generally to other States." Lincoln still did not make Negro suffrage mandatory, but he did not reject the idea either. As with other reconstruction issues, he left the matter open.

It appears obvious in what direction Lincoln was evolving. And that was toward full political rights for the Negro, not away from them. Certainly Secretary of War Edwin M. Stanton, Attorney General James Speed, and other champions of Negro suffrage thought the President now appreciated the need for southern blacks to vote and thus to protect themselves from their former masters. After Lincoln's last Cabinet meeting, Attorney General Speed told Salmon Chase, also an advocate of Negro enfranchisement, that the President "never seemed so near our views."

By war's end, Lincoln seemed on the verge of a new phase of reconstruction, a tougher phase that would call for some form of Negro suffrage, more stringent voting qualifications for ex-Confederates (as hinted at in his 1864 Message to Congress), and probably an army of occupation for the postwar South. At his last Cabinet meeting, Lincoln and his secretaries unanimously agreed that such an army might be necessary to prevent the rebellious southern majority from overwhelming the small Unionist minority in Dixie and maybe even re-enslaving the blacks. In other words, the President was already considering in April, 1865, what Congress would later adopt in the days of "Radical Reconstruction." Perhaps a new and tougher program was what Lincoln had in mind in the closing line of his last speech: "It may be my duty to make some new announcement to the people of the South. I am considering, and shall not fail to act, when satisfied that action will be proper."

He never got the chance to make an announcement. But given his position on reconstruction at war's end, it seems absurd to maintain that Lincoln was ready to restore the South with tender magnanimity. True, in his Second Inaugural Address, he'd said that he would bind the nation's wounds "with malice toward none" and "charity for all." He would be charitable in the sense that he wouldn't resort to mass executions or even mass imprisonment of southern insurrectionists. He would not even have the rebel leaders tried and jailed, although he said he would like to drive them out of America, to "open the gates, let down the bars, scare them off." But as he pondered the problems of reconstruction, Lincoln clearly wanted to bring the South into the mainstream of American republicanism, to install a free-labor system there for blacks as well as whites, to establish public schools for both races, to look after the welfare of the freedmen, to grant them access to the ballot and the courts—to build a new South dedicated like Lincoln to the Declaration of Independence. These were all consonant with Lincoln's core of unshakable convictions about the meaning and purpose of the American experiment, a set of convictions he had held since long before the Civil War.

Lincoln's approach to reconstruction was bound to put him on a collision course with unreconstructed rebels. It is folly to think that they would not have opposed him as obstinately as they resisted Congress two years later. After all, Lincoln stood for everything they had fought against for four long years. He *was* the hated Yankee. Under him they could look forward to an occupying army, Negro political rights, and disenfranchisement for almost the entire prewar and wartime southern leadership—all of which they were certain to despise and resist. In sum, even if Lincoln had lived, reconstruction would have been a painful ordeal for his country and the most difficult problem of his second administration. He knew that, and he said so repeatedly in those final days of April, 1865.

The historical Lincoln, as I have tried to approximate him, was a flawed and complex man who had the gift of vision that let him see things few others ever see. When I say that he was flawed, I am not profaning his memory, as many of my correspondents have accused me of doing. On the contrary, the historical Lincoln comes out more heroic than the immortal Man of the People, because we see him overcoming his deficiencies and self-doubts, often against tremendous odds. Lincoln's long struggle against adversity—inner adversity as well as the terrible problems of his day—is something anybody can identify with and learn from. We can learn from Lincoln's life that even those who rise to supreme heights have personal dilemmas—identity crises, ambivalences, hurts, setbacks, and even a loss of will—which they have to anguish over and work their way through. When I think back over his life, back over his embattled presidency, I am still astonished that he survived the burdens of his office. But he not only survived them; he prevailed. He fought the war through to a total Union triumph, a triumph for popular government and a larger concept of the inalienable rights of man. He summoned Americans both North and South, Americans both black and white, to dedicate themselves to a new birth of freedom, so that government of, by, and for *all* the people would not perish from the earth.

Part Five

FINAL ACT

❧

*Is not here indeed the point
underlying all tragedy?*

WALT WHITMAN

1: THE THEATER

Ford's Theater is the most authentic Lincoln shrine we have, and I try to visit there whenever I can, to recall and relive that terrible night in 1865 so that I might appreciate again what really happened there and what it meant to the country—then and ever since.

Heading for the theater in Washington's noisome traffic, I always have an uncanny feeling, for a visit to Ford's is really a journey back in time. I never have any sensations at the Lincoln Memorial, because its god of marble and stone is not the Lincoln I have come to know. I can't help but think that the historical Lincoln would have recoiled at sight of that giant statue of himself, sitting regally on its thronelike chair. No, that was not the Lincoln of *my* story. My Lincoln had been a man of rich humanity. That Lincoln had said "Mr. Cheermun," had referred to his White House office as "the shop," and had worn small, wire-rimmed spectacles when he prepared his state papers. That Lincoln astonished novelist Emerson Bennett, who observed him in various presidential poses—from a gentle, judicious statesman to a "towering, angry Chief of the Nation, enforcing his order to the Provost Marshal General with swinging arms, shaking fists and stamping feet." That Lincoln said his "ear bones" ached to hear a good peal of honest laughter, engaged in preposterous repartee with Secretary of State William H. Seward, and still told stories on himself. One of his favorites was about two Quaker women discussing the end of the war. "I think," the first said, "that

Jefferson Davis will succeed." "Why does thee think so?" asked
the second. "Because Jefferson is a praying man," the first replied.
"And so is Abraham a praying man," the second rejoined. "Yes,"
said the first woman, "but the Lord will think Abraham is joking."

In truth, humor was one of the few ways he could find escape
from the unending grind of his office. Beyond his carriage rides,
he "had no notion of recreation as such," Seward recalled, and
"found his only recreation in telling or hearing stories in the
ordinary way of business—often stopped a cabinet council at a
grave juncture, to jest a half-hour with the members before going
to work; joked with every body, on light & on grave occasions.
This was what saved him."

Well, that and his rare evenings out to the theater. When
Lincoln could spare the time, he and Mary would dress up, climb
into the presidential carriage, and venture forth to attend Ford's,
Grover's, or one of the other thriving theaters in town. Mary
adored the theater, and Lincoln found it a "wonderful" way to
relax. He preferred Shakespearean productions—not the tragedies, which he liked to read, but the comedies with their risqué
scenes, earthy dialogues, and delicious absurdities.

Ford's Theater is situated on Tenth between E and F Streets
N.W. Approaching it today is like stepping abruptly back into
Lincoln's time, back into another Washington more than a century ago. The old red-brick theater has been so thoroughly restored that both the front and the interior—the lobby, stage,
furnishings and flags, even the state box—look now just as they
did that Good Friday of 1865, when the Lincolns came here with
Clara Harris and her fiancé, Major Henry Rathbone, to enjoy a
performance of the English comedy *Our American Cousin*.

The theater closed after that night and did not reopen until
1968, after a $2.7 million refurbishing. Today it is a meticulously
restored three-story building that is both a museum and a functioning theater. Reproductions of the 1865 cane-bottomed chairs
fill the main floor and the two balconies of the theater; the flag-
draped state box, which is viewed through a window at the rear,

contains the original sofa, as well as a replica of Lincoln's rocker. The museum in the basement of the building not only features Lincoln memorabilia and the diary, dagger, and derringer of John Wilkes Booth, but also offers a shelf of excellent books about Lincoln and the assassination. With the help of Thomas Reed Turner's *Beware the People Weeping,* William Hanchett's *The Lincoln Murder Conspiracies,* George S. Bryan's *The Great American Myth,* Dorothy Meserve and Philip B. Kunhardt's profusely illustrated *Twenty Days,* and other modern studies of Lincoln, we can easily imagine what it was like to be outside the theater on that night of nights, awaiting the arrival of the presidential party as other bystanders were doing.

It was a foggy evening, and gaslights on the street corners glimmered eerily in the drifting mist. Because of last-minute visitors, the Lincolns did not leave the White House until 8:15, and the play had already begun by the time the presidential carriage came churning up muddy Tenth Street and stopped at a box on the curb where the ladies could climb down to the sidewalk without soiling their shoes.

Although in high spirits that morning (the last major Confederate force was expected to surrender in North Carolina at any time), Lincoln looked tired now, worn down by the awesome task of reconstructing his war-torn land. In truth, it was to get his mind off reconstruction and "have a laugh over the country cousin" that Lincoln had come to the theater. We follow the two couples— Mary on Lincoln's arm, pretty young Clara on Rathbone's—up a winding stairway and across the dress circle at the back of the first balcony. We gaze over rows of wooden chairs at a deep stage fronted by an orchestra pit. Two other balconies loom overhead, and gas lamps bathe the auditorium in a golden light.

A thousand people packed the theater that night—among them, high army brass and assorted Washington socialites. When they spotted Lincoln, the audience gave him a standing ovation and the orchestra struck up "Hail to the Chief." The presidential party swept around the back row of chairs, passed through a door

and down a gloomy hallway to the state box, which directly over-
looked the stage. Had we been in the audience on the main floor,
we would have seen Lincoln sink into a rocking chair provided by
the management, with Mary seated beside him and Rathbone, an
ebullient fellow with a walrus mustache, and Miss Harris to their
right. Then, as it is today, the front of the box was adorned with
drapes, a framed engraving of George Washington, and brilliant
regimental and Union flags. On stage, Harry Hawk, the male lead,
ad-libbed a line, "This reminds me of a story, as Mr. Lincoln
would say."

As the play progressed, Mary, wearing a gray silk dress and a
bonnet to match, rested her hand on Lincoln's knee and called
his attention to the situation on stage, and he laughed heartily
from time to time. At one point, as if a cold wind had blown over
him, he got up long enough to put on his overcoat.

Had we left during the third act and gone out to the lobby, we
would have noticed a man talking with the doorkeeper, a nervous
man in his late twenties, with ivory skin, thick black hair, black
mustache, and lustrous eyes, and dressed in a black felt hat and
high boots with spurs. It was John Wilkes Booth, a prominent
Shakespearean actor with militant Confederate sympathies.
Booth believed that most Americans hated Lincoln so adamantly
that they would hail his assassin as a national hero. And Booth was
here this night to become that hero.

Booth had grown up in Maryland, the scion of a famous acting
family that included his father, "Junius the Elder," and two brothers, Junius, Jr., and Edwin. "A singular combination of gravity and
joy," as a sister described him, John had studied drama and made
his stage debut in Baltimore and then had toured southern cities
like Richmond and Montgomery, where he had established himself as a rising young star. He told his sister Asia that he wanted
most of all to be known as a southern actor, beloved of the fine
gentlemen and fluttering ladies in crinoline who applauded him
in the southern theater. Strikingly handsome, he mesmerized
audiences in North and South alike with his spectacular leaps,

heroic speeches, and unpredictable oscillations between tenderness and violence.

When war came, Booth took the malignant southern view of Lincoln, blaming *him* for fomenting the conflict, *him* for putting the bayonet to the southern people and their sacred institutions. Yet he did not enlist in the rebel cause—"I promised mother I would keep out of the quarrel," he told Edwin later, "and I am sorry I said so." He argued bitterly with his brothers, both Union men, and anybody else who challenged him. He professed his loyalty to the old Union—"How I loved the *old flag* can never be known"—but by 1863 that flag had changed. Under Lincoln it had become the emblem of *"bloody deeds,"* of military arrests and draft riots in the North, of abolition and massive killing in Dixie, and Booth could not bear what was happening to the country. As Lincoln resorted to severe war measures to crush the rebellion, Booth's hatred for him smoldered and blazed. "You will see Lincoln made a King in America," he swore to Edwin. And he became obsessed with the Confederate cause and the glory of slavery. In his mind, he *was* a Confederate, as surely as some plantation son battling with Robert E. Lee.

"If the North conquer us," he gesticulated to Asia, "it will be by numbers only."

"If the North conquer us," Asia said gently, "we are of the North."

"Not I!" Booth cried. "Not I—so help me holy God! My soul, life, and possessions are for the South!"

"This country was formed for the *white,* not for the black man," he wrote in 1864. "And, looking upon *African slavery* from the same standpoint held by the noble framers of our Constitution, I, for one, have ever considered it one of the greatest blessings (both for themselves and us) that God ever bestowed upon a favored nation."

Wherever his career took him, to stages in New York, Boston, Philadelphia, and Washington, Booth cursed and castigated the tyrant in the White House. And in Baltimore, his hometown, he found a great many irreconcilables who shared his views. It was here that assassination threats had boiled up in 1861, here that a mob had fallen on Union troops, here that Lincoln had early clamped down the shackles of martial law, here that Booth found an atmosphere of anti-Lincoln hatred that reinforced his own.

He found that in many other towns and cities, too, where opposition newspapers regularly blazed with anti-Lincoln cartoons, lampoons, and editorial invective. "If he is elected to misgovern for another four years," raged one Democratic sheet in 1864, "we trust some bold hand will pierce his heart with dagger point for the public good."

By the late autumn of 1864, with Lincoln reelected and rebel armies on the defensive everywhere, Booth became increasingly distraught. He felt guilty for not fighting with Dixie against Lincoln's armies. Out of his guilt, out of his obsessions with Lincoln, out of the whole atmosphere of violence and anti-Lincoln hatred that fed him, Booth resolved to act. He would perform a breathtaking feat that would help the South; it would be the most spectacular performance of his life. He would kidnap Lincoln, haul the tyrant to Richmond, and hold him for ransom of all rebel prisoners. Oh, that would make a name for him in this war, that would get needed manpower for Dixie, that would help Lee and Davis fight on. "The South can make no choice," Booth wrote a male intimate. "God is my judge. I love *justice* more than I do a country that disowns it; more than fame and wealth; more (Heaven pardon me if wrong), more than a happy home." The old Union, he asserted, was doomed. "I look now upon my early admiration of her glories as a dream. My love (as things stand to-day) is for the South alone. Nor do I deem it a dishonor in attempting to make for her a prisoner of this man, to whom she owes so much of misery." Booth ended his letter: *"A Confederate doing his duty upon his own responsibility."*

In late 1864 and early 1865, he gathered up a motley band of six young conspirators from the dregs of the Baltimore and Washington area, holding them spellbound with theatrical pronouncements about their destiny. There were curly-haired Samuel Arnold and slight, reticent Michael O'Laughlin, former rebel soldiers and old chums of Booth's from Baltimore. There was hawk-nosed, boy-faced John Surratt, who once had studied to be a Catholic priest, sporting a tuft of whiskers on his chin. There was dim-witted George Atzerodt, a hulking wagonmaster with a scraggly beard and a German accent. There was little Davy Herold, described as "light and trifling" by those who knew him, a former pharmacist's clerk at a Washington drugstore where the Lincolns bought their medicines. And there was six-foot Lewis T. Powell (alias Wood, alias Paine), a glowering drone from Florida who had fought in the rebel army at Gettysburg, ridden with Mosby's irregulars, and drifted north to Baltimore, where Booth found him roaming aimlessly. All of them had served the Confederacy in some capacity and all remained rebel sympathizers. Atzerodt, Herold, and Powell, looking up to Booth with stupefied reverence, would do almost anything he asked. Booth had also alerted Confederate sympathizers in lower Maryland about his intentions, for he might need their help in carting Lincoln into Virginia.

In Washington, the conspirators pored over maps and formulated plans. From hidden places around the White House, they watched the President come and go. They trailed him on his carriage rides about the city, observed his outings to the theater. On March 4, 1865, Booth himself was in the inaugural crowd at the capitol, looking down on Lincoln from up behind the railing of the right buttress. "What an excellent chance I had to kill the President," he boasted afterward.

In mid-March, Booth and his cohorts made an abduction attempt, but it fizzled when Lincoln failed to materialize where they lay in wait. After that, Arnold, O'Laughlin, and Surratt turned away from Booth, and the kidnaping plot fell apart. Booth started drinking heavily—on some evenings he downed an entire quart of brandy within two hours. As Lincoln's forces pounded at the collapsing Confederacy, Booth became more and more agitated, wild-looking, and dangerous. When news of Appomattox sent Washington into paroxysms of joy, he plunged into black gloom.

On the night of April 11, Booth and Davy Herold were in the audience on the White House lawn, awaiting an address by the President. It was a misty evening, but even so one could see the new illuminated dome of the Capitol. In the distance, across the Potomac, Lee's Arlington plantation was aflame with colored candles and exploding rockets, as scores of ex-slaves sang "The Year of Jubilee." Lincoln appeared at an upstairs window and read his speech by candlelight. It was about reconstruction. When he endorsed limited Negro suffrage in Louisiana and expressed sympathy for the black man's desire for the vote, Booth turned to Herold in a rage. "That means nigger citizenship. Now, by God, I'll put him through."

By Good Friday, Booth had worked out a demonic plot to murder the President. It was not personal revenge that motivated him, certainly not money (he had an annual income of $20,000), but a warped sense of justice. Better, he reasoned, for Lincoln to perish than for white America to sink into dishonor, into racial mixing and Yankee dictatorship. "Our country owed all our troubles to him," Booth wrote in his memorandum book, "and God made me the instrument of His punishment."

And he wanted the world to know who had performed the act. For he was certain that the country and posterity itself would vindicate him. So he wrote in a letter to the editor of the Washington *National Intelligencer,* a letter Booth sealed and carried in his pocket. He had signed it: "Men who love their country better than gold or life: J. W. Booth, Paine, Herold, Atzerodt."

For Booth had dragged his faithful lackies into his scheme, directing that Atzerodt kill Vice-President Andrew Johnson and Powell Secretary of State Seward (little Davy Herold was to assist them), thus with Booth exterminating the top three executive officials in the land.

At 11:30 Friday morning, Booth appeared at Ford's Theater, where he took his mail. He learned from Harry Ford, co-owner of the theater, that the Lincolns were to attend *Our American Cousin* that night. Sometime in the afternoon, either Booth or one of his cronies went to the state box and completed preparations for the final act. The visitor apparently bored a peephole in the box door so that Booth could peer through at Lincoln while he sat in the rocking chair.* The visitor also fixed the door at the end of the hallway that led to the first balcony: he chipped plaster from the frame so that a bar could be inserted to lock the door from the inside.

A little after four, Booth rode a fast bay mare out of Pumphrey's Livery Stable and headed for Pennsylvania Avenue. There he stopped to talk with an actor friend. A column of rebel prisoners had just toiled by, and the friend asked if Booth had seen them. "Yes," Booth replied. Then he slapped his forehead dramatically. "Great God," he exclaimed, "I have no longer a country." He produced his letter to the editor of the *National Intelligencer* and asked his friend to deliver it on the morrow. The man agreed (but on the morrow he tore the letter open, read the contents, and burned it).

Sometime that afternoon, Booth turned up at the desk of the Kirkwood House, where Vice-President Johnson was staying. Booth handed the clerk a card, unaddressed, with a note jotted on it: "Don't wish to disturb you. Are you at home? J Wilkes Booth." The clerk thought he said the name Johnson—something that would contribute vastly to what one historian has labeled "The Great American Myth," namely, that men high in the government, maybe even the Vice-President himself, were involved in Booth's assassination plot. In point of fact, Booth was a friend of Johnson's personal secretary and intended the card for him. Moreover, the Vice-President himself was a target in Booth's grisly scenario.

At eight, Booth and his three accomplices rendezvoused at the Herndon House, situated less than a block from Ford's at Ninth

*For a discussion of this point, see the reference notes.

and F streets. Here they rehearsed the plan to murder Seward and
Johnson while Booth shot the President. At about 9:30 Booth
reined up in the alley behind Ford's Theater and left his mare in
the care of scene shifter Edman Spangler, who later turned it over
to a messenger boy. Dressed in his dark hat and high riding boots
with spurs, Booth entered Ford's through the back door, crossed
under the stage, and emerged into another alley that led to Tenth
Street. He stopped at a saloon for a whiskey and a chaser, then
went out into the drifting mist and walked past the presidential
carriage.

From the lobby of Ford's, ablaze with lights, we can see him
approach the doorkeeper with a theatrical gesture. When the
doorkeeper mechanically reached for a ticket, Booth took his hand
by two fingers. "You don't want a ticket, Buck," he said, and asked
the time. The doorkeeper directed him to a clock in the lobby.
It was ten past ten.

Crossing the lobby, Booth opened the door to the main floor
of the theater and surveyed the audience and the state box. He
could see Lincoln's face when he leaned forward and glanced
around at the audience, as though he had recognized somebody.
Booth watched the play with more than professional curiosity: he
knew every line and every scene by memory and had calculated
the best moment to strike, when the two actresses had exited and
Harry Hawk was on stage alone.

Booth turned and climbed the stairs humming a tune, crossed
the dress circle, and entered the narrow hall to the state box,
closing and barring the door. The hallway was dark and empty.
John Parker, Lincoln's guard that night, a lazy oaf who served on
the Metropolitan Police Force, had left his post in the hallway and
had either sat down in the gallery to watch the play or gone
outside for a drink. Doubtless Booth peered through the peephole
in the door to the state box. In the narrow beam of light, he could
see the back of Lincoln's head. Mary was sitting close with her
hand in his, and Major Rathbone and Miss Harris were staring
raptly at Hawk, who was now by himself on stage. "Don't know

the manner of good society, eh?" the actor called out. "Wal, I guess I know enough to turn you inside out, old gal—you sock-dologizing old mantrap."

At exactly that moment, Booth entered the box and fired his derringer point-blank at Lincoln's head. Had we been back in the audience, we would have heard a muffled report from the President's box and seen a scuffle there, as Booth slashed Rathbone's arm with a dagger. Then he leaped from the box, only to catch his spur in the Treasury flag and crash to the stage, breaking his left shinbone just above the ankle. The audience was astonished. Why, it was the actor John Wilkes Booth. Was this part of the play? An improvised scene? Crying "Sic semper tyrannis!" ("Thus be it ever to tyrants!"), Booth lunged at Harry Hawk, then limped out the back door and galloped away into the night.

Inside was pandemonium. We can almost hear Miss Harris screaming, "The President is shot!" and Mary Lincoln shrieking from the box in terror, "Help! Help! Help!" People were yelling, shoving one another into the aisles, and rushing for the exits. In all the commotion, two doctors fought their way to the state box and one resuscitated Lincoln with mouth-to-mouth respiration. But he never regained consciousness, for Booth's bullet had destroyed his brain and lodged behind his right eye.

A throng of twenty-one men carried Lincoln out of the theater, and we can retrace their path across Tenth Street to a boarding-house owned by William Petersen, a German tailor. Like Ford's Theater, the interior of the Petersen house has been historically renovated, enabling us to relive the final hours of what Walt Whitman called "O Moody, Tearful Night." As if civil war had not been atonement enough, for the first time in the history of the Republic a President had been assassinated, a calamity that demolished forever William H. Seward's contention that "assassination is not an American practice or habit, and one so vicious and desperate cannot be engrafted into our political system."

By candlelight in the Petersen House, the group of men bore Lincoln down a narrow hallway to the room of a War Department clerk named William T. Clark. Here they laid the President diagonally across a short four-poster bed, on a red, white, and blue coverlet with fierce eagles at each corner. On the way over, Lincoln had lost blood and brain matter, and his right eye was badly swollen now and discolored. Another boarder lit a gaslamp that hissed and illuminated the little room in a ghastly green. As we stand in the doorway, we can almost see the doctors laboring at Lincoln's side, see Charles Sumner, the President's personal friend, taking his hand now and bowing his head in tears. We can see Andrew Johnson (Atzerodt had lost his nerve and never sought him out), roused from his sleep at the Kirkwood House, "awed to passive docility" by the incomprehensible novelty of his new position. We can hear Secretary of War Edwin M. Stanton taking testimony from witnesses in the second of two parlors at the front. With the President dying and the government at a standstill, Stanton was the only ranking official who had the presence of mind to take over. Close to breaking down himself, Stanton interrogated witnesses with the help of a federal judge and two other men. Within four hours, the evidence pointed conclusively to Booth as Lincoln's assassin. Meanwhile word came that someone (this was Powell) had tried but failed to murder Seward and that Washington was in a reign of terror, with lynch mobs roiling in the streets and soldiers and police firing on people who even looked suspicious. One soldier killed a man for saying, "It served Lincoln right." At once Stanton put the city under martial law and organized dragnets to bring in Booth and all other suspects. For Stanton and other officials crowded into the Petersen House, this thing went beyond Booth. For them, it was a monstrous Confederate plot to seize Washington and annihilate all the heads of the government.

As the Secretary of War came and went in the Petersen House, barking out orders, mobilizing troops and police, Mary Lincoln wept hysterically in the front parlor, while outside men and women, black people and white, waited in the rain as the President died. At last, at 7:22 A.M., April 15, the Surgeon General pulled a sheet over Lincoln's face and Stanton muttered that he now belonged to the ages. The news went out to a shocked and grieving nation that Abraham Lincoln, sixteenth President of the United States, had been shot and killed in Washington, one of the final casualties of a war that had broken his heart and had now claimed his life, gone to join the other Union dead he himself had so immortalized.

Beyond the hallway of the Petersen House, we can see Robert Lincoln, the oldest son, helping his mother into a carriage, a crowd closing around as it lurched away. The bedroom emptied now, as the doctors and attendants carried Lincoln's body out to a hearse that would take him back to the White House. We can hear a man give a shout for Jefferson Davis, whereupon the crowd surged forward and almost beat him to death. Finally the police cleared muddy Tenth Street, leaving only the sentinels at the front of Ford's Theater.

The clerk's little bedroom seems empty and lifeless now. But the bloodstained pillow remains an eternal reminder of what happened here. We leave the room by a side door, walk down through the Petersen House, and emerge into modern Washington, whose noisy streets and congested sidewalks strike us like a physical blow. When I come out of the Petersen House, I always find it hard to believe that I am in the twentieth century. Drawn back to Ford's Theater, I keep expecting the paved street to turn into liquid mud. I keep hearing the noises of that unforgettable night—shouts, the clatter of hooves, the rumble of soldiers storming the theater with bayonets fixed. I stand there, rooted to the spot, stricken with the realization that the thing has really just happened, that the events of that Friday and Saturday are frozen here, timeless, shattering, and irrevocable.

2: AFTERMATH

In the museum of Ford's Theater, in the midst of visitors with cameras and tourist maps, we find several artifacts and photographic exhibits that suggest the drama of the events unleashed by Lincoln's murder. By Sunday, April 16, a huge manhunt was under way in the Washington-Maryland area, as Stanton pressed all War Department resources, soldiers, civilian personnel, and Secret Service men into the pursuit of Booth and his accomplices. Within a week, War Department agents had apprehended Powell, an inebriated Atzerodt, Arnold, O'Laughlin, and scene shifter Edman Spangler, locking them all in double irons in the hold of a monitor anchored in the Potomac. In their zeal to get all suspects, authorities also arrested Mary Surratt, John's mother and a Confederate sympathizer, who ran a Washington boardinghouse where Booth and his fellow conspirators often met. Surratt himself escaped to Canada and eventually made his way to Italy.

Meanwhile Booth and Davy Herold were still at large, with rewards of $20,000 apiece on their heads. After shooting Lincoln, Booth had ridden across the Navy Yard Bridge and fled into backcountry Maryland. Herold overtook him there, and the two headed for the dying Confederacy, helped through lower Maryland by rebel sympathizers who gave them food and supplies. Dr. Samuel A. Mudd of Bryantown, an acquaintance of Booth's and also a Confederate sympathizer, even set his injured leg and furnished him a pair of crude crutches. On the fugitives went, racing from one hiding place to another in the thickets and swamps, as

swarms of soldiers, detectives, and Stanton's Secret Service men
closed in on them. Once troops rushed by so close that the hidden
fugitives could hear their rattling sabers.

Finally, with the assistance of a former Confederate under-
ground mailrunner, Booth and Herold slipped across the Potomac
and made their way to Richard H. Garrett's tobacco farm near
Port Royal on the Rappahannock. Here, in the early morning of
April 26, a column of federal troops and War Department detectives cornered the fugitives in a tobacco barn and ordered them
to surrender. Herold emerged with his hands up, but Booth was
defiant. "Well, my brave boys," he shouted, "you can prepare a
stretcher for me."

At that, they set the barn ablaze to smoke him out. Through
the open slats of the building, they could see Booth limping
toward the door with a carbine in one hand and a revolver in the
other. Somebody opened fire—probably Sergeant Boston Corbett
of the Sixteenth New York Cavalry—and Booth staggered and
fell. Several officers dragged him from the smoking barn and laid
him mortally wounded on the grass outside. "Tell my mother,"
Booth whispered—"tell my mother I die for my country." Two
hours later he was dead. On that same day, the last rebel army in
the East surrendered to Sherman in North Carolina, an event
Lincoln had eagerly awaited on the final day of his life.

The officers sewed Booth up in a bag and conveyed him and
his personal effects to Washington and Secretary of War Stanton.
Among Booth's things was a compass, a little Catholic medal, a
pocket knife, and a leather-bound memorandum book—often
called Booth's diary—which was to excite a storm of controversy
and wild speculation in later years. This document revealed no
devastating secrets about Booth's life and murder of Lincoln,
incriminated no government officials in his plottings, as I shall
discuss later. Thirty-six pages were missing from the diary, but the
officers who brought it to Washington later testified that the
pages were gone when they took it from Booth. According to
William Hanchett, a present-day expert on the assassination,

Booth himself removed the pages and used them mainly to send as notes.

Stanton turned the diary over to Judge Advocate General Joseph Holt, who kept it in his possession throughout the ensuing trials. The Judge Advocate General did not introduce it in court, nor did the defense attorneys ask that it be introduced. "There was nothing in the diary," Holt later told a congressional committee, "which I could conceive would be testimony against any human being, or for anyone except Booth himself, and he being dead, I did not offer it to the Commission."

Stanton, in the meantime, was deeply concerned about how to dispose of Booth's body. Frankly, the Secretary worried that rebels and rebel sympathizers might glorify it. His apprehension is understandable, for some rebels had audaciously praised what Booth had done. "God Almighty ordered this event," shrieked the Dallas *Herald*. "Abe has gone to answer before the bar of God for the innocent blood which he has permitted to be shed," echoed the Chattanooga *Daily Rebel* in a statement reprinted in the North. Even southern journals that tried to be temperate could not restrain their bitterness. And if the spot of Booth's burial became known? What would disloyalists and rebel sympathizers do then? What might they say? Stanton shuddered at the thought, shuddered at how offensive it would be to him and "the loyal people of the country" if Booth's remains became "the instrument of rejoicing at the sacrifice of Mr. Lincoln." Well, he would not let that happen. He had the body taken to the grounds of the Washington Arsenal and secretly buried under the floor of a former penitentiary building.

And it *was* Booth buried there. All of his intimate theater friends had identified his body for the government, as had a prominent Washington surgeon who had operated on him the previous year. In 1869, after the passion over Lincoln's assassination had subsided, the War Department released Booth's body to his family, who had it identified again and interred in Green Mount Cemetery in Baltimore. But ever since, fantastic stories have circulated that "the real Booth" escaped to Oklahoma, to England, or some other improbable place. It is all unmitigated nonsense. The real Booth died at Garrett's tobacco farm.

As for Booth's cohorts, Judge Advocate General Holt, Stanton, and President Johnson insisted that the assassination was a war-related act and therefore had the prisoners tried in secret before a military tribunal of nine officers. It was similar to the kind of military courts that had long functioned under Lincoln's wartime authority. Charged with conspiracy to kill Lincoln were Powell, Atzerodt, and Herold, who had stayed with Booth through the assassination scheme; Arnold and O'Laughlin, who had participated in the abortive kidnaping plot; Spangler and Dr. Mudd, who had aided and abetted Booth; and matronly Mary Surratt, who had operated the boardinghouse where the conspirators had frequently congregated. The military proceedings began on May 10, with Holt as prosecutor.

Critics then and thereafter denounced the prosecution of civilians in a secret military court as blatantly illegal and "a horrible miscarriage of justice." I am not going to defend military courts, but one can understand why the Johnson administration resorted to them in the emotion-charged atmosphere of May, 1865. The nation still reeled in shock and rage over Lincoln's murder, and a great many people in and out of government still thought it a diabolical Confederate plot. And the extolling of it in certain rebel newspapers did not disabuse them of that notion. Booth's five bona fide accomplices, moreover, were not ordinary civilians standing trial in peacetime. All of them had served the Confederacy, three as soldiers. Too, the Civil War was not yet over—the last rebel army was still at bay out in the Trans-Mississippi Department when the trials commenced. In this context, as one scholar has recently argued, it seems absurd to think that a civilian court would have reached a different conclusion from that of the military commission.

At the end of June, the court voted the death sentence for Powell, Atzerodt, Herold, and Mary Surratt, although she was probably innocent. The court did recommend clemency for Mrs. Surratt because of her sex and age. But President Johnson, who signed all four orders of execution, claimed that he never saw the mercy plea for Mrs. Surratt. Judge Holt, on the other hand, insisted to the end of his life that Johnson not only read the recommendation, but asserted that she had "kept the nest that hatched the egg." And so it was decided. On July 7, under a blazing sun, Mary Surratt and Booth's hapless minions hanged together. There is a striking blown-up photograph of the scene in the museum of Ford's Theater.

The court voted life imprisonment at hard labor for Arnold, O'Laughlin, and Dr. Mudd, and six years at hard labor for Spangler. As for Dr. Mudd, his pro-Confederate sympathies, acquaintance with Booth, and role in Booth's flight "made it apparent that under the circumstances he was fortunate to have escaped more severe punishment," as a careful student of the conspiracy trials has written. Later the four convicted men found themselves on a penal island off the Florida coast, where O'Laughlin subsequently died. In 1869, President Johnson pardoned the other three and ordered them released.

Meanwhile, in a quieter time, John Surratt returned to the United States and stood trial in a civilian court, which acquitted him because of a hung jury. He settled in Baltimore, became an auditor, and in 1870 gave a public lecture in which he denied any complicity in Lincoln's assassination, but bragged about his part in the abduction plot. What had motivated him? "Where is there a young man in the North with one spark of patriotism in his heart who would not have with enthusiastic ardor joined in any undertaking for the capture of Jefferson Davis and brought him to Washington? There is not one who would not have done so. And so I was led on by a sincere desire to assist the South in gaining her independence. I had no hesitation in taking part in anything honorable that might tend towards the accomplishment of that object."

The kidnaping of the President of the United States was something *honorable?* In Surratt's quixotic ramblings we can almost hear the voice of John Wilkes Booth speaking from the grave.

A schoolmate said of Booth that "it was a 'name in history' he sought. A glorious career he thought of by day and dreamed of by night. He always said he would 'make his name remembered by succeeding generations.' " And that he did, with a vengeance. For Booth was the first in an American rogues' gallery of assassins who were to gun down James A. Garfield, William McKinley, John F. Kennedy, Martin Luther King, Jr., and Robert F. Kennedy. Yes, John Wilkes Booth was the prototype of the messianic misfits with whom we have become familiar in modern America, of Lee Harvey Oswald, James Earl Ray, and Sirhan Bishara Sirhan, each of whose murderous acts traumatized the country. What they did has left us all with the realization that it can happen anywhere, any time: another gunshot, another gust of cries, another public figure lying dead of an assassin's bullet. We have come a light year's distance from the pre-Booth America, when Lincoln's old friend and bodyguard, Ward Hill Lamon, could argue that assassination was "so abhorrent to the genius of Anglo-Saxon civilization, so foreign to the practice of our republican institutions," that it could not happen here. An enormous American innocence died with Booth's shot at Ford's Theater, and we have never again been the same.

Each year, more than half a million people visit Ford's. I wish it were millions. I wish we had a national Lincoln holiday—it is a public disgrace that we do not—on which the country might ponder what it lost at Ford's Theater, what ended here—and what began.

3: STANTON

Around the core of fact about Lincoln's assassination has grown an elaborate web of conspiracy theories, some bordering on lunacy (the papal-plot theory comes to mind), all testifying to the desperate human need to see vast intrigues behind events too large to comprehend.

In the case of Lincoln's murder, the most popular and persistent conspiracy theory points to Secretary of War Edwin M. Stanton as the ringleader of a government plot that involved Thaddeus Stevens and other so-called radicals, or advanced Republicans. Over the years, proponents of this theory have fervently argued that Stanton was an unscrupulous schemer who wanted to punish the conquered South, as the advanced Republicans did, and that a tender and forgiving Lincoln stymied them. So Stanton conspired with Stevens and his cronies to murder Lincoln and clear the way for a harsher reconstruction program than the President planned. And Booth, to use modern argot, became their hit man.

Here is how the plot supposedly worked. Stanton prevented his own chief clerk from escorting Lincoln to Ford's Theater, so that the President would be left unguarded except by the incompetent Parker, whom Stanton or others in the conspiracy arranged to become Lincoln's special guard that night. Thus, when Parker vacated his post (as Stanton had figured he would), Booth had unimpeded access to the state box to shoot the President. After he did so, Stanton had Washington's communications severed and deliberately obstructed the pursuit, leaving improperly guarded the one road the assassin was certain to take out of the capital. In the end, though, one of Stanton's detectives (not Boston Corbett) shot Booth in the Garrett barn to keep him from talking.

Alas for Stanton, Booth's diary turned up. Since thirty-six pages are missing, purveyors of the Stanton thesis conjecture that the Secretary of War must have hacked them out in order to destroy incriminating evidence. Then to silence Booth's accomplices, Stanton rigged a secret military trial that sent them swiftly to the gallows. Thanks to his cover-up, Stanton and the other plotters of Lincoln's assassination went free.

Then in 1977 one Joseph Lynch of Worthington, Massachusetts, made the startling announcement that he had discovered the "eighteen" missing pages of Booth's diary while appraising documents of Stanton's heirs. These pages, he said, indicated Booth's intrigues with Lincoln intimates, Stanton specifically. The news media, of course, broadcast Lynch's claims across the Republic; syndicated journalist Jack Anderson devoted an entire column to the story. Spotting a potential box-office windfall, Shick Sunn Classic Productions went to work on a movie based on the "missing" diary pages as well as "recently discovered" Booth letters and other "data." The result was *The Lincoln Conspiracy*, a wretched motion picture which not only belabored the Stanton thesis, but served it up as one of several wide-ranging plots to kill the President. To capture the mass reading market, Sunn Classic also brought out a paperback book by the same title. To make it look legitimate, the company even appended footnotes.

It was all a hoax, as several Lincoln and civil-war scholars pointed out. The news media ignored them—why publicize the boring truth when sensationalism was available? The "missing" diary pages, of course, were never released and doubtless do not exist (there are thirty-six of them anyway, not eighteen as claimed). No newly discovered documents implicating Stanton, or revealing any conspiracies beyond Booth's own, have ever come to light because no such documents exist. As historian Thomas

Reed Turner has stated, those who manufactured *The Lincoln Conspiracy* must "bear a large responsibility for perpetrating this fraud on the American public."

The whole Stanton thesis is a fraud. It rests on the misassumption that Lincoln and the advanced Republicans were at odds over reconstruction and that Stanton stood with them against his chief. No such thing ever happened. As we have seen, the President sided with the advanced Republicans on nearly all crucial reconstruction issues. In short, they had no earthly reason to kill him. There is no evidence that any of them ever even contemplated so monstrous a thing. As we have seen, Lincoln was no softy when it came to reconstructing southern rebels. He was considering an occupying army to keep them in line. Nor was Stanton in conflict with the President in reconstruction matters. On the contrary, he wholeheartedly endorsed Lincoln's military approach to southern restoration, so much so that the President asked Stanton to draft a tentative plan for military reconstruction, which the Cabinet discussed on Good Friday. Finally—and this is a crucial point—Stanton had been exhausted and sick, and he had promised himself that he would step down when the war ended. After Lee surrendered, Stanton took his resignation to the President. "Stanton," Lincoln said with his hands on the Secretary's shoulders, "you have been a good friend and a faithful public officer and it is not for you to say when you will no longer be needed here." Reluctantly, Stanton agreed to remain a while longer, because when it came to reconstruction he thought that Lincoln would need a tough and experienced administrator at his side.

This is a man involved in a heinous plot to murder his own President?

By Lincoln's own testimony, Stanton was "a good friend" and public servant, and he deserves to be remembered that way. He was a short, thick-chested man with a prodigious beard and a constantly irritated look in his bespectacled eyes. A native Ohioan, born of parents with abolitionist leanings, he had become a successful lawyer and a northern Democrat. In the 1840s, he lost a daughter, a wife, and a brother—a succession of tragedies that hurt him permanently and caused him to turn "a stern face to the world," as his modern biographers put it. In 1856, he and his second wife moved to Washington, where Stanton became a government lawyer and James Buchanan's last Attorney General. After the war broke out, Stanton was extremely critical of Lincoln, as were a great many others. But he had exceptional skill and an unswerving loyalty to the Union, which was why Lincoln chose him to replace the inept Simon Cameron as War Secretary.

The President expected a lot of his new Secretary, and Stanton did not disappoint him. Working at a killing pace, he took a department tangled with corruption and inefficiency and transformed it into a superbly competent agency. He saved the government some $17 million in adjusted war contracts, reorganized the entire supply system, and assimilated a mass of technical military data that Lincoln found indispensable.

As an administrator, Stanton was an iron-fisted martinet who drove his staff as hard as he drove himself. "My chief," grumbled one subordinate, "is narrow minded, full of prejudices, exceedingly violent, reckless of the rights and feelings of others, often acting like a wild man in the dark, throwing his arms around. . . . His idea of energy is altogether physical." Brusque, efficient, and brutally honest, Stanton made a lot of implacable enemies. The "outer crust of his harsh manner," said one government official, "was very thin—but it was thick enough to incense the many that could not pierce it."

Lincoln was one who pierced it. "Folks come up here and tell me there are a great many men who have all Stanton's excellent qualities without his defects," the President once remarked. "All I can say is, I haven't met 'em; I don't know 'em." Because of the war, Lincoln and Stanton spent a great deal of time together. In fact, the Secretary of War became one of Lincoln's closest subordinates, accompanying him on his carriage rides, huddling with him in his White House "shop," standing at his side in the War Department during military campaigns. They both loved the Union's volunteer army, and they developed a mutual respect and trust for one another. In all, Stanton was an incorruptible and thoroughly loyal administrator whom Lincoln could count on to obey orders.

Because Stanton lacked a sense of humor, Lincoln could never joke with him as he did with Seward. Contemporaries recalled that when Lincoln was telling a story and Stanton entered the room, the story and the laughter both died. Yet Lincoln had immense affection for this gnomelike man and defended him in characteristic ways. Once when a delegation confronted Lincoln in a huff and reported that the War Secretary had called him a fool, the President responded with mock amazement. "Did Stanton call me a fool?" he said. "Well, I guess I had better go over and see Stanton about this. Stanton is usually right."

By war's end, few men were on such intimate terms with Lincoln as the Secretary of War. Few men could write the President such chatty, personal letters as those Stanton dispatched while Lincoln visited the Virginia front in 1865.

March 25: "We have nothing new here; now [that] you are away everything is quiet and your tormentors vanished. I hope you will remember Gen. Harrison's advice to his men at Tippecanoe, that they 'can see as well a little further off.'"

March 26: "Your military news warms the blood or we would be in danger of a March chill."

April 3: "Allow me respectfully to ask you to consider whether you ought to expose the nation to the consequences of any disaster to yourself in the pursuit of a treacherous and dangerous enemy like the rebel army. . . . Commanding Generals are in the line of their duty in running such risks. But is the political head of a nation in the same condition[?]"

Nobody in government worried more about Lincoln's safety and did more to ensure it than Edwin Stanton. It was Stanton who made certain that a company of Ohio cavalry guarded the President on his carriage rides, Stanton who ordered Pennsylvania troops to encamp on the White House lawn, Stanton who saw to it that the Washington Metropolitan Police Force provided Lincoln constant protection, Stanton who assigned a military escort to accompany the President on his nocturnal walks to and from the War Department, Stanton who surrounded him with detectives on special occasions like the Second Inaugural, Stanton who begged Lincoln to take care of himself and who became agitated and angry when he did not. Lincoln finally consented to a military escort, mainly out of concern for the soldiers. If Stanton learned that they had let him out of their sight, Lincoln told the men, "he would have you court-martialed and shot."

Lincoln protested all the guards and detectives because they made him feel like a king, and he hated it. He kept saying that anybody who really wanted to could murder him, and there was nothing Stanton or anyone else could do to prevent it.

In the closing months of the war, rumors of assassination and abduction plots swept Washington, and Stanton and his department made every attempt to investigate the more plausible reports. But "warnings that appeared to be most definite," recalled Lincoln's personal secretaries, "when they came to be examined proved too vague and confused for further attention." One warning did touch on Booth himself: a War Department clerk named Louis J. Weichmann told a fellow employee that he had seen suspicious activities at the Surratt boardinghouse, where he had a room. The tip made its way up to Stanton, and his department may have put the conspirators under surveillance. Why nothing more came of this is not known. But Stanton was not guilty of negligence. He investigated all the reports he could, did all he could to protect the President. Had he known about Booth's plottings, no man would have moved faster to stamp them out.

Which brings us to the assassination itself. Stanton had nothing to do with assigning John Parker to guard Lincoln; that came about through an administrative fluke in the Metropolitan Police Force. On Good Friday, Stanton did dissuade his chief clerk from accompanying Lincoln to Ford's Theater—but only because Stanton disapproved of the President's theatergoing and wanted him to stay at home in the evenings lest he get himself killed. During those terrible hours in the Petersen House, with Lincoln mortally wounded and the government paralyzed, Stanton did not cover up Booth's trail, was not guilty of "criminal negligence" in getting up a pursuit. As I have tried to show, Stanton was the only high-ranking official who acted. His colleagues, in fact, spoke of his conduct with "undimmed praise." Corporal James Tanner, who helped take down testimony in the Petersen House, said that "through all that awful night Stanton was the one man of steel." Yet no official was more stricken by what had happened. "I knew it was only by a powerful effort that he restrained himself and that he was near a break," Tanner said. When the Surgeon General told him that Lincoln would never recover, Stanton protested, "Oh, no, General; no—no," and sat down and cried.

Somehow he drove himself on, furiously mobilizing the pursuit of Booth, literally running the government. Yet he had the sensitivity to soothe Robert Lincoln when the President's end finally came. Years later, Robert told Stanton's son, "I recall the kindness of your father to me, when my father was lying dead and I felt utterly desperate, hardly able to realize the truth."

Stanton's own grief was inconsolable. Robert recalled that "for more than ten days after my father's death in Washington, he called every morning on me in my room, and spent the first few minutes of his visits weeping without saying a word." The assassination had a profound impact on Stanton. Filled with apprehension, certain that plots against him and his associates lurked everywhere, he kept a guard around his house and seldom left without a strong man to accompany him. Yet the Secretary of War responded tenderly when Mary Lincoln, in her terrible anguish, reached out to him for help and comfort.

This is a man who plotted Lincoln's murder? The whole notion is so preposterous that it boggles the mind that even the rankest cynic could believe it. To borrow Lincoln's famous remark, "Has it not got down as thin as the homeopathic soup that was made by boiling the shadow of a pigeon that had starved to death?"

Yes, the Stanton thesis is a staggering fraud on the public. Yet I am under no illusion that what I've said here will put an end to it. For as long as there is a gullible public with an appetite for sensationalism, there will be hucksters to peddle this crass and irresponsible tale. There will be more crackpot conspiracy books, more films like Sunn Classic's, more television shows like CBS's *They've Shot Lincoln!*, which was aired in 1972 and which rode the Stanton thesis through cheap rhetorical questions and innuendo. But I will say this about what has been done so far. Every television and movie producer, every publisher, manuscript appraiser, and news editor, every script writer, journalist, historian, and harebrained conspiracy buff who has helped promote this shoddy business is guilty of slandering a decent man, a Union patriot, and a loyal friend and subordinate of Abraham Lincoln.

4: WITHOUT HIM

Perhaps nobody in the Lincoln story—not even Stanton—has been more vilified than the President's wife. We are all familiar with the hostile portrait of Mary. She was a shrew who offended Lincoln's friends, seldom invited people to dinner, and drove poor Lincoln out of the house with her hectoring. During the Civil War, she reigned as a kind of First Bitch whose shrieks made the White House tremble. William Herndon, who hated Mary Lincoln, began the vicious characterization of her that infests the Lincoln literature and that many Americans still regard as true. Even the most recent Lincoln biography, by Oscar and Lilian Handlin, presents Mary as a hysteric who raged at everybody except her children.

In the White House, as in Springfield, Mary had her problems, but she was no harridan. Modern studies like Ruth Painter Randall's *Mary Lincoln, Biography of a Marriage*, and Justin and Linda Turner's *Mary Todd Lincoln, Her Life and Letters*, have given us more sympathetic portraits, helping us to understand the sensitive and troubled woman who stood by Lincoln's side throughout the cataclysm of civil war. As First Lady, Mary functioned in a role for which she was eminently qualified. Visitors at White House functions saw a President's wife who was elegantly fashionable, dressed in elaborate gowns cut low enough to display her ample bosom, tending to her guests with impeccable social grace. Ben: Perley Poore, the prominent journalist and Washington observer, thought her the most charming White House hostess since Dolley Madison.

Yet Mary suffered from the war as much as her husband did. Opposition newspapers smeared the First Lady, too, depicting her as a country hussy who belonged in the barnyard rather than the White House. Worse still was the malicious gossip. Because members of her family sided with the Confederacy, grotesque rumors flew about that the First Lady was a rebel spy who handed over state secrets to the enemy. Of course, Mary did no such thing. She loved the Union and thought all Confederates were traitors, as Lincoln did. Yet the rumors persisted, and they hurt her deeply.

What hurt her most, though, was the death of twelve-year-old Willie Lincoln, in February, 1862. Mary's whole life was her husband and children; she had already lost little Eddie Lincoln before the war; and now Willie too was gone. Mary's grief was so devastating that she suffered a nervous breakdown and lay in her room for three endless months, weeping uncontrollably and crying out for Willie to come back to her. Elizabeth Keckley, Mary's Negro seamstress and confidante, did what she could to ease Mary's anguish. And so did her husband, who feared that she might go insane. With their care and help, Mary recovered enough to leave her bedroom. But she gave away all of Willie's toys and anything else that might remind her of him, and she never again set foot in the room where he died.

To escape her "furnace of affliction," she took flowers to wounded soldiers in Washington's hospitals and found employment for southern blacks who streamed into the capital. Thanks partly to Elizabeth's influence, Mary developed a deep compassion for "all the oppressed colored people" and urged her husband to help them.

Yet the war drove the Lincolns apart, creating tensions and distances between them (as it would have done to any first couple). Mary still cared deeply for her husband, worried that he wasn't getting enough to eat, fretted about his health and safety—"oh God," she would say to Elizabeth, what if she lost Lincoln, too? She saw so little of him anymore, and he was usually weary and withdrawn when she did see him. Because he spent almost all his waking hours at his job, she turned to a salon of male friends for companionship. She had long suffered from migraine headaches, and they were worse now, blinding her with pain and causing outbursts of temper that filled her with remorse when they were over. Shopping expeditions to New York proved wonderful therapy for her migraines. But she spent so extravagantly that she plunged into debt. By 1864, she owed some $27,000 and confessed to Elizabeth Keckley how terrified she was that Lincoln might find out.

And then there were her jealousies. She had gone through menopause, and it left her more insecure than ever. She could not bear to let Lincoln out of her sight, or to see pretty young women flirting with him at White House receptions. An ugly incident occurred near the end of the war, when the Lincolns visited the front in Virginia. Another woman rode beside Lincoln during a troop review, and Mary flew into a tirade, giving the woman a tongue-lashing that humiliated her husband and made a spectacle of herself. The entire episode left a deep wound between Lincoln and Mary.

By Good Friday, though, they had made amends and had never during the war felt so close and tender to one another. They shared breakfast, planned their outing to Ford's Theater that evening, and took an intimate carriage ride together. Lincoln was in high spirits because the conflict was almost over, and he talked about what he and Mary would do when his second term ended. "We must both be more cheerful in the future," he told Mary;

"between the war and the loss of our darling Willie, we have both been very miserable." She developed a headache later and may have had doubts about attending the theater. But Lincoln wanted to go, and Mary relented because she had never "felt so unwilling to be away from him." In the state box at Ford's, she sat close to her husband and slipped her hand into his.

Booth's derringer destroyed two lives that night. The sudden gunshot, the shock of Lincoln slumping into her arms, the maelstrom of screams, pressing faces, grabbing arms, hysterical weeping—all shattered Mary beyond repair. "Oh, my God," she wailed as the doctors led her out of the Petersen House, "and have I given my husband to die?" She was so paralyzed from grief that she could not attend Lincoln's funeral, or accompany the special train that bore him and Willie home together, home to Springfield. For more than a month, she lay in her White House bedroom in wild and desolate despair. She would see no one beyond her sons Robert and Tad, her doctor, Lizzy Keckley, and Secretary of War Stanton. While she wept in her room, cried for Lincoln to take her with him, people roamed through the executive mansion at will, slashing curtains and cushions, cutting away pieces of velvet carpet for souvenirs, carting off china, silverware, and furniture. Mary herself had supervised a complete renovation of the White House in 1861, and now vandals were pillaging it, and she hurt too much to care.

On May 23, clad in black, she descended the White House stairs for the last time and climbed into a waiting carriage with her sons and Lizzy. There were no crowds to see Mary off, no speeches or public farewells. Scarcely even a friend came to say goodbye. Unable to go home to Springfield, unable to face the house on Eighth and Jackson, she headed for Chicago by train, taking along sixty cartons filled with her personal possessions. Already vicious rumors were afloat that it was *Mary* who had looted the White House—why else would it take sixty cartons to move her out? On the train ride west, Mary hardly spoke, her head aching from migraine.

Immersed in a Chicago hotel room, she wrote tear-stained letters to her friends. "Day by day," she said to Mary Jane Welles, "I miss, my beloved husband more & more, how I am, to pass through life, without *him* who loved us so dearly, it is impossible to say. This morning, I have been looking over & arranging a large package of *his* dear, loving letters to me, many of them written to me, in the 'long ago,' and quite yellow with age, others, more recent & *one* written from his office, *only* the Wednesday before, a few lines, playfully & tenderly worded, notifying, the hour, of the day, *he* would drive with me! Time, my dear Mrs. Welles, has at *length* taught & convinced me, that the loved & idolized being, comes no more, and I must patiently await, the hour, when 'God's love,' shall place me, by *his* side again—where there are *no more* partings & no more tears."

Without him, she felt she "had nothing, *was* nothing." While private donors helped settle some of her debts, she still owed thousands of dollars to merchants and bankers in the East. She desperately feared that she would sink into poverty and shame, unable to pay her creditors or care for herself and her sons. Lincoln's estate came to around $85,000, which by law went equally to Mary, Robert, and Tad. Because Mary was a woman and this was the Victorian era, an old male friend of Lincoln's took charge of the estate and invested the principal in lucrative government securities. Mary's share of the interest amounted to $1,500 to $1,800 annually—a considerable sum in those days. But to Mary it was "a clerk's salary." How could she ever solve her money worries on such a pittance? How could she ever buy herself a home? She prevailed on congressional friends like Charles Sumner and Simon Cameron to secure a government pension for her. Too, she insisted that she was entitled to her husband's remaining presidential salary. At last, two weeks before Christmas, 1865, the leaders of this "*grateful* nation," as she bitterly called them, voted her exactly $25,000—one year of Lincoln's salary.

Always impulsive in financial matters, Mary spent most of the money on an expensive home in Chicago, but later had to give

it up because she could not afford to maintain it. Installed in
another Chicago hotel, she became increasingly reclusive, embittered about her circumstances, and profoundly hurt. Life had
dealt cruel blows to Mary, and she felt at times as though she were
out of control in the deep waters encircling her.

By now, Josiah G. Holland's myth-building life of Lincoln had
appeared, and Holland had sent Mary a copy. By now, William
Herndon, Lincoln's law partner and Mary's *bête noire,* had denounced Holland's book and vowed to write one of his own about
the "real" Lincoln. In November, 1866, in Springfield, Herndon
gave a public lecture on Lincoln's romantic life, announcing to the
world that his partner had loved "Miss Ann Rutledge with all his
soul, mind and strength." Her tragic death, Herndon theorized,
had made Lincoln melancholy and fatalistic, had led him into
marriage with a woman he never loved, and yet had taken him to
supreme heights in politics.

Mary was mortified. "This is the return for all my husband's
kindness to this miserable man!" she wrote a Lincoln friend. "Out
of pity he took him into his office, when he was almost a hopeless
inebriate and . . . he was only a drudge, in the place." Now this
ingrate was trying to take away her "last comfort," and she demanded that he be stopped. She called Herndon a "dirty dog" and
vowed that if he ever uttered another word he would find his life
"not worth living for." In retaliation, Herndon later branded Mary
as a liar given to mad fits, a "she wolf" whose relationship with
Lincoln was "unfortunate." While Lincoln intimates sided with
Mary in this war, millions of Americans came to accept Herndon's
opinions. Moreover, his story of Ann Rutledge appealed to Victo-
rian fantasies, giving Lincoln's image a romantic new dimension.
Thanks to Herndon's promotional skills, a great many Americans
embraced it as one of the world's great love stories.

As Ann's star rose, Mary Lincoln fell deeper into adversity. In
1867, in an effort to solve her financial woes, Mary decided to sell
her White House wardrobe and contacted a couple of New York
brokers to act in her behalf. She even enlisted Elizabeth Keckley
in her plan, which called for the brokers to auction the clothes

without saying they were hers, so as to avoid publicity. It turned into a nightmare. The brokers were unscrupulous Barnums who tried to make a fortune at Mary's expense. First they advertised that it was *her* wardrobe for sale and exhibited it for the public to stare at and pick over. When nobody bought anything, the brokers then dreamed up the ghoulish idea of sending Mary's wardrobe—including the blood-stained dress she had on when Lincoln died—on a tour around the country and maybe even to Europe. The scheme fell through, but not before hostile papers like the New York *World* held Mary up for scathing ridicule.

Mary was scandalized. "I pray for death this morning," she wrote Elizabeth Keckley. "Only my darling Taddie prevents my taking my life." But the worst was still to come. In 1868, Elizabeth published her memoir, *Behind the Scenes: Thirty Years a Slave and Four Years in the White House.* Though sympathetic to Mary (it was intended to exculpate the former First Lady), Keckley's frank book reported "the old clothes scandal" in detail, revealed the extent of Mary's wartime debts, and even included personal letters Mary had written her. For Mary, this was an outrageous breach of confidence. How could Lizzy betray her like this? Mary was so angry and hurt that in her correspondence she never again mentioned Elizabeth, except to dismiss her once as *"the colored* historian."

Mary fled to Europe with Tad, hoping to escape the humiliation of the old-clothes episode, the allegations of Herndon, the betrayal of Lizzy. She was ill, too, referring delicately to her troubles of a "womanly nature"—the gynecological disorder that had plagued her since Tad's birth. Maybe the soothing mineral waters of Europe's spas would ease her weakness of limb, her chills and migraines. In Germany, she put Tad in a boarding school and rented a room for herself in a Frankfurt hotel. A female friend who visited Mary was appalled to find her living in a "small cheerless desolate looking room" with only one window and a single candle for light.

Mary's letters in this period reveal a woman increasingly alone, increasingly shut off from family and friends. While in Frankfurt, she learned that Stanton had died and she was overwhelmed with sorrow. Then she discovered that $100,000 had been privately raised for Stanton's survivors and that similar help had gone to the family of a deceased Union general. Such generosity for *them*, yet nothing for the widow of the President of the United States, nothing at all.

Vexed about her "American affairs," Mary continued to write Sumner and other congressmen for federal assistance. In her behalf, they pushed and lobbied for a yearly pension, but her enemies, besides pointing out that she already had enough money, argued that she didn't deserve it because she had been a Confederate sympathizer during the late war. But in July, 1870, Congress finally awarded her a pension of $3,000 annually (later raising it to $5,000 and adding a $15,000 donation), and Mary resolved not to utter another "murmuring word" on the subject. By now, evidently with Robert's help, Mary had settled her debts and was a relatively wealthy woman, with assets totaling $58,756. Yet she had no sense of money and continued to fret about her finances, certain that she was on the brink of poverty and destitution, certain that she was too poor to maintain a home.

Feeling disoriented and ill (the spas could not assuage her pain), she packed her things, fetched Tad, and in May, 1871, set out for home on an America-bound steamer. By now, her youngest son was a manly eighteen and completely devoted to her. How she cherished "Taddie." He had such "a lovely nature," was "all love and gentleness." In his "tender treatment of me at all times," she said, "& very especially when I am indisposed—he reminds me so strongly of his beloved father." Mary was proud of Robert, too, who was married now and becoming a successful Chicago attorney. But with Robert on his own, it was Taddie she clung to for comfort and companionship. In her aching eyes, he alone stood between her and a void.

On their arrival in Chicago, they had a family reunion with Robert in his "charming" new place on Wabash Avenue. But Tad was not feeling well—he had caught a chest cold at sea, and it had gotten worse. Back at the hotel with Mary, he fell dangerously ill, his chest so congested that he had to fight for his breath. Unable to lie down, he had to sit upright in a chair. "With the *last* few years *so filled* with sorrow," Mary wrote a woman friend, "*this* fresh anguish bows me to the earth. I have been sitting up so constantly for the last ten nights, that I am unable to write you at length." The physicians did what they could for Tad, but Robert said he had never seen "such suffering." On July 15, as he and Mary looked on helplessly, Tad slumped forward in his chair, dead of what physicians later called "compression of the heart."

Mary managed to attend a brief funeral service in Robert's house, but was not aboard the train that took gentle Taddie down to Springfield, to be placed in a tomb beside his father. For the fourth time, Mary lay immobilized with grief. "I feel that there is no life to me, without my idolized Taddie," she wrote. "One by one I have consigned to their resting place, my idolized ones, & now, in *this* world, there is nothing left me, but the deepest anguish & desolation."

Her desolation grew worse with Herndon's ongoing allegations. Now he claimed that her husband had been *illegitimate.* How could she stop this man? She felt powerless to stop him, and it tortured her. She just wanted to die, to join Lincoln and Taddie in their grave. Like someone smote a physical blow, she grabbed out for Robert, trying desperately to hold on. She became obsessed with the idea that he was going to die, that her one remaining son was to be taken from her. While on a trip to Florida, she convinced herself that Robert was gravely ill and sent a frantic telegram to his law partner, who went to Robert at once, only to find him entirely well in his office.

When Mary returned to Chicago, Robert begged her to stay at his house. When she refused, he rented two rooms in a Chicago hotel—one for each of them—and tried to look after Mary himself. Her erratic conduct shocked and embarrassed him. She carried $57,000 worth of securities in her skirt pocket. In her misery, she spent money recklessly, putting down $450 for three watches, $600 for lace curtains, $700 for jewelry, even buying seventeen pairs of gloves and three dozen handkerchiefs. And her head ached worse than ever: it felt, she said, as though "an Indian" were pulling wires out of her eyes.

In the hotel at night, she would come to Robert's door in her bedclothes, sobbing that somebody was after her. Once, only half dressed, she mistook the elevator for the lavatory and refused to come out. When Robert and a hotel employee tried to get her back to her room, Mary flung their hands away and shrieked that Robert was trying to murder her.

Robert was beside himself. He had a reputation to think about. He was also genuinely worried about Mary's safety and state of mind. Frankly, he thought she was going mad. To protect his mother, to prevent her from squandering any more of her money, Robert petitioned the Cook County Court to have Mary committed on grounds of insanity. Lured to the hearing by Leonard Swett, Lincoln's old friend, Mary was taken quite by surprise. Who had advised Robert to do this? she demanded of Swett. In court, though, she endured the trial with determined dignity, as a parade of physicians and other witnesses described her bizarre behavior and unanimously testified that she was unbalanced. The jury agreed, and the name of "Mary Lincoln" appeared in the Lunatic Record of the Cook County Court, page 596.

After the verdict, Robert came to her with tears streaming down his face, and he took her hand. "O Robert," she said, "to think that my own son would ever have this done." For Mary, this was a final, devastating betrayal. That night, for the first time in her life, she tried to kill herself with a lethal dose of camphor and laudanum. But her druggist had substituted a harmless ingredient for the laudanum, and she did not die. The next day, thoroughly miserable, she rode with Robert himself to a private sanitarium west of Chicago.

With an airy room and the freedom to go for walks and rides, Mary was not physically uncomfortable here. But the news of her incarceration had flashed across the country, and she seethed with resentment, schemed to get out. She was no maniac. She was Mrs. Abraham Lincoln. She would prove that to Robert and all her enemies and detractors.

She found ready allies in Myra and Judge James Bradwell of Chicago, both dedicated feminists; the Bradwells in turn enlisted the help of Elizabeth and Ninian Edwards of Springfield—Mary's sister and brother-in-law—and pressed the sanitarium to let her live with them. Less than four months after she entered it, the sanitarium released her in the Edwards's custody. When the court in a second trial ruled her sane, Mary felt exonerated. She wrote "Robert T. Lincoln" and demanded the return of her things. "You have tried your game of robbery long enough," she said, and signed the letter "Mrs. A. Lincoln."

She stayed a year with the Edwardses, fled to Europe again, then in 1880 came back to Springfield for good, back to their home on the hill, back to her room there. Ill, partially blind, and crippled from a back injury, Mary spent her final days in this shuttered room, seldom venturing out, seldom seeing anyone. In May, 1881, Robert came to ask his mother's forgiveness and love. With him was his daughter, who was named after Mary. Incapable of saying no to her and Robert together, Mary promised to forgive and forget. Then they were gone and Mary was alone again in her dimly lit room. She kept the curtains closed, her eyes unable to tolerate any light beyond that of a single candle. Outside, children played in the streets, and some whispered that a crazy woman lurked behind the window with the curtains drawn. But Mary was beyond that world now; it could no longer hurt her. She lingered in the room where the candle burned, drifting with the days, caressing her wedding ring with its inscription "Love Is Eternal," and counting over her memories of past happiness. She lived in the past now, in a gentler time when she had first come to Springfield and stayed in this house . . . when she had loved so to dance with all the "gay" gentlemen . . . when she had met and married a tall, awkward young attorney who had the most congenial mind she had ever known . . . when she had carried his sons and made him a home. Then at night Mary would rise, blow out the candle, and slip into bed, lying carefully to one side in order not to disturb "the President's place" beside her.

ACKNOWLEDGMENTS

I am grateful to the following people for helping me prepare this volume: M. S. "Buz" Wyeth, Jr., my long-time editor at Harper & Row; Terry Karten, my supportive second editor there; Gerard McCauley, my long-time agent; Eva Langlois, my indispensable assistant; Sally Ives, my imperturbable typist; and Frank J. Williams, President of the Lincoln Group of Boston, and Mark E. Neely, Jr., Director of the Louis A. Warren Lincoln Library and Museum, who shared with me their vast knowledge of Lincoln and who read the manuscript and offered constructive comments. In addition, Frank Williams and his gracious wife Virginia welcomed me into their home—with its rich Lincoln collection —for weekends of inspiring Lincoln talk. I am also indebted to Ralph G. Newman, founder of the Abraham Lincoln Book Shop of Chicago and a devoted Lincoln scholar, for his generosity, counsel, and friendship over the past eight years. My gratitude, too, to Lincoln College in Lincoln, Illinois, for awarding me an honorary doctorate in humane letters, and to Pat Newman, Willard Bunn III, Christopher N. Breiseth, Daniel R. Weinberg, Harold M. Hyman, James T. Hickey, Gabor S. Boritt, Charles B. Strozier, and my many other friends in the Lincoln community for enlightening conversation and past kindnesses. Members of the Amherst Creative Biography Group, including Dorothy Clark, Peter Eddy, Sandra and Bill Katz, William Kimbrel, Elizabeth Lloyd-Kimbrel, Ann and Michael Meeropol, Will Ryan, and

Leslie Stainton, heard part of this book during our biweekly readings, and I appreciate their helpful criticism. Finally, I want to offer a special thanks to the University of Massachusetts, Amherst, for supporting my efforts at creative biographical writing and research.

REFERENCES

Part One: Myth

1: MAN OF THE PEOPLE

The quotation "Myths tell us" is from X. J. Kennedy, *Literature: An Introduction to Fiction, Poetry, and Drama* (Boston, 1983), 610. On the Christ-like Lincoln, the quotation "Oh, friends" is from Lloyd Lewis, *Myths after Lincoln* (paperback ed., New York, 1957), 95; the quotation "We mourn for the loss" from James M. McPherson, *The Negro's Civil War* (paperback ed., New York, 1967), 308; the quotation "To the deeply emotional and religious slave" from David Donald, *Lincoln Reconsidered* (paperback ed., New York, 1956), 148. For the Holland school of mythology, see Holland's own work, *The Life of Abraham Lincoln* (Springfield, Mass., 1866), and Donald, *Lincoln Reconsidered*, 148–54; Lewis, *Myths after Lincoln*, 333–34; and Roy P. Basler, *The Lincoln Legend* (reprint ed., New York, 1969), 8–9. My discussion of Herndon draws from David Donald, *Lincoln's Herndon* (New York, 1948), 218–41, 296, 303–4, 306–7, 316–20, 344–73; Donald, *Lincoln Reconsidered*, 154–57, 160–61; and Lewis, *Myths after Lincoln*, 334–35. Donald's biography of Herndon also has an excellent discussion of Ward Hill Lamon's *Life of Abraham Lincoln* (1872), which drew from Herndon's materials. For further discussions of the Ann Rutledge myth, see Basler, *Lincoln Legend*, 147–63; and J. G. Randall, *Lincoln the President: From Bull Run to Gettysburg* (paperback ed., New York, 1945), 321–42. Quotations "cause a squirm" and "Atheist! Atheist!" are from Lewis, *Myths after Lincoln*, 336, 303; the quotation "composite American ideal" from Donald, *Lincoln Reconsidered*, 163.

For the background and historical context of Carl Sandburg's *Abraham Lincoln: The Prairie Years*, see Herbert Mitgang (ed.), *The Letters of Carl Sandburg* (New York, 1968), 225–37; Alfred Harcourt, "Forty Years of Friendship," *Journal of the Illinois State Historical Society*, XLV (Winter, 1952), 395–97; North Callahan, *Carl Sandburg: Lincoln of Our Literature* (New York, 1970), 23, 75–95; and Alfred Haworth Jones, *Roosevelt's Image Brokers: Poets, Playwrights, and the Use of the Lincoln Symbol* (Port Washington, N.Y., 1974), 7–37. I also benefited from Robert W. Johannsen's unpublished paper "The Poet as Biographer: Carl Sandburg's Prairie Years," read at a symposium on Carl Sandburg as a Lincoln biographer, Jan. 21, 1978, at Knox College in Galesburg, Ill. The quotation "Like him" is from Callahan, *Sandburg*, 101; the quotation "both poets withall" from Sherman, "Carl Sandburg's Lincoln," *New York Herald Tribune Books*, Feb. 7, 1926.

The best accounts of Whitman and Lincoln are in Justin Kaplan, *Walt Whitman: A Life* (New York, 1980), 28–30, 258–61, 271–72, 300–1, 308–9, and Kaplan's unpublished paper "After Whitman," which was also read at the Knox College symposium and which is excellent on the connection between Whitman and Sandburg. The quotation "only distinguished epic poet" is from Kaplan's paper. For more on Whitman's Lincoln, see Basler, *Lincoln Legend*, 267–71, and Daniel Aaron, *The Unwritten War: American Writers and the Civil War* (New York, 1973), 69–72.

As for Sandburg's own comments about his work, the quotation "In Lincoln" is from Sandburg, *Abraham Lincoln: The Prairie Years* (2 vols., New York, 1926), 1: viii; the quotation "take Lincoln away from the religious bigots" from Wayne Gard, "Carl Sandburg Interprets Young Lincoln," *The Literary Digest International Book Review*, IV (Feb., 1926), 189; the quotation "felt as if in a trance" from Mitgang, *Letters of Carl Sandburg*, 255–56; the quotations "All-American" and "democracy can choose a man" from Sandburg, *Abraham Lincoln: The War Years* (4 vols., New York, 1939), 2: 332–33.

For the critical reaction to Sandburg's Lincoln, see Johannsen, "The Poet as Biographer"; and Jones, *Roosevelt's Image Brokers*, 51–62. The Benét quotation is from the *Atlantic Monthly* (Dec., 1939), 22; the Hill quotation from the Kansas City *Star*, Dec. 2, 1939; the Commager quotation from the *Yale Review*, XXIX (Winter, 1940), 374; the Sherwood quotation from the *New York Times Book Review,* Dec. 3, 1939. Another favorable appraisal is Benjamin P. Thomas, *Portrait for Posterity* (New Brunswick, N.J., 1947), 285–310.

There were negative reactions, of course. Historian Milo Quaife, in the *Mississippi Valley Historical Review,* XIII (Sept., 1926), 287–91, thought the *Prairie Years* sheer fiction, "a literary grab bag" that could never be accepted as history. For Edmund Wilson, Sandburg's biography was the "cruellest thing that has happened to Lincoln since he was shot by Booth." Wilson, *Patriotic Gore: Studies in the Literature of the American Civil War* (New York, 1962), 115. In my book, *Our Fiery Trial: Abraham Lincoln, John Brown, and the Civil War Era* (Amherst, Ma., 1979), 101–9, I discuss the errors, apocrypha, and fictionalizing that mar Sandburg's work as biography.

The sources of my discussion of the *Prairie Years* are as follows: the quotation "He suggests a bard" is from Roscoe C. E. Brown, *North American Review,* CCXXIII (June, 1926), 33; Sandburg's folk tales about young Lincoln and his quotations about Lincoln and Ann Rutledge, all from Sandburg's *Lincoln: The Prairie Years,* 1:50, 51–52, 73, 138, 140–41, 189–90 (see also 12, 16, 33, 40, 41–42, 43, 56–59, 71 ff., 187, and 290 for other fictional passages); the Wilson quotation in *Patriotic Gore,* 116; Sandburg, *Lincoln* (one-volume ed., New York, 1954), 38–40, 45–46; Sandburg's statement that he was sorry he had fallen for the Rutledge legend, Johannsen, "The Poet as Biographer"; quotations "two shifting moods," "stubby, homely words," "the Strange Friend," "something out of a picture book for children," and "a mind, a spirit, a tongue" from Sandburg, *Lincoln: The Prairie Years,* 1:177, 2:105, 284, 428, and 1:480; quotation "fabulous human figure" from Sandburg, *Lincoln* (one-volume ed.), 296.

My discussion of the *War Years* draws from the following sources: the Sherwood quotation from the *New York Times Book Review,* Dec. 3, 1939; Sandburg's Lincoln as a people's hero from *Lincoln: The War Years,* 2:562, 587, 589–92, 646, also 3:300, 383, 391, 567–68, and 4: 216–17; Sandburg's Lincoln and the Emancipation Proclamation from ibid., 3:20, 22, 25, and 4:216–17; Sandburg's Lincoln, the so-called radicals, and the South and reconstruction from ibid., 4:217, also 2:-559–60, and 3:82, 642; quotations "To a deep river" and "greatest general" from ibid., 4:297, 376–77; quotation "baffling and completely inexplicable" from Mitgang, *Letters of Carl Sandburg,* 490.

2: ARCH VILLAIN

See in particular Don E. Fehrenbacher, "The Anti-Lincoln Tradition," *Papers of the Abraham Lincoln Association,* 4 (Springfield, Ill., 1982): 7–28, from which I extracted the quotation "bad man." The quotation "scholarly, ringing" is from Lewis, *Myths after Lincoln,* 99; the quotation "hundred years hence" from the New York *Herald,* Apr. 17, 1865.

My account of the secessionists' and Confederates' Lincoln draws from Michael Davis, *The Image of Lincoln in the South* (Knoxville, Tenn., 1971), 41–104; my own *With Malice Toward None: The Life of Abraham Lincoln* (New York, 1977), 187; and Thomas Reed Turner, *Beware the People Weeping: Public Opinion and the Assassination of Abraham Lincoln* (Baton Rouge, La., 1982), 90–99. The quotation "the most execrable measure" is from Dunbar Rowland, *Jefferson Davis, Constitutionalist: His Letters, Papers, and Speeches* (Jackson, Miss., 1923), 5: 409–11; the quotation "All honor to J. Wilkes Booth" from John Q. Anderson (ed.), *Brokenburn: The Journal of Kate Stone, 1861–1868* (Baton Rouge, La., 1955), 333; the quotation "God's judgment day" from the Houston *Tri-Weekly Telegraph,* Apr. 25, 1865.

For the countermyth in the postwar and new South: the quotation "Is it insanity" is from George Edmonds [Elizabeth Avery Meriwether], *Facts and Falsehoods concerning the War on the South* (Memphis, Tenn., 1904), 49–50; the quotation "whole story of his career" from the *Southern Magazine* 11 (Sept., 1872), 374; the quotation "gawky, coarse" from Basler, *Lincoln Legend,* 57; the quotation *"amounts to a patent perversion"* from Davis, *Image of Lincoln in South,* 169; the quotation "The real monument" from Fehrenbacher, "Anti-Lincoln Tradition," *Papers of the Abraham Lincoln Association,* 4: 22.

For the countermyth outside the South, see Masters, *Lincoln: The Man* (New York, 1931), passim. Masters wrote at a time when it was popular for biographers to use psychology to debunk their subjects. The California political scientist to whom I refer is Dwight G. Anderson, whose *Abraham Lincoln: The Quest for Immortality* (New York, 1982) is a modern rerun of Masters and typical of the kind of fanciful psychologizing that infests recent historical literature. See, for example, George B. Forgie, *Patricide in the House Divided: A Psychological Interpretation* (New York, 1979), which argues that Lincoln both revered and resented the Founding Fathers (they had garnered all the glory) and deliberately brought on the crisis of the Union in order to escape his dilemma. As a friend of mine said, "If you believe that, you'll believe anything."

Vidal's syphilitic Lincoln is in Vidal, "Lincoln: His Ambition Was a Little Engine That Knew No Rest," Los Angeles *Times*, Feb. 8, 1981.

3: WHITE CHIEF AND HONKY

For Lincoln as White Chief: Davis, *Image of Lincoln in South*, 148–52, has a trenchant discussion of Dixon's Lincoln, but see also Basler, *Lincoln Legend*, 47, 220–21, 240. The Vardaman quotations and his excerpts from Lincoln's Charleston speech are in the *Congressional Record*, 63d Cong., 2d sess., 51 (Jan. 22–Feb. 6, 1914), 3036, 3038–40, and 65th Cong., 1st sess., 55 (July 24–Aug. 29, 1917), 6061–64. For Martin Luther King's hate mail citing Lincoln: the quotation "It should do you lots of good" is from "A disgusted White Man" to King, Aug. 5, 1960, Martin Luther King., Jr., Collection, Mugar Memorial Library, Boston University; quotation "I don't believe in lynchings" from "KKK" to King, May 2 [no year], *ibid.*

For King's views of Lincoln, see my own *Let the Trumpet Sound: The Life of Martin Luther King, Jr.* (New York, 1982), 120, 159, 207–9, 256–57, 263, 272, and *Builders of the Dream: Abraham Lincoln and Martin Luther King, Jr.* (the Fifth Annual R. Gerald McMurtry Lecture, Fort Wayne, Ind., May 20, 1982). Like historians Franklin and Quarles, King did not share the anti-Lincoln attitudes of many modern black intellectuals. The quotation "overwhelmed me" is from James Forman, *The Making of Black Revolutionaries* (New York, 1972), 47; the quotation "one of the most far-reaching pronouncements" from Quarles, *Lincoln and the Negro* (New York, 1962), 150. See also Franklin, *The Emancipation Proclamation* (paperback ed., New York, 1965), particularly 13, 29, 98–99, 131–32, 143, 145.

Malcolm X was also part of the 1960s black backlash against Lincoln. "He probably did more to trick Negroes than any other man in history," Malcolm said. See Robert Penn Warren, *Who Speaks for the Negro?* (New York, 1965), 262. The Lester quotation is from his *Look Out Whitey! Black Power's Gon' Get Your Mama!* (New York, 1968), 58; the Bennett quotations from his article "Was Abe Lincoln a White Supremacist?" *Ebony* (Feb., 1968), 35–42. Bennett's assertion that the Emancipation Proclamation had "all the grandeur of a real estate deed" is a loose paraphrase of Richard Hofstadter's description of it as having "all the moral grandeur of a bill of lading." Hofstadter, *The American Political Tradition and the Men Who Made It* (New York, 1948), 131. Echoing Bennett, black scholar Nathan Irving Huggins, *Slave and Citizen: The Life of Frederick Douglass* (Boston, 1980), 77, even denied that Lincoln was an antislavery man. The Harding quotations are from *There is a River: The Black Struggle for Freedom in America* (New York), 220, 223, 225, 226, 231–32, 234–40, 255, 256, and xix. The Frye quotation is from Kennedy, *Literature*, 610.

Part Two: Many-Mooded Man

1: RESURRECTING LIFE

The Michelet quotation is in Norbert Guterman, *A Book of French Quotations* (New York, 1963), 277.

2: A MATTER OF PROFOUND WONDER

Lincoln's looks: the quotation "lay floating" and "howdy" from James G. Randall, *Mr. Lincoln* (New York, 1957), 30, 28; the quotation "I have never seen a picture" from Richard N. Current, *The Lincoln Nobody Knows* (New York, 1958), 5; the quotation "His face is certainly ugly" from Lillian Foster, *Way-Side Glimpses* (New York, 1860), 221.

On Lincoln's personality, the quotation "many mooded man" is from Donald, *Lincoln's Herndon*, 305; the quotation "He was, take him all in all" from Holland, *Life of Lincoln*, 241, and also *The Southern Review* (Apr., 1873), 328; the quotation "Lincoln's nature" from Emanuel Hertz, *The Hidden Lincoln* (New York, 1938), 159; the quotation "He was the most reticent" from Reinhold H. Luthin, *The Real Abraham Lincoln* (Englewood Cliffs, N.J., 1960), 122; the quotation "he was not, a demonstrative man" from Justin G. and Linda Levitt Turner, *Mary Todd Lincoln: Her Life and Letters* (New York, 1972), 293.

For Lincoln and his parents and frontier background, see the excellent analysis in Charles B. Strozier, *Lincoln's Quest for Union: Public and Private Meanings* (New York, 1982), 3–30, 50–65. The quotation "my mother is a bastard" is from Current, *Lincoln Nobody Knows*, 22, but see also Paul M. Angle (ed.), *Herndon's Life of Lincoln* (paperback ed., New York, 1961), 46–47; the quotation "never did more in the way of writing" from Abraham Lincoln, *Collected Works* (ed. Roy P. Basler and others, 9 vols., New Brunswick, N.J., 1953–55), 4:61, hereafter *CW*.

For Lincoln's reading, literary bent, and way with words, see Roy P. Basler, "Abraham Lincoln's Rhetoric," *American Literature*, 11 (1939): 170–71; Edmund Wilson, *Patriotic Gore: Studies in the Literature of the American Civil War* (New York, 1962), 120–23; Louis A. Warren, *Lincoln's Youth: Indiana Years* (Indianapolis, Ind., 1959), 10–14; and Paul M. Angle, "Lincoln's Power with Words," *Papers of the Abraham Lincoln Association*, 3 (Springfield, Ill., 1981): 9–25. The quotations *"the absence of all business"* and "Let reverence for the laws" are from Lincoln, *CW*, 1:265 and 112; the Wilson quotation in *Patriotic Gore*, 117; the quotation "By nature a literary artist" from Albert J. Beveridge, *Abraham Lincoln, 1809–1858* (2 vols., Boston, 1928), 1:302; Lincoln's poem in *CW*, 1:378–79; the Stowe quotation in Herbert Mitgang (ed.), *Abraham Lincoln: A Press Portrait* (Chicago, 1971), 377; the quotation "moved by some great & good feeling" from Randall, *Mr. Lincoln*, 31; the quotation "he was given to raising" from Paul Simon, *Lincoln's Preparation for Greatness* (Norman, Okla., 1965), 213. The quotations about the frontier influences on Lincoln's manner of speech are from Beveridge, *Lincoln*, 1:53–54; George Templeton Strong, *Diary, 1835–1875* (ed. Allan Nevins and Milton H. Thomas, 4 vols., New York, 1952), 3:188, 204–5; and Benjamin P. Thomas, "Lincoln's Humor: An Analysis," *Papers of the Abraham Lincoln Association*, 3:33–34.

Lincoln and mathematics: the quotation "Their ambition" from Lincoln, *CW*, 1:113; the story about Lincoln and Euclid's geometry from Paul M. Angle, "Lincoln's Power with Words," *Papers of the Abraham Lincoln Association*, 3:12.

For Lincoln's depression and search for identity, see the sophisticated analysis in Strozier, *Lincoln's Quest for Union*, 35–88. The quotation "I have no other" is from Lincoln, *CW*, 1:8; the quotation "Well, I feel just like the boy" from P. M. Zall, *Abe Lincoln Laughing: Humorous Anecdotes from Original Sources by and about Abraham Lincoln* (Berkeley, Cal., 1982), 22. For Lincoln and Ann Rutledge, see my references above under "Man of the People." Lincoln's letters to Mary Owens are in *CW*, 1:78–79, 94–95. The quotation "was deficient" is from Mary Owens Vineyard to Herndon, May 22 and June 22, 1866, Herndon-Weik Collection, Library of Congress. The Speed quotation is from Angle, *Herndon's Life of Lincoln*, 170, but also see Hertz, *Hidden Lincoln*, 159.

For Lincoln and Mary Todd Lincoln, see Ruth Painter Randall, *Mary Lincoln: Biography of a Marriage* (Boston, 1953), 3–85, and Turners, *Mary Todd Lincoln,* 3–34, 475. The quotation "the most congenial mind" from Katherine Helm, *The True Story of Mary, Wife of Lincoln* (New York, 1928), 76; the quotation "he would listen" from Elizabeth Edwards's first statement [n.d.] and second statement, Sept. 27, 1898, Herndon-Weik Collection; the quotation "I am now, the most miserable man" from Lincoln, *CW,* 1:229; Lincoln's letters to Speed about their romantic troubles in ibid., 259–61, 265–66, 267–68, 269–70, 280–81, 282, 288–89; the quotation "except my marrying" from ibid., 305; the quotation "lover–husband" from Turners, *Mary Todd Lincoln,* 534; the quotation "probably ended sexual intercourse" from Strozier, *Lincoln's Quest for Union,* 88.

3: ALL CONQUERING MIND

Lincoln's preoccupations with death and insanity: Lincoln's recitation of "Mortality" and his poem on Matthew Gentry are in *CW,* 2:90, and 1:5–86. My version of "Mortality" is from *The Home Book of Verse,* Vol. II (ed. Burton Egbert Stevenson, New York, 1940), 3409. For Lincoln and liquor, see Beveridge, *Lincoln,* 1:82–83, 534. The quotation "all conquering mind" is from Lincoln, *CW,* 1:279.

For Lincoln's humor, Zall, *Abe Lincoln Laughing,* is the most scholarly and reliable collection of Lincoln stories; but also see Thomas, "Lincoln's Humor," *Papers of the Abraham Lincoln Association,* 3:- 29–47. The quotations "whistle down sadness" and "I laugh because I must not weep" from Henry C. Whitney, *Life on the Circuit with Lincoln* (Boston, 1892), 171, 146–47; the quotation "I tell you the truth" from John F. Farnsworth's testimony in Sandburg, *Lincoln: The War Years,* 3:305; the quotation "seemed to diffuse" from Lamon, *Lincoln,* 478–79; the quotation "He can rake a sophism" from Thomas, "Lincoln's Humor," *Papers of the Abraham Lincoln Association,* 3:46; humor on the Mexican War and state sovereignty from Zall, *Abe Lincoln Laughing,* 144, 55–56; the quotation "Has it not got down" from Lincoln, *CW,* 3:279; the quotation "every one of his stories" from Zall, *Abe Lincoln Laughing,* 5; the quotation "he saw ludicrous elements" from Thomas, "Lincoln's Humor," *Papers of the Abraham Lincoln Association,* 3:36; the quotations "the strongest example," "This is an indictment," and "burst of spontaneous storytelling" from Zall, *Abe Lincoln*

Laughing, 69, 43, 5; the quotation "with their hands" from Basler, *Lincoln Legend,* 125; the story of an old Englishman, the Negro dialect joke, and the Swett joke from Zall, *Abe Lincoln Laughing,* 147, 42, 40; the quotation "akin to lunacy" from Charles Minor, *The Real Lincoln* (Richmond, 1904), 29–30; the quotation "on a certain *member*" from David C. Mearns, *The Lincoln Papers* (2 vols. in 1, reprint ed., New York, 1969), 169; Lincoln's story, "Bass-Ackwards," in *CW,* 8:420; the joke on his looks from Zall, *Abe Lincoln Laughing,* 21. For Lincoln wrinkling his nose and scratching his elbows, see the *Letters of Horace H. Furnass* (2 vols., Boston, 1922), 1:126. Henry Villard, quoted in Randall, *Mr. Lincoln,* 213, said that Lincoln "shook all over . . . and when he felt particularly good over his performance he followed his habit of drawing his knees with his arms about them, up to his very face."

4: MR. LINCOLN

The best studies of Lincoln's law career are John J. Duff, *A. Lincoln, Prairie Lawyer* (New York, 1960), and John P. Frank, *Lincoln as a Lawyer* (Urbana, Ill., 1961). The quotation "I have news" is from Lincoln, *CW,* 2: 106; Lincoln's finances in Harry E. Pratt, *The Personal Finances of Abraham Lincoln* (Springfield, Ill., 1943); the quotation "resolve to be honest" from Lincoln, *CW,* 2:82.

For Lincoln on alcoholics, see ibid., 1:271–79; on women's rights, ibid., 48. The quotation "In this statement" is from Roy P. Basler's essay in Cullom Davis and others (eds.), *The Public and the Private Lincoln: Contemporary Perspectives* (Carbondale, Ill., 1979), 42; Herndon's quotation on the Irish in his article in the New York *Tribune,* Feb. 15, 1867; Lincoln's remarks on the Know-Nothings in *CW,* 2:323.

Part Three: Advocate of the Dream

1: THE BEACON LIGHT OF LIBERTY

For Lincoln and the Declaration of Independence, see Lincoln, *CW,* 2:266 and 4:168–69, 235–36, 240, 266. The quotations "profitable lesson" and "got through the world" are from ibid, 2:124. The best study of Lincoln's economics is G. S. Boritt, *Lincoln and the Economics of the American Dream* (Memphis, Tenn., 1978). The quotations "The legitimate object," "better their conditions," and "the liberty party" are from Lincoln, *CW*, 2:220–21, 3:312, and 2:276.

Lincoln's views on slavery before 1854: the quotation "founded both" from ibid., 1:75; the quotations "continual torment" and "had the power" from ibid., 2:320; the quotation "sort of Negro livery stable" from ibid., 2:253, 237–38; the quotation "noblest political system" from ibid., 276; the quotation "there should be nothing" from ibid., 3:3–7, also 2:492, 513–14; the quotations "just what we would be" and "human sympathies" from ibid., 2:255, 264; the quotation "a captive people" from ibid., 132. See also Don E. Fehrenbacher, *Prelude to Greatness: Lincoln in the 1850s* (Stanford, Cal., 1962), 24–25, 85.

2: THIS VAST MORAL EVIL

For Lincoln's reactions to the Kansas-Nebraska Act, see the speeches in Lincoln, *CW*, 2:247–83, 398–410, which include his Peoria address. My description of the great southern reaction draws from the *Illinois Daily State Register*, July 30, Aug. 19, Oct. 15, 1856; Muscogee (Alabama) *Herald* as quoted in ibid., Oct. 15, 1856; George Fitzhugh, *Cannibals All! or Slaves without Masters* (ed. C. Vann Woodward, Cambridge, Mass., 1960), 252; Lincoln, *CW*, 2:341 and 3:53–54, 205; Beveridge, *Lincoln*, 2:436–39. Lincoln's remarks about slave traders are in *CW*, 2:322.

Lincoln's "House Divided" speech, ibid., 461–69, outlines the stages of the slave-power conspiracy as Lincoln saw it. But see also ibid., 2:341 and 3:53–54, 204–5; Beveridge, *Lincoln*, 2:563–64; Fehrenbacher, *Prelude*, 79–95; and Eric Foner, *Free Soil, Free Labor, Free Men: The Ideology of the Republican Party before the Civil War* (New York, 1970), 73–102. Whether or not there was a southern conspiracy isn't so significant as the fact that Lincoln and the Republicans *thought* there was, for that is what shaped their actions. I am trying to stress the point that people respond to events according to their perception of reality. Therefore, what people *believe* is true is quite as important as what *is* true when it comes to reconstructing the past or understanding the present.

Lincoln's quotations "vast moral evil," "*central idea,*" "the bread that his own hands have earned," and "stripes, and unrewarded toils" are from his *CW*, 2:494, 385, 520, 320. My own work *With Malice Toward*

None narrates the Lincoln-Douglas debates from Lincoln's point of view, whereas Robert W. Johannsen, *Stephen A. Douglas* (New York, 1973), 641–79, relates them from Douglas's perspective. The speeches of both men are gathered in Lincoln, *CW*, vols. 2 and 3, and in Paul M. Angle (ed.), *Created Equal: The Complete Lincoln-Douglas Debates of 1858* (Chicago, 1958). Douglas's remarks about Lincoln and Negroes are from his speeches at Chicago and Ottawa.

Lincoln had touched on racial equality and intermarriage in earlier stump battles with Douglas (see, for example, *CW*, 2:266, 405, 407–8). My discussion of Lincoln's views on the subject derives from the following sources: Lincoln's position on legally enforced discrimination in Illinois from Mark E. Neely, Jr., *The Abraham Lincoln Encyclopedia* (New York, 1982), 217; the quotation "Lincoln of history" from Don E. Fehrenbacher, "Only His Stepchildren: Lincoln and the Negro," *Civil War History*, 20 (Dec., 1974), 303; Lincoln's quotations on Negroes in *CW*, 2: 501, 3:16, 145–46, 301, and 5:372–73; Current's observations in Davis and others, *Public and Private Lincoln*, 144. For Lincoln and Springfield and Sangamon County in 1858, see Christopher N. Breiseth's excellent analysis in ibid., 101–20.

Some white historians agree with Bennett and Harding that Lincoln was a white supremacist. See George M. Fredrickson, "A Man but Not a Brother: Abraham Lincoln and Racial Equality," *Journal of Southern History*, 41 (Feb., 1975), 39–58; Strozier, *Lincoln's Quest for Union*, 173–75, 178–79; and Kenneth M. Stampp, *The Imperiled Union: Essays on the Background of the Civil War* (New York, 1980), 128. Other Lincoln scholars, including the present author, disagree with this argument and have been at great pains to place Lincoln's public utterances of the 1850s in historical context and to show how much he grew and changed in the war years. See Fehrenbacher, "Only His Stepchildren," *Civil War History*, 20, 293–310; the essays of Breiseth and Current in Davis and others, *Public and Private Lincoln*, 101–20, 137–46; Current, *Lincoln Nobody Knows*, 214–36; Quarles, *Lincoln and the Negro;* and Franklin, *Emancipation Proclamation.*

3: MY DISSATISFIED FELLOW COUNTRYMEN

Lincoln on the stump derives from Lincoln, *CW*, 3:368–69, 375–76, 380, 387–88, 390–91. For Lincoln and the Republican vision of America, see ibid., 3:462–63, 477–81, and Lincoln, *Collected Works—Supple-*

ment, 1832–1865 (ed. Roy P. Basler, Westport, Conn., 1974), 43–45, hereafter *CWS;* the quotation "This is a world" from Lincoln's Cincinnati speech, the quotation "if constitutionally we elect," and Lincoln's Cooper Union speech, all from Lincoln, *CW,* 3:376, 440–41, 453–56, 501–52, and 535–55.

For Lincoln and the 1860 nomination: the quotation "taste *is* in my mouth" from ibid., 4:45, also see 34, 36, 38, 43, 46, 47, and 3:375; how Lincoln got nominated from Lincoln, *CWS,* 54–55, Willard L. King, *Lincoln's Manager: David Davis* (Cambridge, Mass., 1960), 137 ff., Fehrenbacher, *Prelude to Greatness,* 155–59, from which I took the quotation "could not win," and Stampp, *Imperiled Union,* 136–62; the quotations "class," "caste," and "despotism" from Lincoln, *CW,* 3:375.

My account of Lincoln, the South, and secession draws from Davis, *Image of Lincoln in the South,* 7–40; the quotation "the South, the loyal South" from the Atlanta *Southern Confederacy* as reprinted in the *New York Times,* Aug. 7, 1860; the quotation "the people of the South" from Lincoln, *CW,* 4:95; David M. Potter, *The Impending Crisis, 1848–1861* (New York, 1976), 405–47, 485–513, and *Lincoln and His Party in the Secession Crisis* (New Haven and London, 1942), 9–19, 139–42; Stampp, *Imperiled Union,* 163–88, 191–242; Steven A. Channing, *Crisis of Fear: Secession in South Carolina* (New York, 1970), 17–57, 229 ff.; Allan Nevins, *The Emergence of Lincoln* (2 vols., New York, 1950), 2:287 ff.; the quotation "Slavery with us" from Channing, *Crisis of Fear,* 291; quotation "To remain in the Union" from Montgomery *Mail* as reprinted in the Nashville *Banner,* Nov. 11, 1860; the quotation "loud threats" from Thurlow Weed, *Autobiography* (Boston, 1883), 605–14; the quotations "Why all this excitement?" and "complaints?" and Lincoln's First Inaugural Address from Lincoln, *CW,* 4:215–16, 262–71. See also James G. Randall, *Lincoln the President: From Springfield to Bull Run* (paperback ed., New York, 1945), 178–206.

Lincoln and Fort Sumter: the quotation "all the troubles" from Orville H. Browning, *Diary* (ed. Theodore Calvin Pease and James G. Randall, 2 vols., Springfield, Ill., 1927–33), 1:476; the quotations "no attachment to the Union" and "irrevocably gone" from Stephen A. Hurlbut to Lincoln, March 27, 1861, the Robert Todd Lincoln Collection of the Papers of Abraham Lincoln, Library of Congress, hereafter RTL; Lincoln, *CW,* 4:423–26; Richard N. Current, *Lincoln and the First Shot* (New York, 1963), 43 and passim.; Stampp, *Imperiled Union,* 177–88; Potter, *Lincoln and His Party,* 337–66; quotations "an ingenious sophism" and "With rebellion" from Lincoln, *CW,* 4:433–37; the quotation "*professed* Union men" and Lincoln's references to Lee, Johnston, Magruder, and southern insurrectionists from ibid., 4:427, 43 and 6:264, 265, 8:121; the quotation "all conquering *mind*" from ibid., 1:279.

Part Four: Warrior for the Dream

1: THE CENTRAL IDEA

The quotation "You are nothing" is from A. G. Frick [?] to Lincoln, Feb. 14, 1861, Chicago Historical Society; the quotation "miserable traitorous head" from clipping in Edmund J. McGarn and William Fairchild to Lincoln, Apr. 20, 1861, RTL; the quotation "clear, flagrant, and gigantic case" from Lincoln, *CW*, 6:264; the quotation "not at all hopeful" from Orville Browning to Lincoln, Aug. 19, 1861, RTL, and Browning, *Diary*, 1:488–89; Lincoln's message to Congress and quotations "nothing in malice," "I happen temporarily," and "material growth" from Lincoln, *CW*, 4:426–39, 5:346, 7:512, 3:477–79, 5:52–53; Boritt, *Lincoln and the Economics of the American Dream*, 195–231; the quotation "remorseless revolutionary struggle" from Lincoln, *CW*, 5: 49.

There is a popular argument in the academies that Lincoln was a "Whig in the White House," adhering to some theoretical Whig formula about a restricted presidency beyond what was necessary to save the Union. This argument rests on the assumption that Lincoln had left the Whigs reluctantly in 1856 and that ideologically he remained attached to the old party. This does not accord with the evidence. Lincoln was no reluctant Republican. By 1856, he had become convinced that old party labels—even his own Whig label—severely impeded the mobilization of anti-Nebraska forces and that a new free-soil party was imperative. The Republicans now loomed as the new major party of the future, and Lincoln readily enlisted in their antiextensionist cause. In fact, he gave the keynote address for the organization of the Republican party in Illinois. He never said, in a single surviving record, that he regretted the demise of the Whigs. Indeed, they had become obsolete in the battles over slavery that dominated the 1850s. In Republican ranks, Lincoln no longer had to consort with proslavery southerners, as he had with the Whigs. In Republican ranks, he belonged to a party that forthrightly denounced slavery as a moral wrong and that shared his views on the American experiment and the inalienable rights of man. In Republican ranks, Lincoln found an ideological home for all of his principles—political as well as economic. And no man, as I pointed out in the text, defended Republican dogma more eloquently and unswervingly than he. Thus, when he gained the presidency, Lincoln was a *Republican* in the White House, not a Whig. Among other things, it was not a Whig who employed all the pressures and prestige of the White House to get the present Thirteenth Amendment through a recalcitrant House of Representatives (as I describe in the text). Nor was it a Whig who raised Republican ideology to the lofty heights of the Gettysburg Address.

As for some Whig theory of the presidency, it is improbable that any such thing existed for a minority party which, in its twenty-four- or twenty-five-year history, managed to elect only two chief executives, both of them professional soldiers and political amateurs who died during their first year in office. The Vice-Presidents who replaced them—if anybody can remember their names—hardly left their marks on the job. The "Whig in the White House" argument appears in Donald, *Lincoln Reconsidered*, 187–208, and is carried to almost absurd lengths in Boritt's otherwise superior study, *Lincoln and the Economics of the American Dream*.

2: DEATH WARRANT FOR SLAVERY

The quotation "Lincoln would like to have God" is from Quarles, *Lincoln and the Negro*, 84. My discussion of the pressures on Lincoln to free the slaves is based on the following sources. The advanced Republicans: my own "The Slaves Freed," *American Heritage* (Dec., 1980), 74–78; David Donald, *Charles Sumner and the Rights of Man* (New York, 1970), 17 ff.; Hans L. Trefousse, *The Radical Republicans, Lincoln's Vanguard for Racial Justice* (New York, 1969), 171–73, 203–22; Franklin, *Emancipation Proclamation*, 1–28, 124; Detroit *Post and Tribune, Zachariah Chandler* (Detroit, 1880), 253; George Washington Julian, *Political Recollections, 1840–1872* (Chicago, 1880), 153, 165–66, 223; Edward Magdol, *Owen Lovejoy, Abolitionist in Congress* (New Brunswick, N.J., 1967), 299–302; the quotation "never allowed himself" from Noah Brooks, *Washington, D.C., in Lincoln's Time* (ed. Herbert Mitgang, Chicago, 1971), 33; quotations "perhaps the most energetic," "queer, rough," and "first blast" from Hans L. Trefousse, *Benjamin Franklin Wade, Radical Republican from Ohio* (New York, 1963), 180, 131, 181; the quotation "cooked by Niggers" from Trefousse, *Radical*

Republicans, 31; the quotation "more advanced Republicans" from Detroit *Post and Tribune, Chandler*, 222.

Frederick Douglass: Douglass, *Life and Times* (reprint of revised 1892 ed., New York, 1962), 336; McPherson, *Negro's Civil War*, 38–40; also Philip S. Foner (ed.), *The Life and Writings of Frederick Douglass* (4 vols., New York, 1975), 3: 13–21.

The need for slave soldiers: ibid.; the quotation "You need more men" from Donald, *Sumner*, 60; the quotation "Let the slaves" from Arna Bontemps, *Free at Last: The Life of Frederick Douglass* (New York, 1971), 224.

Lincoln's response to the pressures: the quotation "I think Sumner" from Fawn M. Brodie, *Thaddeus Stevens, Scourge of the South* (paperback ed., New York, 1966), 155; the quotation "too big a lick" from Donald, *Sumner*, 60; Lincoln's gradual emancipation plan in *CW*, 5: 145–46, 317–19, and Charles M. Segal (ed.), *Conversations with Lincoln* (New York, 1961), 165–68; the quotations "milk-and-water gruel" and "I utterly spit at it" from Brodie, *Stevens*, 156.

My account of the congressional attack against slavery comes from the following: the Stevens profile from ibid., 68, 86–93, 193; the quotation "I trust I am not dreaming" from McPherson, *Negro's Civil War*, 44; the quotation "his pride of race" from Foner, *Life and Writings of Douglass*, 3: 24; the quotation "would never prosper" from Douglass, *Life and Times*, 336.

The quotation "strong hand on the colored element" is from Lincoln, *CW*, 7: 281–82. Gideon Welles, "History of Emancipation," *Galaxy* (Dec., 1872), 842–43, and Welles, *Diary* (ed. John T. Morse, Jr., 3 vols., Boston, 1911), 1:70–71, describe the carriage ride in which Lincoln discussed emancipation. Lincoln's letter to Greeley is in *CW*, 5:388–89. For interpretations of the letter similar to my own, see Quarles, *Lincoln and the Negro*, 128, and V. Jacque Voegeli, *Free but Not Equal: The Midwest and the Negro in the Civil War* (Chicago, 1967), 46.

Lincoln's preliminary Emancipation Proclamation is in *CW*, 5:433–36. The quotation "We shout for joy" is from Foner, *Life and Writings of Douglass*, 3:25; the quotation "Hurrah" from Trefousse, *Wade*, 187; the quotation "contained precisely" from Brodie, *Stevens*, 158; Sumner's remarks in his *Complete Works*, (20 vols., reprint of 1900 ed., New York, 1961), 9:199–200, 247. For a discussion of emancipation and Lincoln's message to Congress, Dec., 1862, see my own *With Malice Toward None*, 325–26, and Franklin, *Emancipation Proclamation*, 81. The Democratic response is in ibid., 81–82; the quotation "From the genuine abolition view" from Douglass, *Life and Times*, 541–42. The final proclamation is in Lincoln, *CW*, 6:28–30. The quotation "my name" is from Segal, *Conversations with Lincoln*, 234–35; the quotation "let us not cavil" from Franklin, *Emancipation Proclamation*, 113; the quotation "played his grand part" from Julian, *Political Recollections*, 226, also 250; the quotation "the sunlight" from the *Liberator*, Jan. 9, 1863; the quotation "The time has come" from McPherson, *Negro's Civil War*, 50.

3: THE MAN OF OUR REDEMPTION

The quotation "of minor significance" is from Randall, *Mr. Lincoln*, 347. See my comments on the "insignificant" and "free-no-slaves" argument in *Our Fiery Trial*, 137–38. The quotation "events of the war" is from Sandburg, *Lincoln: The War Years*, 4:217; the quotation "the colored population" from Lincoln, *CW*, 6:149.

The best studies of Lincoln and black troops are Dudley T. Cornish, *The Sable Arm: Negro Troops in the Union Army, 1861–1865* (paperback ed., New York, 1966), and Quarles, *Lincoln and the Negro*, 153–83. The quotation "ALL SLAVES" is from ibid., 166; the quotation "with clenched teeth" from Lincoln, *CW*, 6:410; the Negro soldier and the "Sambo" image in John T. Hubbell, "Abraham Lincoln and the Recruitment of Black Soldiers," *Papers of the Abraham Lincoln Association*, 2 (Springfield, 1980): 20–21.

For Lincoln and colonization, see the excellent summary in Neely, *Abraham Lincoln Encyclopedia*, 63; the quotation "entirely a fantasy" from Neely, "Abraham Lincoln and Colonization: Benjamin Butler's Spurious Testimony," *Civil War History*, 25 (March, 1979): 77–83. George M. Fredrickson, "A Man but Not a Brother: Abraham Lincoln and Racial Equality," *Journal of Southern History*, 41(Feb., 1975), 39–58, is simply wrong in arguing that Lincoln continued "to his dying day to deny the possibility of racial harmony and equality in the United States and persisted in regarding colonization as the only real alternative to perpetual race conflict." For Lincoln's desire to frighten rebel leaders out of the country, see Benjamin P. Thomas, *Abraham Lincoln* (New York, 1952), 517.

On the reaction to Lincoln's Proclamation, the quotation "brink of ruin" is from Browning, *Diary*, 1:610–13, 616; the quotation "an act of justice" is from the Proclamation itself; Lincoln's assertion that blacks who had tasted freedom would never again be slaves in *CW*, 6:358; the quotation "a coarse, but an expressive figure" from ibid., 6:48–49; the quotation "He is stubborn" from Brodie, *Stevens,* 201; the quotation "His mind acts slowly" from Magdol, *Lovejoy,* 401. Lincoln's abortive peace proposal to Jefferson Davis is in Lincoln, *CW,* 7:517–18; see also John G. Nicolay and John Hay, *Abraham Lincoln, A History* (10 vols., New York, 1890), 9:221.

For Lincoln and the Thirteenth Amendment, see Albert G. Riddle, *Recollections of War Time* (New York, 1895), 323–24, and Julian, *Political Recollections,* 250. The quotation *"if slavery is not wrong"* is from Trefousse, *Radical Republicans,* 299, and Lincoln, *CW,* 7:281; the quotations "stand here and denounce" and "the greatest measure" from Brodie, *Stevens,* 204; the quotation "It seemed to me" from Julian, *Political Recollections,* 251; the quotations "great moral victory" and "King's cure" from Lincoln, *CW,* 8:254–55; the quotation "people over the river" from Segal, *Conversations with Lincoln,* 17.

Lincoln's Second Inaugural is in *CW,* 8:332–33. For Lincoln, Douglass, and the blacks, see Douglass's article in the New York *Tribune,* July 15, 1885; Douglass, *Life and Times,* 347–49, 484–86; Quarles, *Lincoln and the Negro,* 196–205, 233; Randall, *Mr. Lincoln,* 363–68; the quotation "similarity with which I had fought" from Boritt, *Lincoln and the Economics of the American Dream,* 174.

4: NECESSITY KNOWS NO LAW

On Lincoln's emergency measures, see Harold M. Hyman, *A More Perfect Union: The Impact of the Civil War and Reconstruction on the Constitution* (New York, 1973), 50–64; the quotations "their ability," "without authority of law," and "These measures" from Lincoln, *CW,* 5:240–43, 4:429; the quotation "all the acts, proclamations" from J. G. Randall and David Donald, *The Civil War and Reconstruction* (2nd ed., revised, Lexington, Mass., 1969), 279.

My account of martial law and military arrests is based on Hyman, *More Perfect Union,* 65–155; James G. Randall, *Constitutional Problems Under Lincoln* (paperback ed., Urbana, Ill., 1964), 118–85; the quotations "most efficient corps" and "Are all the laws" from Lincoln, *CW,* 6:263, 4:430–31; also Benjamin P. Thomas and Harold M. Hyman, *Stanton: The Life and Times of Lincoln's Secretary of War* (New York, 1962), 157–58, 280–81, 375; Welles, *Diary,* 1:321.

For the Vallandigham case, see Frank L. Klement, *The Limits of Dissent: Clement L. Vallandigham and the Civil War* (Lexington, Ky.,

1970), 102 ff., and Bruce Catton, *Never Call Retreat* (Garden City, N.Y., 1965), 102–4, 172–74; the quotation "I see nothing before us" from ibid., 104; Lincoln's open letter in Lincoln, *CW*, 6: 260–69.

On Lincoln and confiscation, the quotation "the traitor" is from Lincoln, *CW*, 5:328–31. Randall, *Mr. Lincoln*, 349, asserts that Lincoln "shrank from enforcing the confiscation acts," but the evidence belies this claim. The President not only ordered General John C. Frémont, commander of Missouri, to abide by the first confiscation act, but insisted in his Annual Message, Dec. 3, 1861, that he had faithfully enforced it. Moreover, as I point out in the text, Lincoln compelled conquered rebel states to obey all congressional laws relating to slavery before those states could be reconstructed.

On the 1864 election, the quotation "The election was a necessity" is from Lincoln, *CW*, 6:101; the Stowe quotations are from Mitgang, *Lincoln, A Press Portrait*, 377, 378.

5: THE WARRIOR

T. Harry Williams, *Lincoln and His Generals* (New York, 1952), remains the standard study of the subject and one of the best Lincoln books in existence. I have, however, learned from Warren W. Hassler, *Commanders of the Army of the Potomac* (Baton Rouge, La., 1962), which is sympathetic to McClellan and extremely unflattering to Lincoln and Stanton; from Randall, *Lincoln the President: From Bull Run to Gettysburg* (paperback ed., New York, 1945), which is also sympathetic to McClellan; and from a spate of modern biographies of individual generals too numerous to list. But see in particular the biographies of Grant by William S. McFeely and Bruce Catton, and of Sherman by James M. Merrill, John Bennett Watters, and B. H. Liddell Hart.

The quotation "I am thinking" is from Browning, *Diary*, 1:523; the quotation *"good many bloody struggles"* and Lincoln's "general idea of the war" from Lincoln, *CW*, 1:510, 5:98–99; the quotation "pain me very much" from Lincoln, *CW*, 5:286; the quotation "fighting, and *only* fighting" from Randall, *Lincoln the President*, 87; the quotation "we may as well" from John Hay, *Lincoln and the Civil War in the Diaries and Letters of John Hay* (selected by Tyler Dennett, reprint of 1939 ed., New York, 1972), 46; the quotation "He is an admirable engineer" from Williams, *Lincoln and His Generals*, 178; the quotation "Beware of rashness" from Lincoln, *CW*, 6:79; Hooker's remark about the rebel army from

Williams, *Lincoln and His Generals*, 238; the quotation "My God!" from Allen T. Rice (ed.), *Reminiscences of Abraham Lincoln by Distinguished Men of His Time* (New York, 1888), 402; the quotation "hurt this enemy" from Hay, *Diaries* (Dennett, ed.), 46, also 218–19; the quotation "hold on with bull-dog grip" from Lincoln, *CW*, 7:499; the quotation "We are not only" from Merrill, *William Tecumseh Sherman* (Chicago, 1971), 258, 266; the quotation "There is many a boy" from Stephen E. Ambrose, "William T. Sherman," *American History Illustrated* (Jan., 1967), 57. In sum, said Chauncey Depew, Lincoln "knew the whole situation better than any man in the administration, and virtually carried on in his own mind not only the civic side of the government, but all the campaigns." Rice, *Reminiscences*, 428–29.

6: TOWARD A NEW BIRTH OF FREEDOM

My interpretation is similar to that in Peyton McCrary, *Abraham Lincoln and Reconstruction: The Louisiana Experiment* (Princeton, N.J., 1978). McCrary's is now the standard book-length study of Lincoln's approach to southern restoration, replacing William B. Hesseltine, *Lincoln's Plan of Reconstruction* (Tuscaloosa, Ala., 1960), which is dated both in its scholarship and its preconceptions. Several older historians, especially those in or from the South, have faulted McCrary's inescapable conclusions that Lincoln stood with his advanced Republican colleagues on critical reconstruction questions; apparently these historians prefer the mythical version. Those who approach McCrary's book with an open mind will find it exhaustive, accurate, and persuasive, without the kind of pro-southern sentimentality that mars older writings on the subject.

McCrary's work, like my own, is part of a growing body of modern scholarship that has reassessed Lincoln's stance toward the freedmen, conquered Dixie, and Congress and the advanced Republicans. See, for example, Harold M. Hyman, *Lincoln's Reconstruction: Neither Failure of Vision nor Vision of Failure* (the Third R. Gerald McMurtry Lecture, Fort Wayne, Ind., May 8, 1980), and Hyman, *More Perfect Union*, 209–15, 276–81; Herman Belz, *Reconstructing the Union* (Ithaca, N.Y., 1969), particularly 147, 162–63, 258–62, 290–91; Donald, *Sumner*, 179–209; Trefousse, *Radical Republicans*, 280–304; Quarles, *Lincoln and the Negro*, 185 ff.; and Bruce Catton, *Never Call Retreat*, 288–95. Wrote the venerable Catton: "Mr. Lincoln is usually pictured as occupying a middle role between opposing extremes in this situation [the need for revolutionary change in Dixie], but actually he was not. He was at one of the extremes himself." He disagreed with the advanced Republicans "only on the method by which the change was to come."

On phase two of Lincoln's approach, the quotation "a radical extension" is from Belz, *Reconstructing the Union*, 291–92. On phase three, Lincoln's Proclamation of Amnesty and Reconstruction, appended to his Message to Congress, Dec. 8, 1863, is in Lincoln, *CW*, 7: 49–56; see also 6:358, 7:89–90, 8:106–7. The quotation "how to keep the rebellious populations" is from Hay, *Diary* (Dennett ed.), 113; the quotations "opposing elements," "which accepts as sound," and "to now abandon them," from Lincoln, *CW*, 7:51; Lincoln's Message to Congress, Dec. 6, 1864, from *ibid.*, 8:152. Lincoln's reference to the southern ruling class and "odious and detested" slave dealers is in *ibid.*, 2:322.

For Lincoln's closeness to advanced and moderate congressional Republicans, see Lincoln's own remarks in Hay, *Diary* (Dennett ed.), 113, and Hyman, Belz, Donald, and Trefousse, cited above. The quotation "like *two* schoolboys" is from Turners, *Mary Todd Lincoln*, 185.

On Lincoln and the welfare of the freedmen, the quotation "laboring, landless, and homeless class" is from Lincoln, *CW*, 7:55 and 6:265; see also 6:49. Lincoln warned that he would not tolerate abuses of southern blacks and that white authorities must recognize their permanent freedom and provide for their education. But he dropped the apprenticeship idea entirely, as I state in the text. See ibid., 7:145, 217–18 and 8:20, 30–31, 107, 402. For the refugee system, consult Voegeli, *Free but Not Equal*, 95–112; Quarles, *Lincoln and the Negro*, 188–90; Cornish, *Sable Arm*, 112–31; and Bell I. Wiley, *Southern Negroes, 1861–1865* (Baton Rouge, 1938), 199–259.

On Lincoln and Negro voting rights, the quotations "the very intelligent," "better for the poor black," "saving the already," and "as bad promises" are from Lincoln, *CW*, 7:243 and 8:107, 402, 404. For differing accounts of the compromise, see Donald, *Sumner*, 196–97, Belz, *Reconstructing the Union*, 258–62, 290–91, and McCrary, *Lincoln and Reconstruction*, 287–89. Lincoln's last speech is in *CW*, 8:399–404. The quotation "never so near our views" is from David Donald (ed.), *Inside Lincoln's Cabinet: The Civil War Diaries of Salmon P. Chase* (New York and London, 1954), 268. See also McCrary, *Lincoln and Reconstruction*, 304.

For Lincoln's last Cabinet meeting, see Thomas and Hyman, *Stanton*, 357–58, 358n., and my own *With Malice Toward None*, 427–28. The quotation "It may be my duty" is from Lincoln, *CW*, 8:405; the quotation "open the gates" from Thomas, *Lincoln*, 517. Belz, Hesseltine, and others have argued that in April, 1865, Lincoln considered a new approach to reconstruction, that he hoped to work through existing rebel legislatures to effect civil reorganization. There is no convincing evidence to support this. See my own "Toward a New Birth of Freedom: Abraham Lincoln and Reconstruction, 1854–1865," *Lincoln Herald*, 82 (Spring, 1980): 296.

Part Five: Final Act

1: THE THEATER

The profile of Lincoln's humor and humanity draws from Zall, *Abe Lincoln Laughing*, 6, 151; the Seward quotation is from Randall, *Mr. Lincoln*, 237. My sketch of Booth and the assassination is based on George S. Bryan, *The Great American Myth* (New York, 1940), 75–185, 201–2, which is still the most reliable account of the murder; Thomas Reed Turner, *Beware the People Weeping: Public Opinion and the Assassination of Abraham Lincoln* (Baton Rouge, 1982), 18–64; Louis J. Weichmann, *A True History of the Assassination of Abraham Lincoln and of the Conspiracy of 1865* (ed. Floyd E. Risvold, New York, 1975), 3–216, plus John Surratt's Rockville Lecture, ibid. 428–40; Ralph Borreson, *When Lincoln Died* (New York, 1965), 15–46, containing excerpts from eyewitnesses; Dorothy Meserve and Philip B. Kunhardt, Jr., *Twenty Days* (New York, 1965), 11 ff.; Luthin, *Real Lincoln*, 610–18, 625–50; David M. DeWitt, *The Assassination of Abraham Lincoln and Its Expiation* (New York, 1909), 1–54; and Benn Pitman (comp.), *The Assassination of the President and the Trial of the Conspirators* (Cincinnati, 1865). The Booth quotations are from Bryan; the quotation "If he is elected to misgovern" from La Cross (Wis.) *Democrat*, Aug. 29, 1864; the quotation ("assassination is not an American habit") from Frederic Bancroft, *Life of William H. Seward* (New York, 1900), 2: 418; the quotation "awed to passive docility" from Luthin, *Real Lincoln*, 656; the quotation "served Lincoln right" from *Lincoln Lore* (Apr., 1961).

As for the peephole in the state-box door, nobody saw Booth bore it or chip the plaster from the frame of the outer door. But circumstantial evidence points to Booth, since an iron-handled gimlet was found in his room at the National Hotel after the assassination. Authorities assume that he used this instrument to fix the outer door and to make the peephole, then scraping it clean with a small knife. Booth had such free access to Ford's, was so well known to the people there, that he could easily have made his preparations without attracting attention. See Luthin, *Real Lincoln*, 627–28, and DeWitt, *Assassination of Lincoln*, 42, a volume based on contemporary testimony and official records and reports.

The chief government witness against Booth's accomplices, Louis J. Weichmann, whose *True History of the Assassination* was only recently published, contended that the facts indicate that somebody involved in the assassination plot was in the state box earlier that day, boring the hole in question, making the mortise in the outer door frame, and leaving a wooden bar for Booth to insert into it and thus to lock out people from the auditorium.

In 1963, however, a National Park Service pamphlet, *Restoration of Ford's Theater, An Historic Structures Report*, hurled new evidence into the peephole controversy. The pamphlet quoted Frank Ford, son of theater-owner Harry Ford, who wrote in 1962 that workmen acting on his father's instructions had made the hole, so that the guard that night could peer through at the President without disturbing him. People can believe that if they want to. But I am suspicious of hearsay evidence offered almost a century after the event. Therefore I am inclined not to accept Frank Ford's claim until it can be substantiated by contemporary evidence.

2: AFTERMATH

My sources for Booth's death, diary, and body are Bryan, *Great American Myth*, 228–314; Turner, *Beware the People Weeping*, 74–75, 100–24; Luthin, *Real Lincoln*, 665–71; and William Hanchett, *The Lincoln Murder Conspiracies* (Urbana, Ill., 1983). The quotations "Well, my brave boys" and "Tell my mother" are from Bryan, *Great American Myth*, 264, 265; the quotation "There was nothing in the diary" from Turner, *Beware the People Weeping*, 75; the quotation "God Almighty ordered" from Mitgang, *Lincoln, A Press Portrait*, 476; the quotation "Abe has gone to answer" from the Chattanooga *Daily Rebel* as reprinted in the Philadelphia *Evening Bulletin*, May 10, 1865.

The best analysis of the conspiracy trials is Turner, *Beware the People*

Weeping, 138–52. See also Turner, "What Type of Trial?" *Papers of the Abraham Lincoln Association,* 4:29–50. The Surratt quotation is from Weichmann, *True History,* 431; the quotation "it was 'a name in history' " from Luthin, *Real Lincoln,* 612; the Lamon quotation is from his *Recollections of Abraham Lincoln, 1847–1865* (Chicago, 1895), 262, 272. See also James W. Clarke, *American Assassins: The Darker Side of Politics* (Princeton, N.J., 1982).

3: STANTON

For the various theories, consult Hanchett, *The Lincoln Murder Conspiracies.*

On the lecture circuit and in the classroom, I am repeatedly asked about Stanton's connection with the assassination. "Did he engineer it?" "Was he involved?" The Stanton thesis began with Otto Eisenschiml, *Why Was Lincoln Murdered?* (Boston, 1937) and *In the Shadow of Lincoln's Death* (New York, 1940). See the excellent critiques in William Hanchett, "The Eisenschiml Thesis," *Civil War History,* 25 (Sept., 1979): 197–217, and Turner, *Beware the People Weeping,* 6–9. The Sunn Classic motion picture came out in 1977, as did its paperback, *The Lincoln Conspiracy,* written by David Balsiger, Sunn's "Director of Research Development," and Charles E. Sellier, Jr., "Senior Vice President of Production." For scholarly exposés of this atrocious work, see William C. Davis, "Behind the Lines: Caveat Emptor" and "Behind the Lines: 'The Lincoln Conspiracy'—Hoax?," *Civil War Times Illustrated* (Aug. and Sept., 1977), 33–37, 47–49; and Turner, *Beware the People Weeping,* 13–16.

My profile of Stanton draws from the following sources: the quotations "Stanton, you have been," "stern face," and "My chief" from Thomas and Hyman, *Stanton,* 354, 41, 378; the quotation "the outer crust" and "Folks come up here" from Bryan, *Great American Myth,* 129, 130; the quotation "Did Stanton call me a fool?" from Thomas, "Lincoln's Humor," *Papers of the Abraham Lincoln Association,* 3:40; Stanton's letters to Lincoln in Lincoln, *CW,* 8:373–74, 375, 384–85; the quotation "he would have you court-martialed" from Thomas and Hyman, *Stanton,* 394–95; the quotation "warnings that appeared" from John G. Nicolay and John Hay, "Abraham Lincoln: A History of the Fourteenth of April," *Century Magazine,* 39 (1890): 431; Weichmann's warning and the quotations "undimmed praise," "through all that night," "I knew it was only" from Turner, *Beware the People Weeping*, 69–72, 55, 56, 63; the quotation "I recall the kindness" from Thomas and Hyman, *Stanton*, 638. Turner's chapter on Stanton in *Beware the People Weeping* is an excellent scholarly exoneration. See also Mark Neely, Jr., "Vindication," *Lincoln Lore* (May, 1982).

4: WITHOUT HIM

My profile of Mary is based on the works of Randall and the Turners, cited in the text. See also David Donald, "Herndon and Mrs. Lincoln," in Donald, *Lincoln Reconsidered*, 37–56; Mary Elizabeth Massey, "Mary Todd Lincoln," *American History Illustrated* (May, 1975), 4–9, 44–48; and Elizabeth Keckley, *Behind the Scenes* (reprint ed., New York, 1968), along with my appraisal of it in *Our Fiery Trial*, 139.

The quotation "We must both" is from Turners, *Mary Todd Lincoln*, 218; the quotation "felt so unwilling" from Milton H. Shutes, *Lincoln and the Doctors: A Medical Study of the Life of Abraham Lincoln* (New York, 1933), 132–34; the quotation "Oh, my God" from Howard H. Peckham, "James Turner's Account of Lincoln's Death," *Abraham Lincoln Quarterly* (Dec., 1942), 176–83; the quotations "Day by day," "had nothing," "*grateful* nation," "This is the return," "dirty dog," "not worth, living for," "she wolf," "I pray for death," "*the colored* historian," "womanly nature" from Turners, *Mary Todd Lincoln*, 257, 238, 304, 413–14, 416, 440, 472, 474; the quotation "small cheerless" from Randall, *Mary Lincoln*, 417; the quotation "murmuring word" and Mary's description of Tad from Turners, *Mary Todd Lincoln*, 573, 250–51, 523, 590; the quotations "I feel that there is no life" and "O Robert" from Randall, *Mary Lincoln*, 425, 431; and Mary's letter to Robert in Turners, *Mary Todd Lincoln*, 615–16.

INDEX